Milton
and the Rhetoric
of Zeal

Medieval and Renaissance Literary Studies

MILTON

AND THE

Rhetoric

of

Zeal

THOMAS
KRANIDAS

DUQUESNE UNIVERSITY PRESS
PITTSBURGH, PENNSYLVANIA

Published in the United States of America by:
DUQUESNE UNIVERSITY PRESS
600 Forbes Avenue
Pittsburgh, Pennsylvania 15282

Library of Congress Cataloging-in-Publication Data

Kranidas, Thomas.
    Milton and the rhetoric of zeal / Thomas Kranidas.
       p. cm.—(Medieval & Renaissance literary studies)
    Summary: "Describes a rhetoric of radical excess that developed
among the Puritan wing of English Protestantism during the
sixteenth and seventeenth centuries and from which Milton's
radically aggressive style of prose emerged"—Provided by publisher.
    Includes bibliographical references and index.
    ISBN 0–8207–0361–3 (alk. paper)
    1. Milton, John, 1608–1674—Prose. 2. Milton, John, 1608–1674—
Technique. 3. English language—Early modern, 1500–1700—Rhetoric.
4. Christianity and literature—England—History—17th century.
5. Politics and literature—Great Britain—History—17th century.
6. Christian literature, English—History and criticism. 7. Radicalism—
Great Britain—History—17th century. 8. Puritans—England—
Intellectual life. I. Title. II. Medieval and Renaissance literary studies
    PR3592.P7K73 2005
    828'.408—dc22
                        2004023895

For my children:
Stephen, Tommy, Anne and Carrie
and
for my wife, Carole

Contents

PREFACE

My first reading of Milton's prose came as an undergraduate at the University of Washington in the fall of 1948, in the midst of one of the first postwar witchhunts in an American state university. The anxiety and disappointed idealism that followed World War II were developing into the Cold War and were soon to spawn the venomous McCarthy Era of irresponsible accusations and proscriptions. In the spring of that year, the Washington State Un-American Activities Committee—the "Canwell Committee" took its name from its chairman—had investigated "communist activity" on campus. My friends and I considered that committee more or less rabid, and Edwin O. Guthman of the *Seattle Times* proved us more or less right in the series of stories which won him the Pulitzer Prize for National Reporting in 1950.

Among those investigated was my first Milton professor, Garland Ethel. Professor Ethel had become something of a campus hero that summer when he admitted to brief membership in the Communist Party but declined to "name names," the tag line for what many of us construed as squealing on one's fellows. At the hearings, which we attended whenever we could, Ethel made campus history when he was asked to give the names of colleagues who had attended "Communist cell" meetings with him; Dr. Ethel said he wanted to make a statement from Shakespeare's *Hamlet,* one which proved to have no Polonian ambivalence in this context: "This above all: to thine own self be true, And it must follow, as the night the day, Thou canst not then be false to any man"; and he refused to "name names" (Hamlet, 1–3.82–84). Chairman Canwell was outraged; he pounded his gavel in counterpoint to Ethel's recitation of the Shakespeare text while loudly chanting into the microphone, *"We'll—Have—No—Shake— Speare—Quo—Ted—Here!"* Dr. Ethel was cited for contempt. Unlike three of his colleagues Ethel was not fired.[1] That Fall I took my first Milton course from him. The readings of *Areopagitica* and *Samson Agonistes* were especially memorable in that class. The One Just Man was ideal *and* real. However much that naïveté was to be diluted later, the experience of that summer and fall influenced the way I look at heroic gestures against the odds, moved me to read Milton with at least a political memory, and to take his confrontational prose seriously.

Some years later I read all the prose when, again at the University of Washington, I did my dissertation, on Milton's decorum, under Arnold Stein, a very different kind of reader of Milton, but one who particularly encouraged me after he read my chapter on three groups of the prose: the anti-prelatical tracts, the divorce tracts, and the three Latin defenses. In that reading and writing I found a great and somehow personal pleasure in the very range of styles, perhaps even in the impropriety, of the early work. A thesis, and later a book, became a study of how and why Milton violated the standards of a safe decorum which emphasized conformity rather than appropriateness. Toward the end of rewriting my dissertation as *The Fierce Equation*—but too late to make it a part of that book—I came on the work of Thomas Brightman and the tradition of zeal that he fostered, particularly in the 1630s and 1640s. The essay "Milton and the Rhetoric of Zeal" was a first statement of my findings. I have been expanding on that essay for 30 years, quite happily, with the support of friends (slightly bemused), colleagues and institutions.

John Milton was heir to a rhetorical tradition of zeal, of inspired truth-telling that could include displays of outrage and intolerance, unreasonable passion, and coarseness. But under that crudeness lay the heart of Puritan zeal and in a real sense the power of Puritanism, the energy of a focused belief system that liberated and empowered the individual. The Bible was the center of that system, but for Milton, and for many others like him, it was a Bible read with the individual assurance of the authority, God-given, to interpret. Mere fundamentalism is not the issue. Milton's faith in Scripture liberated him to read it independently, and his faith liberated him to challenge, analogically, the conventional limits of systems, of the institutions of the church, of marriage, of education, of public dissemination of information, of kingship and of poetry and theology.

This study presents first the sources and the display of the rhetorical tradition of zealous religious discourse. The scriptural sources of this tradition are identified as useful very early in Christian history; I move quickly over these early stages to emphasize the Protestant assessment and ultimately the virtual cooption of that tradition for the ideological wars of the later sixteenth and seventeenth centuries. I identify Revelation 3.16 as a particularly effective text for the Puritan agenda and suggest the avenues of argument that text provided, especially the identification of the Church of England with the lukewarm Church of Laodicea and the rejection of ethical and aesthetic moderation as an ideal in Christian polemic. Then I examine two of the major arguments that the established Church continuously invoked against Puritan zeal, "Decency," and "Indifference" which is the traditional Christian *adiaphora*. During this period Archbishop Laud made the argument for Decency, the defined appropriateness allowed by Indifference, a critical part of his campaign to reform the Church of England; as a consequence, Puritan attacks on that reform are powerful and insistent, ranging from sober to riotous. I then turn to the pulpit as a major site for the convergence of these arguments.

The first chapter is also something of an anthology of Puritan zealous writing, an attempt to show its ubiquity, its variety, its cumulative organization of energy into a lethal weapon of discourse. The Irresistible Force of this rhetoric overwhelms, at least for a significant period, the Immovable Object of English moderation, moderation in religion and in language. Milton contributes to the high drama of this conflict, and of course he reflects it.

The rest of the study is an attempt to give a reading of the antiprelatical tracts, especially as they function within this tradition. The tradition contextualizes these tracts, allowing the reader to see them not only as historical documents but as significant steps in Milton's literary progress toward mastery of styles, toward the recognition of the necessary coexistence of the circumstantial and the ideological, of the interpenetrability of the sublime and the ridiculous. The early tracts are indeed *antiprelatical*, but, in their development, in the individual and proclaimed way in which they accumulate and interpret detail, they become also literary documents in the emerging career, personal and institutional, of the poet of *Paradise Lost. Of Reformation* is in part a sublime document of national aspiration; it is also a document that quite brazenly proclaims its author's moral self-confidence and his literary ambitions. The plangent sublimity coexists with scabrous polemical passages; both are enabled by the rhetoric of zeal. If none of the four tracts that follow quite reach the passion and eloquence of the first, they each in various ways and to differing degrees of success aspire to the goals of the first tract: the search, and ultimate claim on, kerygmatic authority, the responsibility and the right to proclaim and to expound God's word.

The coda that concludes this book may seem a bit of private indulgence, but I think it makes a legitimate point about the thesis argued here and about the process of this argument. The rhetoric of campus activism in the United States during the 1960s paralleled the rhetoric of Puritan zeal in its virulence and in its deliberate violation of Establishment decorum. For both historical periods the identifiable stages of this deliberate politics of indecorum have an interesting similarity.

I read, or at least skimmed, some thousands of tracts in the Thomason Collection of the British Library, and hundreds more from the same period at the Henry E. Huntington Library and in the McAlpin Collection of the Union Theological Seminary, great libraries with superb resources generously shared. I looked especially for the tropes I had identified as those of Puritan zeal, and I noted relevant additional tropes and images that recurred in the discussions of contemporary ecclesiology and politics, and especially in discussions of the discourse of polemical theology. My method is historical, with a touch of the New Historicist in a respect for nonliterary discourse, the broadsides and satires from which Milton would adopt the language of street controversy. This language he would use when he thought it useful to his purposes—the disruption of the opposition's argument, the illumination of the subject, the enlightenment of those hitherto deemed unteachable, and of course, with the necessary bluntness of polemic, the destruction of Prelacy.

When I started this inquiry, I felt like a pioneer, one, to be sure, following a trail blazed by William Haller, Arthur Barker and Don M. Wolfe, but nevertheless a pioneer. Now I feel a bit like a camp-follower. I note the work of the younger writers in the field at the end of chapter 1. Here I will mention only three who have been of special importance to me. The late Joan Webber was a friend before she turned to creating the brilliant and seminal *The Eloquent "I,"* and we corresponded on her chapter on Milton. I learned more from her than she did from me. I met Thomas Corns in 1982 and benefited from his erudition and skill; his comments on chapter 1 and on the coda of this study were extremely useful. I continue to learn from him. Stanley Fish has enlivened Milton studies more than anyone since C. S. Lewis. Though I take issue with him in this study, I respect his scholarship and appreciate his friendly encouragement.

My deepest debts are the most personal ones. I was fortunate in doing my dissertation under Arnold Stein, one of the most elegant readers of seventeenth century poetry of his generation, and, under his shy severity, a warm and encouraging mentor. I had the extraordinary privilege of having Owen Barfield as close friend, the great gift of observing one of the truly wise men of the twentieth century in his daily intellection, his passionate and continuous living in and reconstruing of Classical and English literature. I would have abandoned this project early on had it not been for Jeanne Clayton Hunter. She encouraged and assisted me out of her friendship, her love for Milton, and her remarkable sympathies for English Puritanism. Her knowledge of John Preston, for example, proved immediately useful, as did her readings of John Calvin and of George Herbert. Nearing the end of my writing, I had the important help of Carol Barton, my student, my colleague in this inquiry, and my friend, who took my computer ignorance in hand; she did not cure it but she compensated for it with her generous help. But her help was much more than technical; it included stylistic and factual suggestions of value to me, and general incitements to endurance. She made it possible for me to finish.

My wife, Carole Kessner, has, through her love and through her scholarly example, made the profession of scholarship a shared experience of "meet help" and "fit conversation." My children, to whom this book is also dedicated, have been continuously loving and supportive of a father too often "otherwise engaged."

I am grateful for generous support from the following: The John Simon Guggenheim Foundation gave me the opportunity to work for a year at The British Library. The National Endowment for the Humanities and the Henry E. Huntington Library allowed me a seven-month stay at the latter's Eden for Scholars. At the very end of this enterprise, I enjoyed the courtesy and efficiency of the Renaissance Center of the University of Massachusetts at Amherst, of the New York Public Library, and the Columbia University Library. The State University of New York at Stony Brook allowed me generous research grants and sabbaticals throughout most of my 30-year stay on that campus, including a final one-year research leave; for advice on the last grant, I thank Professor Paul Dolan. Among my colleagues Professor Rose Zimbardo was always encouraging and helpful with suggestions on early drafts. I co-taught a course with my historian colleague, Professor Karl Bottigheimer, in which I learned some of the limitations of my discipline and some of the legitimate disagreements between the "literary" and the "historical" approaches. I am grateful to my feisty and wonderful students, who didn't sit still for too much doctrine—literary or theological. Forty something years of teaching them Milton and Shakespeare at the university level has been a major blessing of my life.

For some 30 years I have had the privilege and pleasure of meeting with colleagues in the Milton Seminar where ideas flowed and collegiality flourished. It has been a special pleasure to see this particular manifestation of the "Milton industry" belie that tag and continue to express itself as a humane and humanistic enterprise, however embarrassed some of the younger members will be to have me put it that way. To members of that group I give thanks for their eminent examples, their stimulation, and their friendship.

Duquesne University Press has been encouraging and efficient in all its dealings with me. I wish to thank Professor James Egan for a meticulous and generous reading of the manuscript and a series of valuable suggestions for improvement. I wish also to thank Albert Labriola and Susan Wadsworth-Booth for wise interventions and my editor Kathy Meyer for her courteous and skillful supervision.

Chapters 2, 3, and 4 are substantial revisions of essays previously published. I wish to thank *ELH, Milton Studies,* and *The Huntington Library Quarterly* respectively for permission to reprint sections from those essays. The early version of "Milton and the Rhetoric of Zeal" appeared in *Texas Studies in Literature and Language* in 1964; an early overview of the topic appeared in *Studies in Philology* in 1965; for permission to reprint whatever remains of those essays I am grateful to the editors of the respective journals. I am grateful to the Yale University Press for permission to quote extensively from their landmark edition, *Complete Prose Works of John Milton.*

A NOTE ON TEXTS

I have retained original spellings in most of my early texts, while regularizing *i*'s, *j*'s, *u*'s, *v*'s, and long *s*'s. For background material in the first chapter, I have used modern editions where possible, including those for Bishop Hall, but in chapter 4 I use earlier editions for Hall, in order to retain the intensely personal flavor of the debates. I use the Yale edition of Milton's prose throughout and *The Riverside Milton*, edited by Roy Flannagan, for poetry.

ONE

The Rhetoric of Zeal

*Yea, looke what an edge is to a Razor, look what wine is
to mans spirit, what the soule is to the body, wings to a bird, winde
to sayles, what mettle is to a horse, looke what vivacity and vigour is
to any creature; that is zeale to a Christian. It is that that acts his
soule, the vigour, activity, the fervency of his affections; that is zeale.*
—Stephen Marshall, *Divine Project,* 29[1]

The English "Wars of Truth" were intoxicated with
language. The exhilaration of print, with its capacities
for a larger and more varied audience; the opportunities
it offered for anonymity, for sustained display, for self-
aggrandizement; the sharp edges of the contrasting positions
it admitted to its colloquy; the almost infinite possibilities of
intermediation;[2] and, most powerfully, the sheer importance
of the debates it made possible: all these contributed to a
rhetoric of astounding variety, and often of raging intensity.
For an English Protestant like John Foxe, printing was a miracle
sent by God to facilitate Reformation: "How many printing
presses there be in the world, so many blockhouses there be
against the high castle of St. Angelo, so that either the pope

1

must abolish knowledge and printing or printing at length will root him out."[3]

Whatever the reasons for the ensuing mid-seventeenth century conflicts—economic, political, religious—the stakes seemed immense to those involved. With almost equal self-assurance, both sides claimed God's approval in their struggles for ideological dominance, for control of the national church, for political and social appropriation. Most urgent was the conflicted search for eternal life itself.

One is faced with a vast discourse of intense self-importance. Some of it is dreadful; some of it is historically fascinating; a little of it is noble. In evaluating that discourse—specifically, in confronting John Milton's polemical prose—one can no longer assume the standards of a Western tradition long committed to clarity, perspicuity, and decorum—the last term still an unstable one. From at least Aristotle onward, the rhetoricians had argued toward rational control, toward moderation and clarity, indeed toward a coolness that could at times simulate heat but would at no time surrender to it.[4] The open hand of rhetoric was twin to the tight fist of logic, and the one could easily metamorphose into the other. The "clunch fist of logic (good to knock down a man at a blow) can so open itself as to smooth and stroke one with the palm thereof."[5] Decorum moderated judiciously between the punch and the stroke.

Like the language of many of his fellow activists, Milton's language defies moderation and praises surrender to anger under the aegis of zeal: ζῆλος, *zeilos,* means a kind of emulatory rivalry, as opposed to a hostile φθόνος, *phthonos,* or envy. From the beginning, the Christian use of the term had a powerful ambivalence. In 2 Corinthians, Paul praises "the forwardness of your mind . . .; and your zeal hath provoked very many"; two chapters later he speaks of his "godly jealousy" for those whom he has espoused to Christ (2 Corinthians 9.2, 11.2).[6] But in Romans, he has warned that though the people Israel "have a zeal for God, it is not according to knowledge. For they being ignorant of God's righteousness, and going about to establish their own righteousness, have not submitted themselves unto the righteousness of God" (10.2–4).

Even in his early prose, Milton is aware of Paul's warnings, his consciousness of the difference between righteous zeal and self-righteousness. That awareness stays with him and produces a number of elaborate apologias. At his most traditionally analytic, he will recognize this range of meanings in *De Doctrina*. "An eager desire to sanctify the divine name, together with a feeling of indignation against things which tend to the violation or contempt of religion, is called ZEAL," he writes,[7] citing examples from Psalms 69 and 119, Romans 12, and the figures of Lot, Moses, Phinehas, Elijah, Jeremiah, Christ, Stephen, Paul, and Barnabas in illustration. "Opposed to zeal is the lukewarm, as, for example, Eli, I Sam. 29 and 3.13, and in the Jewish leaders, John 12.43, and in the Laodiceans, Rev. 3.15, 16," this last a crucial association for contemporary polemics. The distinctions are important to Milton: "ignorant and imprudent zeal is . . . opposed to true zeal," as is "zeal which is too fervent. . . . And hypocritical and boastful zeal" (*CPW*, 6:697–98). Yet self-consciousness does not preclude an extraordinary display of an aggressive and consuming zeal for the Lord in his early prose and poetry, a zeal poised perilously close to self-righteousness but, I would argue, distinct from it. The idea energizes Milton's entire canon.

The *OED* sets out the difficult dynamics of the term:

1. In biblical language, rendering L. *zelus* (or *aemulatio*), Gr. ζῆλος, denoting ardent feeling or fervour (taking the form of love, wrath, "jealousy," or righteous indignation), with contextual tendency to unfavourable implications (emulation, rivalry, partisanship). . . .
4. Intense ardour in the pursuit of some end; passionate eagerness in favour of a person or cause; enthusiasm as displayed in action.[8]

It is that *ardor* that I emphasize here, an ardor consciously and even defiantly deploying itself as the vehicle for vatic mission and national destiny. That ardor recognizes and dismisses the cries of alarm, from faint to traumatic, over the misuses of zeal.

The poles of the argument are established by the pertinent biblical texts. The Puritans[9] cite five passages especially. The first is from the song of Barak and Deborah in Judges 5, a song which celebrates the courageous and unambiguous activism of Jael while condemning those who tarried or stood aside. This text is cited hundreds of times in the controversial literature of the period: "Curse ye Meroz, said the angel of the LORD, curse ye bitterly the inhabitants thereof; because they came not to the help of the LORD, to the help of the LORD against the mighty" (Judges 5.23). The eminent Stephen Marshall based his most famous sermon on this text, a sermon reputed to have been preached 60 times.[10]

Psalm 69 is less exclusively Puritan property, but verse 9 was frequently invoked in injunctions to censure of, or strong action against, the Church Establishment:

> I am become a stranger unto my brethren, and an alien unto my mother's children.
> For the zeal of thine house hath eaten me up; and the reproaches of them that reproached thee are fallen upon me. (8–9)

The frame of beleaguered faith in this passage serves the Puritan idea of election against the odds as well as it serves the Miltonic idea of the one just man (or angel) standing in righteousness against a host of iniquity. One remembers Noah . . . Abraham . . . Abdiel:

> Among the faithless, faithful only hee;
> Among innumerable false, unmov'd,
> Unshak'n, unseduc'd, unterrifi'd
> His Loyaltie he kept, his Love, his Zeale;[11]

The third scripture text which opposes the middle ground and the postponement of action is Elijah's words to the people in 1 Kings 18.21: "How long halt ye between two opinions? If the LORD be God, follow him: but if Baal then follow him." "Halting" as it is used in this passage—wavering, refusing to make a decision—becomes a pejorative, even a contemptuous, term, as it is in Arthur Salwey's *Halting Stigmatiz'd:* "It is a very evill thing to halt in Religion. It is a very evill thing to be either a *Neuter,* or an *Uterque,* or a Waverer in Religion. Neutralitie, without controversie, is not to be endured. . . . As the *Neuter* is abominable, so the halting *Uterque* is not to be indured."[12] Harder to appropriate for immediate political purposes, but frequently cited by the proponents of zeal was the familiar text from Matthew 12.30 and Luke 11.23, often introductory to an attack on "neuters," or paired with an allusion to another zealous text:

> He that is not with me is against me: and he that gathereth not with me scattreth abroade. . . . This thunder-clappe nyppeth, knocketh downe, and all to clattereth al Neutres.[13]
> He *that i[s] not with* me *is against me:* they are cursed bitterly *who come* not out to *helpe the Lord against the mighty.*[14]

The fifth text, and the most politically potent, is Revelation 3.16—the last of Christ's pronouncements to St. John of Patmos concerning the seven churches of Asia Minor:

> And unto the angel of the church of the Laodiceans write; These things saith the Amen, the faithful and true witness, the beginning of the creation of God:
> I know thy works, that thou art neither cold nor hot: I would thou wert cold or hot.
> So then because thou art lukewarm, and neither cold nor hot, I will spue thee out of my mouth. (3.14–16)

The Puritans could not claim exclusive rights to this text, but by the early 1640s they had virtually commandeered it for their own political purposes, as I shall show below.

Against these powerfully disturbing attacks on ecclesiastic discipline and style, the Church of England used one Pauline injunction above all others: "Let all things be done decently and in order" (1 Corinthians 14.40). All of these texts became specific counters in the theological and ecclesiological debates of the Tudor-Stuart period, with a particular urgency in the 1630s, 1640s, and 1650s. And both sides took into account, and sometimes used, the "opposing" texts.

For Milton the most useful of these is the passage from Revelation, a text which served Puritan strategy in two ways: it validated the violence of their rhetoric and of their "Root and Branch" political behavior; and it marginalized the contemporary Church of England, *de facto* the Anglican hierarchy, by identifying it with the lukewarm Church of Laodicea.

LUKEWARMNESS

The Book of Revelation has an ambiguous position in the Canon, with somewhat reluctant acceptance by the Eastern Churches[15] and no canonical status in the Syrian Church. Its phantasmagoric imagery is not unique in Scripture, but it encourages the imagining of violent action more than do the other narratives, of the New Testament especially. In times of instability and danger, the Book of Revelation invites radical interpretation. Consider the frescoes at Iveron monastery on Mount Athos; consider Michelangelo or Dostoyevsky—or Charles Manson.[16] For the faithful of Milton's time this book was a source of mystery and of mysterious instruction. The sheer number of contemporary interpretations of the book testify to its attraction for cleric and layman alike.[17] Nervous concern for the timetables of Apocalypse is apparent in the lists of sermons and in the lists of political interpretations whose main subject was the decoding of Revelation.

My focus here is on the pervasive *incidental* use of images from that text, images which direct the English public toward a radically politicized view of the prophecies it contains. The subject, though trivial-seeming, is a large one, and in this context I can look only at the cluster of ideas that crowds one corner of it; yet that cluster had considerable relevance to the politics in which Milton participated. The Church of England was identified by contemporary Puritans as the antitype of the Church of Laodicea. The abhorrence expressed toward that church by the Christic voice of Revelation 3 becomes paradigm for violent rhetoric and violent behavior by the righteous against the "lukewarm professors."

Modern delicacy has obscured the original force of this passage of Revelation, and specifically of the Greek word ἐμέω, *emeo*, which is translated "vomit" (in the Rheims Bible) or "spew," a synonym. The King James "spew" was usually read as "vomit" up to the mid-seventeenth century. As late as 1680, Henry More, in the midst of a less strenuous approach to the text, can still speak of the lukewarm Christian as "nauseous and loathsome."[18] Today, the New English and Jerusalem Bibles have the inoffensive "spit" (though my 1978 Thomas Nelson edition has "vomit" in the "Read-Along Translation"). The stronger reading in early texts provides horrific warning to the *neuter*, to the *tolerationist*, and to the *moderator*—in short to the proponents of the English *via media*.

The power and danger of zeal are recognized at the beginning of the English Reformation, and its political implications are an early matter of concern. John Bale attacks the "false glosying hypocryte" who is lukewarm and identifies himself as "an exile also in this life for the faythfull testimonye of Jesu Crist."[19] Bishop Jewel, propounder of the Elizabethan Act of Settlement, first praises zeal and then warns against its excesses in a sermon to Queen Elizabeth, republished in the crucial political year 1641: "Zeale . . . is an earnest affection, and vehement love: as is the love of a mother towards her children, or of the naturall childe towards his mother: This zeale cannot abide to see that thing which it loveth, despised or hurt. . . . It taketh away the use of reason: it eateth & devoureth up the heart."[20]

Though he sees zeal's positive uses clearly, the bishop will also cite and emphasize Paul's caution from Romans 10, identifying the bad man who "perswadeth himselfe he hath the zeale of God: and what he doth in selfe-love of his owne fantasie, he will beare in hand he doth it for the love of God" (8–9). The analysis of lukewarmness is sometimes quite elaborate. In his 1595 lectures on the first three chapters, the influential William Perkins identifies "diverse kinds of such

lukewarme Gospellers and Christians": "Papist[s] . . . mediators . . . pacificators," with a special jab at "Temporizers"
who "will follow the Prince, and change their religion with
the time," the fearful lovers of Christ, servers of God and
Mammon, and those who sin even though they love Christ.[21]

The reissue of Jewel's sermon in 1641 suggests the urgency of the debate among Milton's contemporaries and the
incitement to search through the recent past for reinforcing
arguments. The Earl of Clarendon writes of the "printing any
old scandalous pamphlets and adding new to them" in 1641.[22]
The bitterly zealous pamphlets of Marprelate and his numerous progeny were easily available.[23] In counterattack, the
established Church attempted to stabilize and control the
uses of a text that perplexed and confounded, then helped
to shape, the opposing rhetorical strategies of Puritan and
Anglican.

In *Christian Moderation* (1640), Bishop Joseph Hall seeks
to save the argument for the Church of England:

> Far be it from us to allow lukewarmness in the matters of God; a
> disposition, which the almighty professeth so much to hate, that
> he could rather be content the angel of the church of Laodicea
> should be quite cold, than in such a mambling of profession. And
> indeed what temper is so offensive to the stomach as this mean?
> fit only for a medicinal potion whose end is ejection, not for
> nourishment. (*Works*, 6:444)[24]

But, aware of the opposition's exploitation of the text, he urges
moderation:

> We must be zealous; we must not be furious (446). . . . There must
> be then two moderators of our zeal; Discretion and charity
> (447). . . . The form of tongues in the first descent of the Holy Ghost,
> was fiery and cloven; and that was the fittest for the state of the
> first plantation of the gospel . . . now, in the enlarged and settled
> state of his evangelical Church, the same Spirit descends, and
> dwells in tongues, cool and divided, *Cor unum, via una.* (474)

Hall's attempt to contain "primitive" zeal failed, as did
numerous other interventions of "moderatours," including

Francis Bacon (whose *A Wise & Moderate Discourse* Milton cites, from the 1641 edition, in *CPW*, 1:450, 668). Though he disclaims the right to judge the Bishops, Bacon warns the Church that "if any [Bishop] bee neither hot nor cold . . . it is time they returne whence they are fallen."[25] With the magisterial breadth—or is it hedging?—of a good politician,[26] he declares:

> a feeling Christian will expresse in his words a character either of zeale or love: the latter of which as I would wish rather to be embraced, as being more fit for the times; yet is the former warranted also by great examples. But to leave all reverend and religious compassions toward evils, *or* indignation toward faults, to turne religion into a Comedy or Satyr, to search and rip up wounds with a laughing countenance, to intermix Scripture and Scurrility sometime in one sentence, is a thing farre from the devout reverence of a Christian.[27]

A critical distinction between the politic and the zealous emerges in Bacon's advice to James I in *Certaine Considerations* (1604); James is to serve as the "Christian Moderator" who must find "the golden Mediocritie."[28] Bacon's invoking of the golden mean, in this context, is opposed to standard Puritan practice, which attacked the use of the *ethical* ideal in religious controversy and discipline. Such "mediators" are, according to Robert Bolton, outward conformists, who make "moderation in Religion a Saint: . . . They admire, and applaude with much self-estimation of their singular skill, and rare felicitie, in pitching just upon the golden meane, as they conceive, betweene prophanenesse and precisenesse."[29] Bacon's view is opposed to Milton's also in his caution with "the people," as we shall see: "Lastly, whatsoever is pretended, the people is no meet judge or arbitrator; but rather the moderate, quiet, and private assemblies of the learned" (*Certaine Considerations*, 46).

The publication of Bacon's texts was an attempt to bridge the gap between the two parties, but despite the common sources, even initial agreements in definition, Anglican and Puritan split over the uses of "intense ardour" and "discretion." Milton's famous passage confirms the consuming, and eminently political, insistence on zeal as the cutting edge of the later English Reformation:

> And it is still *Episcopacie* that before all our eyes worsens and sluggs the most learned, and seeming religious of our *Ministers,* who no sooner advanc't to it, but like a seething pot set to coole, sensibly exhale and reake out the greatest part of that zeale, and those Gifts which were formerly in them, settling in a skinny congealment of ease and sloth at the top: and if they keep their Learning by some potent sway of Nature, 'tis a rare chance; but their *devotion* most commonly comes to that queazy temper of luke-warmnesse, that gives a Vomit to GOD himself. (*CPW,* 1:536–37)

The style and meaning of this passage are clarified, and made less extraordinary, when we look at Puritan commentaries on Revelation 3.

The most influential and one of the most extended commentaries is Thomas Brightman's *Apocalypsis Apocalypseos,* first published in Frankfurt in 1609.[30] Brightman's use of Revelation 3.16 concurs with other commentators and concretizes the polemical use of the text:

> but that is lukewarme, because it hath a heate which is neare to the stomacks heate, and with which it is best acquainted, is neither perceived & felt when it goeth in, neither is therefore when it is entred in, concocted, but remayneth without working, and at last being troublesome with the long stay of it, is cast out of dores with loathing, like an unprofitable guest.[31]

Brightman's extended discussion of Revelation 3.16–22 suggests that the Puritan attitude toward Anglican moderation is already polemical:

> Now hee calleth that man cold, who can well indure that the dueties of godlines should lie dead, & out of request. . . . Hee calleth him hott, who boyleth with heate and fervency of Spirit, in his due and full regard of Gods worship, being like to boyling water, that seetheth and boyleth (as wee say) in the Pott. . . . For wee

must not think, that to bee hot is vitious in this place, as if it were an inconsiderate zeale, as the case standeth with the habits of morall vertues, wherein both the extreams, straying from the mediocritie, either in excesse or defect, are faults & vices . . . ; but it is a matter of commendation, as being the onely vertue, from which bothe coldnes and *lukewarmenes* swerve. (*Revelation*, 166–67)

The Puritans make a critical distinction between the Aristotelian golden mean and lukewarmness in religion. "*Moderation* doth better in other things, then in the practise of *Religion*, where there cannot be a *minimum*."[32] Religious zeal is an extreme which is not vicious; it is preferable to both the other extreme and the mean. One should note a corollary: the unusual hatred between the mean and both the "good" and "bad" extremes, and a contempt for the mediatorial. Matthew Newcomen describes it in a sermon preached in November of 1642: "And it is a true observation of some, that the nearer any are to a *conjunction* in matters of Religion, and yet some *difference* retained, the *deeper* is the *hatred*; . . . a *Formalist* hates a *Puritan* worse then doth a *Papist*."[33] Conversely, Puritan rage at the Church of England is very often more immediately consuming than is hatred of the Church of Rome:

Behold that mischievous Generall [Satan] sends forth the reserved squadron of Knights of his new order of refined Reconcilers, by whose pretences of friendship and peaceable mediations, he is confident to overthrow the Protestant cause more quickly than by the heads and hands of all former Souldiers.[34]

For the Anglican apologist, the equation of ethical and religious moderation persists: "The true *Protestant* Religion stands like a *vertue* betweene two *vices*, *Popery* and *Separatisme*";[35] "As morall virtue is placed in the middle between two extreames . . . so also true Religion hath her proper seat in the middle between superstition in the excesse, and profanenesse in the defect"; and, confirming the primacy of anti-Puritan rhetoric, the influential Daniel Featley continues, "of the two extreames profaneness is the worse."[36]

The most incendiary emphasis in Brightman's contribution to the politics of zeal is the identification of the Church of England as the antitype of the Church of Laodicea,[37] that "luke-warme vayneglorious Laodicea" to which the biblical verses are directed. As early as 1596 George Gyffard had hinted at this same correlation; in his address "Unto the Christian Reader," he writes that verses 16 through 22 were "no fable, this is not the word of any mortall man, . . . I beseech ye marke well, and let it be deepely printed and ingraven in your hearts which the Lord uttereth here. It may doe us good, for are we not growing lukewarme, even as the Churche to whome this message was sent?"[38] Gyffard avoids the full typological identification, in fact denies the prophetical interpretation of the first three chapters of the Book of Revelation. But the unease shows in the rhetorical question he puts to his brethren, and in his implicit analogy between Laodicea and London: "that citie was very wealthie in worldly substance through wollen cloath" (105). Reluctantly but firmly and repeatedly Brightman equates "lukewarme vayneglorious Laodicea" with the Church of England:

> I that by Gods providence had found these Epistles cast abroad, and understood by the inscriptions to what Churches they were sent, durst not but give them unto you. . . . I have not with dry eyes taken a survay of this *Laodicea*. I could not but poure forth teares and sighes from the bottom of my hart, when I beheld in it, Christ himselfe loathing of us, and provoaked extremely to anger against us. (A2v, 159)

Denying that "any distempered affection of [his] hart . . . hath set [him] on worke to seeke out an odious application of this Epistle," he states bluntly, "The *Counterpaine* ["Anti-type" in the 1611 edition, 103] (I say) of *Laodicea,* is the third reformed Church, namely: *Our Church of England*" (159).

After praising God's bounties toward England, Brightman describes the lukewarmness of the Laodiceans and compares their pastors (whom he describes as "prudent and moderate men") with "such as wee call at this day *statists, or moderate and direct Protestants of State,* and which are commonly known to bee *lukewarme professours"* (167). Though the Church of England cannot be considered cold,

> hott it is not, as whose *outward regiment* is as yet for the greatest part *Antichristian & Romish.* . . . God . . . doth more easily endure that his grace should not bee known, then that it should bee despised. . . . The mediocritie therefore is worst of all, which indeed is honoured of the world, because of that shew it maketh of a certaine moderation and peaceablenes. (168–69)

Brightman does not argue that Christ prefers Rome to England, but rather that he prefers "blinde Papists before those *Angels* onely, who being bewitched with ambition and covetousnes, doe scornfully reject holy reformation" (169). For them, the ejection from Christ's mouth will be terrible, "For what can be more acceptable to a man that is stomack-sicke with eating meate that hee loatheth?" (171). The punishment will not be for the whole Church but for *"all Lukewarme Pastours . . . this whole Hierarchy . . .* that seeke onely for honours and wealth, not the things that bee Christs" (172). However, the Church as a whole is likely to feel "some litle calamitie, as being infected with the contagion of this sinne . . . and there is no man so rude and unexpert, that seeth not plainely that the whole body doth labour of the same disease" (172). The section ends with a fervent prayer: "Stirre up within us the flame of thy love; dissolve I beseech the this our ycenes [icyness], and suffer us not to please our selves as wee doe in this our pietie by the halves" (173). Between 1641 and 1644 there were seven editions of *Reverend Mr. Brightman's Judgments or Prophecies,* and an edition of *The Workes of Thomas Brightman.* But his substantial influence begins earlier. Defense against an attack from abroad is found in *A Shield of Defence* in 1612, which is especially laudatory of his identification of Laodicea with contemporary London.[39] And an interesting criticism of Brightman's Laodicean analogy is found in William Cowper's *Patmos: or A Commentary on the Revelation of Saint John* . . . (1619). In an introductory survey of 42 commentaries on the Revelation, Cowper, Bishop of Galloway, remarks that in Brightman's reading "types properly belonging to Christ, are accommodate to men. . . . It is a griefe to see how the comfort given therein is empaired, the majestie and amplitude thereof restrained, by binding it to particular persons and times."[40] Cowper avoids the mention of the Laodicea-England identification, but it seems clear that it is one of the causes of his grief. And Bishop Hall scolds his "old acquaintance Brightman" for making "those churches of Asia the types and histories of all the Christian churches which should be to the end of the world" (*Works*, 6:444).

The lukewarm/Laodicea trope stays alive through the twenties and thirties as is evidenced by the spirited defenses against it[41] and the assumptions of its valency, as by the eminent John Preston's conflation of two zealot texts:

> but as the stomacke loathes lukewarme water, so God lukewarme religions. As therefore *Eliah* exhorts the people to follow either God or Baal and not to halt between them both; so it's good for us to take heede of mingling truth and falsehood.[42]

The chasm widens between the uses of zeal and the uses of reason; Bolton writes that the "lukewarm professors" "undoe their soules by adoring discretion as an Idoll. . . . And at length most certainely the just execution of that terrible commination, Revel. 3.16, will crush their hearts with everlasting horrour, confusion and woe" (*Directions*, 50–51).

Brightman's work was suppressed during the Anglican censorship, but not forgotten. During the forties he was seen as a prophet who had predicted the corruption of the Church of England, antitype of Laodicea, and its politically volatile corollary, the triumphant virtue of the Church of Scotland, antitype of the Church of Philadelphia.[43] "That worthy Instrument of God Mr. *Brightman*";[44] "that famous light in former times, 30 or 40 yeers since."[45] He is mentioned as prophet and an "able worthy Confessor"[46] and along with Cartwright is named among the "learned and Godly men."[47] Among the citations are those by Thomas Edwards in the popular *Gangraena*, where Brightman is quoted often and at length on the subject of lukewarmness,[48] and Samuel Gibson, who makes the troublesome political comparison that "[The Church of Scotland] had the honour to be in the Antitype to *Philadelphia*, the best of those Churches of *Asia*, when ours was made the Antitype to *Laodicea*, the worst of the seven."[49]

In the 1640s the Church of England was regularly identified by Puritan polemics with the church whose lukewarmness was so loathsome to Christ that he ejected her from his body. By no means a rare figure, the trope was used by Milton's occasional colleagues Edward Calamy and Stephen Marshall, and by Henry Burton, Lewis Hewes, John Lilburne, men whose visibility confirms the ascription as commonplace.[50] By 1647, Brightman's admirers saw triumphant closure for his argument:

> So may wee truly say of this Faithfull man, that being Dead hee yet speaketh by his workes of Faith. Witnesse those on the *Revelation*; Who, though hee was silenced Living, that neither hee nor his Workes might speake in England: Yet now wee see them have liberty to speake; when all those their enemies are prest to silence and shame: As hee by a divine and propheticall Spirit discovered out of the Epistle to the Angell of *Laodicea* (italics reversed).[51]

I am insisting on the common but not uniform assumptions held by seventeenth century polemicists on both sides concerning a scriptural text with immediate political applicability. Not the exclusive franchise of the Puritans, this radical interpretation of a prophetic text surely served their politics better than it did the politics of the Church of England. Three pieces from quite different sources, all of them clerical, summarize the range of influence of this text, and of its imbrication with the other texts of zeal. The first is the little poem "Neutrality loathsome" by Robert Herrick, traditionally the model of the Anglican parson:

> GOD will have all, or none; serve Him, or fall
> Down befor *Baal*, *Bel*, or *Belial*:
> Either be hot, or cold: God doth despise,
> Abhorre, and spew out all Neutralities.[52]

The second is by William Sclater, in a 1641 sermon:

> Now then, be for God, or for *Baal;* abhorre a *Samaritan* mongrell
> disposition; a *Laodicean* lukewarmnes; this halting twixt two
> opinions; this swearing by God, and by Malcham too; this dowbak'd
> lukewarm temper, God threatens to spue out as loathsome and
> with nauseation from his presence. In short, is a man a Minister?
> and is his aime in Preaching, onely by a vainglorious ostenta-
> tion of wit to please man; or to tickle the itch of the wavering
> times; and not (without envy, without soothing partiality) to declare
> the pure doctrine of Christ Jesus, in syncerity.[53]

Milton could have known these texts. He probably knew
this final and important example of Puritan appropriation of
Revelation 3.16, Henry Wilkinson's *A Sermon against
Lukewarmnesse in Religion* (1641). In the "address to the
House," Wilkinson writes that he was suspended for preaching
the sermon, and "released" by the House, which then ordered
the piece printed.[54] The Wilkinson sermon contains the
expected ingredients. First the horror of lukewarmness: "What
lesse to be indured in the stomacke, than indigested meate?
What lesse to be embraced, than vomit? what more to be
loathed?"(3) Secondly, the separation of virtue in religion from
the golden mean:

> What ever may be said of morall vertues, that they consist in the
> middle, yet I am sure, that this kind of Mediocrity hath no place
> here: For our love to God, and zeal to the truth can never be too
> intense. . . . This middle way, this halting betweene two opinions
> is sure to be wrong; the extreames both are sure to be better, and
> one is sure to be right. (5, 7)

Though he does not name the Church of England as
Laodicea, it is clear what discipline Wilkinson has in mind
when he speaks of the "lukewarme professours":

> they are very scrupulous in mint and rue, and very exact in the
> Ceremony; and (as if Religion were a Comedy) they will in voyce,
> and gesture act divine duties, though in their hearts they renounce;
> and in their lives deny the parts they play. . . . Why will they take

so much paines to personate, and act a Christian, and not to be one? (11)

It is the absence of zeal and of sincerity under the voice and, perhaps especially, under the gesture, of ceremony that Wilkinson condemns. Yet he is not naive: "Knowledge withoute zeale puffes a man up and zeale without knowledge is like the Devill in the possessed, which casts him sometimes into the fire, and sometimes into the water: such was the zeale of *Paul* before his conversion" (18). To Puritans like Brightman, Wilkinson, and Milton, the elegant poise of the *via media* was lukewarmness, self-serving and cowardly moderation. They eschewed "halfway" positions as hypocritical, mediation as idolatrous. As Puritans, they acknowledged one and only one Mediator; one and only one undivided commitment: "There are no mediatours of Intercession, neither the blessed Virgin, not Saints in Heaven, nor Angells, no more than these are Mediatours of Redemption. Christ is the one only Mediatour both of intercession and Redemption."[55] No "carnal" mediators and no "carnal" mediations. And no substituted "holy duties":

It is a shrewd [signe] of a lukewarme temper, when men make some conscience of performing holy duties, but they doe them as if they were about some other businesse ... when wee see men halting betwixt Christ and Baal, endeavouring to reconcile betwixt Rome, and the reformed Churches. ... When we see men professing true Religion, and the service of one God, dividing themselves, some betwixt God and Mammon; others betwixt god and their belly; a third betwixt God and some adored *Hellen;* a fourth betwixt God and his *Mecaenas;* a fifth betwixt God and the world. (Wilkinson, 34–36)

From opposed political camps, Herrick and Sclater use the texts of zeal passionately and with absolute assurance of being understood by a broad cultural community. But it is Wilkinson who demonstrates the special political purposes to which Puritan preachers and pamphleteers could—and would—put these texts.

DECENCY

In the face of this passion against the figure of Mother Church, one needs to remember how insistent and often persuasive the attractions of the *via media* could be. Most beautifully, George Herbert describes the moderation of "The British Church," the comely mother poised between the slattern of Geneva and the Whore of Rome:

> I joy, deare Mother, when I view
> Thy perfect lineaments and hue
>
> Both sweet and bright.
> Beautie in thee takes up her place,
> And dates her letters from thy face,
> When she doth write.
> A fine aspect in fit aray,
> Neither too mean, nor yet too gay,
> Shows who is best.[56]

Though Herbert's doctrinal alignments within the elegant web of the *Temple* are still difficult to assess,[57] this poem is a consummate statement of the *via media*. From the lips of Hooker, from the lips of Bishop Hall and of John Donne (in both poetry and prose), from the steady claims of the Church of England against the Brownists, against the sectaries and Marprelates of dissension, came a rhetoric affirming Anglican decency as Christian decorum, as in Archbishop Laud's citing of Cyprian in his Speech in Star Chamber on 14 June 1637:

> it becomes not *me* to answer them with the like, either *Levities* or *Revilings*, but to *speake* and *write* that only which becomes *Sacerdotum Dei*, a *Priest* of God.[58]

Decency emphasized the continuity of traditional practice and an acceptance of indifferent external forms, with mediation as a strong principle. Space, gesture, vestments, furniture, all became mediating functions of Holy Decency, of the sensible and sensuous instigation to proper piety through the Beauty of Holiness.

Early on, Richard Hooker defends sacred space with a shrewd political eye: "the very majesty and holiness of the place, where God is worshiped, hath, *in regard of us* great virtue, and efficacy for that it serveth as a sensible help to stir up the devotion."[59]

Defenses of Decency (implying attacks) continue throughout James's reign, but the controversy explodes during the reign of Charles and the primacy of his archbishop, William Laud.

Laudian reform is dogmatic on the subject of conformity even when it presents its demands with a palliating preface. Laud's celebrated *Conference with Mr. Fisher the Jesuit*, a good case in point, describes a debate that took place in 1622, but was not published until 1624 (with subsequent editions in 1626 and 1639). This later edition was published, Laud tells us, "to vindicate [his] reputation" (10) from the attacks of Puritan Divines. In his address to the king, Laud writes with energetic commitment:

> No one thing hath made Conscientious men more wavering in their owne mindes, or more apt, and easie to be drawne aside from the sincerity of Religion professed in the Church of England, then the Want of Uniforme and Decent Order in too many Churches of the Kingdome. . . . These Thoughts are they, and no other, which have made me labour so much as I have done, for Decency and an Orderly settlement of the Externall Worship of God in the Church. For of that which is Inward there can be no Witnesse among men, nor no Example for men. Now no Externall Action in the world can be Uniforme without some Ceremonies. And these in Religion, the Ancienter they bee, the better, so they may fit Time and Place.[60]

The rational but stubborn tone reflects the Laudian administrative style. Shuttling between an almost gentle persuasiveness and real contempt, Laud makes the same appeal to rationality that Lyndon B. Johnson did when he half-pleaded/half-demanded of the war protesters of the 1960s "Let us reason together." And the outraged response of both Laudian-era Puritans and Vietnam-era protesters was aimed at what struck them as irrelevantly rationalized and patronizingly conciliatory, as hypocritically "decent"—a posture of accommodation rather than a move toward the solution of problems.

There is an extraordinary pathos in much of the Anglican defense of Decency, sincere, angry, and yet bewildered at the ways in which Puritan polemic ignores their argument. *"Will you speake wickedly for Gods defence saith Job,"* wrote Richard Hooker. "Will you dipp your tongues in gall and your pennes in blood, when yee write and speake in his cause?"[61] (Just so, there was pathos—and a little comedy—in the bewilderment of the "Liberal" professoriate of the 1960s at the attacks on stately academic process.) Without denying the logical coherence of Holy Decency, one can still note the early political failure of the argument, and some of the reasons for that failure.

The Canons of 1640 were, in terms of church discipline, "conservative, even reactionary,"[62] and they precipitated the anger of Puritan leaders, political and religious, despite the introductory attempts at conciliation. Canon 7 tolerantly reminds the reader that "in the practice or omission of this Rite [bowing to the East], we desire that the rule of Charity, prescribed by the Apostle, may be observed, which is, That they which use this Rite despise not them who use it not, and that they who use it not, condemn not those that use it" (*CPW*, 1:993). The same Canon prescribes as *fit* and *convenient*, though *indifferent*, the placing of the Communion Table and its railing off, the approach to the table for communion (which "may be called Altar by us" [992]), and bowing toward the East. However nicely the claim for Indifference may have been made, all three of these prescriptions were incendiary to a portion of the Puritan polity, including Milton.

Laud's "Canons and Constitutions Ecclesiasticall"[63] concerning external devotion carried the same mixed message: these things and practices are indifferent but traditional and appropriate; therefore the Church *prescribes* them. Put baldly, despite professions of tolerance, prelatical authority takes precedence over individual conscience in the discipline of Laud's Church of England.

As the issue becomes increasingly politicized, Laud sets his formerly liberal Bishop Hall to defend his policies. At the outset, Hall had been highly accommodating: "As for our Ceremonies . . . they are but ceremonies to us; and such as wherein we put no holiness, but order, decency, convenience."[64] Thirty years later, in "Holy Decency in the Worship of God" (appended to *Christian Moderation*, 1640), his tone is far less lenient:

> many Christians . . . place a kind of holiness in a slovenly neglect, and so order themselves, as if they thought a nasty carelessness in God's services were most acceptable to him. . . . the very dogs are allowed free access and leave to lift up their legs at those holy tables where we partake of the Son of God. . . . *Let all things be done decently, and in order* . . . whereof *order* refers to persons and actions; *decency*, to the things done and the fashion of doing them. (*Works*, 6:492–93)

Consistency was not a primary virtue in these tract wars, not for Hall, not for Milton. The very day's political necessity effected changes in strategy and in conceptions of the discipline itself. This is not to absolve the participants of responsibility for the mutability of their major positions. One can still detect more and less consistency, more and less public honesty. Here Hall neatly combines prelatical and scriptural authority under the aegis of St. Paul who "sends us for the determination of decency, to the judgment of our Right Reason, Undebauched Nature, and Approved Custom" (*Works*, 6:492–93).

One neglected aspect of these stylistic wars is an intentionally crude, often even scatological, comedy.[65] Anglican apologists, from Hall to John Taylor the Water Poet, often use a comedy of outrage, that is, an *outraged* comedy ("the very dogs are allowed access . . ."), and are vilified in kind. Thomas Cheshire vigorously attacks the antiritualists in his sermon at St. Paul's; he complains of a woman "dandling and dancing her child upon the Lords holy Table, when she was gone, I drew near, and saw a great deal of *water* upon the Table; I verily thinke they were not *teares* of devotion, it was well it was no worse."[66] This outrage is deployed effectively, if rather surprisingly, from the Anglican pulpit, mixing easily with more sober matters of doctrine and discipline.

For the Puritans, Martin Marprelate had early defined the decorum for *outrageous* comedy:

> for jesting is lawfull by circumstances, even in the greatest matters. The circumstances of time, place and persons urged me thereunto. I never profaned the word in any jest. Other mirth I used as a covert, wherein I would bring the truth into light, the Lord being the Author both of mirth and gravity. Is it not lawfull in itselfe, for the truth to use either of these ways, when the circumstances doe make it lawfull?[67]

John Bastwick's remarkable and popular *Letany* (1639) provides a prime example of the Marprelate tradition.[68] To many, Bastwick was virtually a saint,[69] one of "those there [three] renowned living martyrs of the Lord Doctor *Bastwick*, Master *Burton*, and Master *Prin*."[70] Their triune martyrdom was a carefully cultivated icon: They "had their eares cut with the Knife made as it were *of the glasse of that glassie sea* and burnt with the fire thereof."[71] To Clarendon, Bastwick was "a half-witted, crack brained fellow . . . with some wit and much malice" (*Rebellion*, 1:266). Both wit and malice show in this description of Archbishop Laud's "decent" progress through the streets of London:

> Againe, if you should meet him, comming dayly from the starchamber, and see what pompe grandeur and magnificence he goeth in; the whole multitude standing bare where ever he passeth, having also a great number of Gentlemen, and other servants waiting on him, al uncovered, some of them cariying up his tayle, for the better breaking and venting of his wind & easing of his holy body (for it is full of holes) others going before him and calling to the folke before them, to put off their hats and to give place crying roome, roome, my Lords grace is coming, tumbling downe and thrusting aside the little children a playing there: flinging and tossing the poore costermongers and souce-wives fruit and pluddings [puddings], baskets and all into the Thames (though they hindered not their passage) to shew the greatnes of his state and the promptitude of their service, to the utter undoing and perishing of those allready indigent creatures . . . yet one can scarce keepe from laughter, to see the [d]rollery of it, and considering the Whole passages of the businesse with the variety of the actions, hearing on the one side, the noyse of the Gentlemen crying roome, &

> cursing all that meet them and that but seeme to hinder their passage & on the other side seeing the wayling mourning and Lamentation the women make crying out save my puddings, save my codlings for the Lords sake, the poore tripes and apples in the meane tyme swimming like frogs about the Thames making way for his Grace to goe home againe. (*Letany*, 6)

John Lilburne wrote that *Letany* "is all full of wit. . . . hee made that booke to make himselfe merry. . . . not much soliditie . . . but onely mirth" (*Triall*, 36). Surely it is brilliant propaganda, propaganda as "a kind of rhetoric. . . . disallowing readers their power to interpret."[72] Here is broad ridicule of the "upstart" Laud and his sycophants; burlesque of his "decent" ceremony that shrewdly transforms it into a vain display; sentimental concern for the children and the poor women cast aside by this great shepherd turned dignitary—a whole scene, almost Jonsonian in its variety and its effect, devoted to destroying the decorum of the Archbishop's progress. "To the Courteous Reader" prescribes the polemical uses of the preceding scene:

> [This will] stirre up in thee a Christian hatred . . . a pious zeale and fervent indignation against all the damnable inventions and barterings of all those Fishmongers. . . . our dayly *letany* praying from *plague pestilence* and *famine,* frome *Bishops Priests* and *Deacons good Lord deliver us.* (*Letany*, 10)

This Marprelate tradition continues to thrive in the 1640s, with the bishops as favorite targets:

> I hope to see some of those bigg bellied Bishops like so many false fellowes, for all their knacks and knaveries, to shake their shanks upon a Gallowes: For if GREGORY once get them under his hands, all their tricks and trumperies will not serve their turne.[73]

The comic insults that Milton inflicts (not always successfully) on his opponents, like the "hot-liver'd grammarians" of *Animadversions* (*CPW,* 1:666), are attempts to demolish Anglican decency through comedy.[74] Implicit in these attacks is a kind of bluff claim that Decency is prissy and unmanly.

"Fools," Milton writes, "who would teach men to read more decently then God thought good to write" (*CPW,* 1:903).

The class issues implicit in Bastwick's invective are taken up by the other side in the reiterated attacks on the ignorant, the tub preachers, the writers of tracts and on whole congregations: "God forbid that wee should live to see God, that is the God of decency, served in such sort and manner, as Plowmen come home from their ploughes."[75] "This is the *misery*; 'tis superstition now adaies for any man to come with more *Reverence* into a *Church* then a *Tinker* and his *Bitch*" (*Star Chamber*, 46–47).

Because of these ecclesiological and political accretions, by the 1640s the "God of decency" has become a thorn intestine to the Church of England. In its *de facto* defining of the indefinite, its mandating of things indifferent, Holy Decency outraged the Puritans, and sometimes even its own ideological neighbors. Lord Falkland, for example, in his important speech on Episcopacy, opposes Root and Branch extirpation but makes a serious charge against decency:

> some Bishops and their adherents . . . have beene the destruction of unitie under pretence of uniformity to have brought in superstition, and scandall, under the titles of reverence, and decency: to have defil'd our Church; by adorning our Churches; to have slackned the strictnesse of that union which was formerly betweene us, and those of our religion beyond the sea, an action as unpoliticke, as ungodly.[76]

Style, the performance style of religious discipline, was political. *Decency* was a call to conservative values affirming tradition and the sense of continuity; it was hierarchical, yet it claimed to minimize distinctions, to mediate between extremes, between Rome and Geneva, between superstition and carelessness, between authoritarianism and license. Its symbol was ameliorative: Mother Church—beautiful, feminine, loving, forgiving.

And it was precisely the Decency of Mother Church that Puritan activists sought to destroy through ridicule and contempt, a kind of masculinist swagger and aggressiveness. Specifically, such rhetoric demolishes Laudian decorum: "you account and call that onely *Decent* in the *worship* of *God*, which either your selfe, or that Whore of *Babylon* hath devised for *Decent*. . . . Will *Christ* (trow you) aporove that for *decent* in his *Spouse*, which is the *Whores* Fashion."[77] Of the 40 words in the passage, 29 are monosyllabic: Henry Burton is *assaulting* Laud, masculine against feminine. Puritans construe Anglican decency as a pseudo-maternal decorum of superficial nurture, while zeal is, in Wilkinson's words, "of a most masculine disengaged couragious Nature, free from all base and servile feares, it yeelds to no encounters, but it is encreased by opposition" (*Lukewarmnesse*, 20–21).

In their first attack on Bishop Hall, SMECTYMNUUS complain of the prelatical party:

> All of their speech is of the *Church, the Church*; no mention of the *Scriptures, of God the Father*; but all of the *Mother the Church*. Much like as they write certain *Aethiopians*, that by reason they use no marriage, but promiscuously company together, the children onely follow the *Mother*, the *Father* and his name is in no request, but the *Mother* hath all the reputation.[78]

Hall responds indignantly to the comparison with "Aethiopian strumpets,"[79] but the trope of pejorative feminizing thrives.[80] Of the adornment of the Scripture, here melded to the Church by the prelates, Milton writes in *Of Reformation* that they thought the

> plaine and homespun verity of *Christs* Gospell unfit any longer to hold their Lordships acquaintance, unlesse the poore threadbare Matron were put into better clothes; her chast and modest vaile surrounded with celestiall beames they overlai'd with wanton *tresses*, and in a flaring tire bespeckl'd her with all the gaudy allurements of a Whore. (*CPW*, 1:557)

Milton will subtly expand this "trope or figure" of the "common Mother" (*CPW*, 1:727) in the *Animadversions* (see chapter 4).

Anglican decency ultimately survived the revolution, outlived, and out-maneuvered, the Good Old Cause. But for many Englishmen of the 1640s, perhaps for most of the Puritans, surely for John Milton, Decency was a specious and hypocritical veneer on a failing religious discipline, as a witty wisp of malice will remind us in *Paradise Lost*, where Satan's disguise as "stripling cherub" ends: "His habit fit for speed succinct, and held / Before his decent steps a silver wand" (3.643–44).

INDIFFERENCE

Behind the concept of the *via media* and decency lay the concept of Indifference. *Ta Adiaphora* still play(s) a significant role in Christian theology. During the English Reformation, the concept was often debated, and more often assumed, as the starting point for defining discipline outside the specific authorizations of Scripture. All parties, all sects, recognized the term, and all defined its usefulness territorially. The Church Fathers wrote on it at length; the Reformers accepted and used it; the Church of England assumed its practicality and utility. Every organized segment of Christianity, one by one, would in fact lay claim to the concept, as each segment matured into a functioning organization with rights to the distribution of assets and honors. Each saw in the doctrine of Indifference the warrant to determine what were and were not "things indifferent" and to express that determination in the enforcement of ritual and architecture, in the ownership and uses of property, and generally in the exercise of para-scriptural authority.

I present here a bare sampling of the literature on Indifference, focusing on its immediate use for the period. Originally intended to obviate or resolve sectarian divisiveness, Indifference instead became another source of contention between Anglican and Puritan, especially in the first half of the seventeenth century. There are some glowing texts that propose the proper definition of Indifference and its application. And there is convincing evidence that the unilateral definition of Indifference becomes more and more acceptable to each group as that group moves toward ecclesiastical hegemony. Henry Robinson reminds us that demands for the enforcement of the Directory for Worship are being made by those who had railed against the enforced use of the *Book of Common Prayer* five years earlier.[81] A Royalist attack on the Solemn League and Covenant shrewdly complains of those "who have alwaies cryed out for Liberty of conscience, not suffering themselves to be limited in a Ceremony or thing indifferent . . . thus Imperiously Tyrranize over other mens Consciences, forcing upon them Oath after Oath, Covenant after Covenant."[82] On the other side, George Gillespie can scold Robinson's *Liberty of Conscience* for its "detestable indifferencie or neutrality,"[83] while quoting Brightman to condemn the Church of England as Laodicea. One person's Indifference is another person's Sin.

The Parker Society Reprints are full of passages which reveal the ideological alignment of the speaker through his attitude toward "scandal," toward the privileging of individual conscience over conformity to an indifferent position. *Scandal* in fact generally comes to mean egregious imposition upon the individual conscience, usually in matters claimed as indifferent. Early on, Tyndale identifies the ambivalences to come and the sheer convenience of the term. The stiff polemical attitude of 1530 shows in his *Answer to Sir Thomas More's Dialogue:* "thing that are but men's traditions, and all indifferent things which we may be as well without as with, may well be put down for this dishonouring of God through the abuse."[84] The more conservative statement comes in 1535: "he that knoweth the intent of the law and of works . . . shall never condemn his brother, or break unity with him, in those things which Christ never commanded, but left indifferent."[85] Archbishop Cranmer's Proclamation of Feb. 6, 1548 reports that Edward VI "chargeth and commandeth, that no manner of person . . . do omit, leave undone, change, alter, or innovate any order, rite, or ceremony commonly used and frequented in the church of England, and *not commanded to be left undone* at any time in the reign of our late sovereign lord, his highness' father" (my italics).[86]

The "indifferent" becomes mandatable by human authority. Martin Bucer's response in *Mynd and Exposition* to this
claim for "Christyan obedyence [in] observacion of all thinges
indifferent, commanded by auctoritie," is firm and proleptic
of the Miltonic position: "The obedience and auctoritie of
Christians consysteth nether in commandinge nor observinge,
but rather royting up all such plants not planted by the
heavenly father."[87] By 1574 the political lines are clearly drawn.
In his celebrated exchanges with Thomas Cartwright,
Archbishop Whitgift defends current church practice. Perhaps
his most effective demonstration is in the eight arguments
from Calvin. God has made plain in Scripture what is necessary
to salvation. He has delegated to His Church non-Scriptural
ceremonies and discipline. A Christian man should obey "such
constitutions" which

> taketh not liberty from the conscience, because they be not made
> to be perpetual and inviolable, but to be altered as time, occasion,
> and necessity, requireth . . . all ought to obey such ordinances, for
> charity's sake . . . if a man do violate them by ignorance or
> forgetfulness, he doth not offend; if by contempt or stubbornness,
> he doth greatly offend. . . . confusion (which is to suffer every man
> to do what he list) is the seed of contention and brawling. . . . the
> true ministers of God be not contentious, neither yet the churches
> of God.[88]

But the neutralist-appearing position, intended to mollify,
to bridge, to embrace the opposition, can turn into an abrasive
fiat: "of ceremonies, none at all [to be refused], which tend
either unto order, comeliness, or edification."[89]

Though the sixteenth century Reformers tried to put a brave
face on the universal acceptability of Indifference, they failed
to eliminate the internal subversive element of individual
conscience. Thomas Wilson's definition shows the potency of
emphasis in the defining of religious terms:

> [Indifferent] Something which is neyther commanded of God, nor
> forbid, but of a middle nature; . . . Wherein yet nothing must be
> appointed to bee done, contrary to order, comelinesse, or
> edification. See Rom. 14, 1 Corinth. 14. throughout. . . . Learned

> Divines affirme . . . that things In-different, . . . ceasse to be such
> when any of these conditions following are annexed unto them. 1.
> Compulsion. 2. Opinion of worship, necessity, or merit. 3. Scandall
> and offence. 4. Enterance, and occasion of abuse, or Idolatry. 5.
> Any hinderance to truth or edification, or obscuring, and darkning
> of Religion and piety by them, though they should containe no
> other evill in them.[90]

All of these "conditions" are potential challenges of the
individual conscience, and all were challenged by those
outside, or gingerly within, the Church of England.

When does discipline move from indifferent to essential?
The debate becomes critical: "they would have us at the
very first dash sweare in a damnable Heresie, that matters
necessary to salvation are contained in the Discipline of our
Church."[91]

Puritans decry *imposition* especially: "If it be a thing
indifferent, why is it then so rigidly imposed, as a thing of
absolute *necessity* to be observed: this destroyes the nature
of a thing indifferent, which the Scripture condemneth."[92]
There is a virtual genre of attacks on the mis-definitions of
Indifferency (on Roman errors as well as those of Canterbury):
one writer refers to "the wildernesse of unbounded Indifferency,"[93] another to the "tyrannous lawes made upon
indifferent things, against our Christian libertie";[94] a third
declares that "The urging of uniformity in all indifferent things
as necessary to unity is a most false principle."[95] John Tombes
connects the imposition of indifferent things to will-worship:

> All wil-worship at first conception hath pretence of order and
> decency, perhaps the things in which it is placed are taken but as
> indifferent, which yet in processe of time gaine opinion of holinesse
> and necessity to that end, and so bring the conscience into
> bondage.[96]

SMECTYMNUUS writes of "a thing indifferent (which
stands as a wall of separation betwixt us and our brethren)";[97]
and, in 1646, Samuel Rutherford glosses the Puritan argument with the blunt "Not to command, [in Scripture] is to
forbid."[98]

The most powerful statement, and one which Milton knew, was that of Robert Greville, Lord Brooke, *A Discourse Opening The Nature Of That Episcopacie, Which Is Exercised In England* (1641). Detailed, measured, and often eloquent, Brooke's *Discourse* (happily reprinted in William Haller's *Tracts on Liberty*)[99] provides evidence for the seriousness of the theological debates *as politics*—extended, impassioned, and practical, concerned with contemporary *usage*, not precept. (The present-day politics of abortion may be the closest analogue.) Don M. Wolfe has summarized the *Discourse* with sympathy (*CPW*, 1:145–48); and he has specifically praised the treatment of Indifferency:

> Brooke wrote with more arresting and original logic than any pamphleteer of his day, Anglican or Puritan. In an absolute sense nothing is indifferent, no gesture, ceremony, or chalice: "but to *our understanding*, some things seeme so, for want of Good light." Since no mind sees the absolute, who is to decide what is indifferent? (*CPW*, 1:146)

Brooke's astuteness extends to the secular: "[The bishops] doe really set Lawes in *State* matters, under the notion of Indifferent; so that the *Subjects Liberty*, or propriety in goods, *They* compasse with their Net of *Indifferencie*; which they make heavie with the plummet of great penalties" (*Tracts*, 2:56). Brooke separates the personal adherence to Scripture from that to things indifferent: "In expounding of Scripture, the *Scripture*; but in finding out what is *indifferent, Recta Ratio* right reason, must be Judge" (*Tracts*, 2:57). Chapter 5 analyzes the Nature of Indifference, concluding: "No Thing, No Act, is *Indifferent* in *Se*, in *Re*, in it selfe, in the thing; but either *necessary* to be done, (if *Best*) or *unlawfull* to be done, if *Bad*, or *lesse Good, pro hoc statu*" (*Tracts*, 2:70).

The argument on indifferency is the center of Brooke's powerful tract, presented with the kind of immediacy that would attract the zealous, especially those needing to point to specific "scandals" that were truly scandalous to a wide Puritan audience:

the Reading of the Booke of *Sports* (first invented by themselves [the Bishops]) that monstrous and prodigious late *Oath,* with divers new *Canons,* not enjoyned by *Parlament,* or any other Legall authority, I might adde their bare bidding forme of Prayer, *Second Service* at the *Altar;* (though it could not be heard) an illegal Oath of *Canonical* Obedience, (blind devotion). . . . placing the Communion Table *Altar-wise;* Railing it in; Bowing to it; Receiving at it etc. . . . their most unchristian *Oath Ex Officio,* (fouler than the foulest dregges of that cruell *Inquisition*) at one blow cutting asunder all the nerves, not onely of *positive,* but *morall, naturall* Lawes; all which (being tender of the least graine of mans liberty) have entrusted with this *Universall* maxime, *Nemo tenctur se prodere,* No man is bound to betraye himselfe. (*Tracts,* 2:60)

This disciplined passion provides a model for Milton's political style. And, as Don Wolfe has suggested, *A Discourse* may have helped to crystallize Milton's incipient Independency. In any case, this powerful piece was one of the few of the period to evidence anything approaching Milton's rhetorical intensity and breadth. On the question of Indifferency, Brooke's analysis became for the Puritans a classic and final statement.

Or did Milton provide a model for Lord Brooke? *Of Reformation* appeared in May of 1641, *A Discourse* in November of that year. There is no need to make the texts compete for precedence, but the similarities are striking on this topic, including an interesting concern for emigration:

What more binding then Conscience? what more free then *indifferency?* cruel then must that *indifferency* needs be that shall violate the strict necessity of Conscience, merciles, and inhumane that free choyse, and liberty that shall break asunder the bonds of Religion . . . I shall beleeve there cannot be a more illboding signe to a Nation . . . then when the Inhabitants, to avoid insufferable grievances at home, are inforc'd by heaps to forsake their native Country.[100]

Perhaps it is only another commonplace, shared by Lord Saye and Seale, who also laments those "thrust out of the Land, and cut off from their native Countrey" because they could not accept the Bishops' imposition of ceremonies termed "indifferent."[101]

Bishop Hall accuses the Puritans of "in-decency" for not observing indifferent practices; Lewis Hewes accuses the Church of England of indecency for not *eschewing* the indifferent.[102] Milton recognizes both the weight and the indeterminacy of the concept when he indentifies "Those burdens impos'd not by necessity . . . but laid upon our necks by the strange wilfulnesse and wantonnesse of a needlesse and jolly persecuter call'd Indifference" (*CPW*, 1:925). Like *Zeal*, like *Decency*, *Indifferency* divides Christian from Christian in the 1630s and 1640s in England, inflaming antagonisms rather than providing neutral space for religious observance and reconciliation.

BLIND MOUTHS

One of the most highly contested sites of the ideological battles of this period is the pulpit, where the spectrum of theological and ecclesiological differences was argued, often with an immediately effective passion. Milton's focus at this time is on the ecclesiological, on church discipline as persuasion. Differences over celebration of the Eucharist were important and cacophonous, but Milton largely ignores them. He prefers the spirited debates on the discipline of the Church to theological debate (which often descended into brawl) on the Eucharist, on paedobaptism, on the numerology of Apocalypse. Is it a disdain for the impractical, the unknowable? Or is it Milton's recognition of those things that God has "suppressed in night / To none communicable in earth or Heaven" (*PL*, 7.120–24)? I suspect the former. For all his taste for the sublime, Milton was a practical man, one acutely aware of man's human domain and his limitations. For him, at this time, the sermon was the confluence of several immediate concerns which involve and stimulate political as well as ecclesiastic argument. The centrality of The Book in European Protestantism ensures the critical importance of the sermon in the exposition and promulgation of Christian enlightenment and ultimately salvation. The resulting concern for the appropriateness and efficacy of style is well put by John Calvin: "when that rough and in a manner rude simplicity doth raise up a greater reverence of it selfe than any Rhetoricians eloquence, what may wee judge but that there is a more mightie strength of truth in the holy Scripture, than that it needeth any Art of words?"[103]

English Protestantism adopted and shared these emphases, translating continental Reformers like John Weigand:

> God hath not rolled up his doctrine in darknesse . . . hee hath set it forth, symply, playnly and most openly, unto all folkes and would have al to understand it. I pray thee, what is more simple and more plain then Christs owne Sermons be? Hee frameth himself after the capacitie of the learners, hee useth such common and homely manner of speech, as the vulgar people doe.[104]

The history of the English sermon continues to be well served, including the genre's potential for challenging ecclesiastical authority.[105] I here emphasize the controversial aspects of the genre in the period of the 1630s and 1640s. I shall try to remember Kevin Sharpe's warning against assuming major political effect from the average printed sermon,[106] while presenting evidence to the contrary. Stephen Marshall's reputation is a formidable example, with quite specific attributions of influence, such as the following: "I believe your bare example in this businesse hath swayed more with many of our Brethren in these parts of *Essex*, then their owne judgements: . . . they have trusted to your eyes and shut their owne."[107] The evidence, from Clarendon and from contemporary scholarship, is substantial.

To present readers, the early seventeenth century sermon means Andrewes and Donne, popular court preachers of enormous learning and style. Puritans attacked the oratorical styles of both men (though, so far as I know, not their persons), Andrewes's for its compression, Donne's for its amplitude— and both for their displays of learning and of art.

Donne's first printed sermon has a particular relevance. Delivered on the 15th of September, 1622, it focuses deliberately on the politics of preaching, a defense of James I's

Directions for Preachers,[108] which was itself a rather angry response to the pulpit criticism of the Spanish marriage proposed for Prince Charles and the reluctant Infanta. Donne's sermon is dedicated to James's notorious favorite, the Duke of Buckingham, in one of the clergyman's more obvious demonstrations of *realpoetik*, with its lavish praise of James and its party-line constriction of the preacher's role. Yet it *is* Donne, a brilliantly argued plea for conformity, for the muting of Puritan zeal:

> for without order, an armie is but a great Ryot; and without this decencie, this peace-ablenesse, this discretion, this order, zeale is but fury, and such preaching is but to the obduration of ill, not to the edification of good Christians. . . . For when there is not an uniforme, a comely, an orderly presenting of matters of faith, faith it selfe growes loose, and loses her estimation; and preaching in the *Church* comes to bee as pleading at the Barre, and not so well.[109]

The *Directions* which Donne defends makes simplistic definitions, but they are definitions which resound into the later decades:

> His Majesty therfore cals us to look, Quid primum, when we received the Reformation in this Kingdom, by what meanes, (as his Majestie expresseth it) Papistry was driven out, and Puritanisme kept out, and wee delivered from the Superstition of the Papist, and the madnesse of the Anabaptists, as before hee expresseth it. (*Sermons*, 4:202)

The doctrine which effected "this great cure," Donne tells us, "is contained in the two *Catechismes* in the 39. *Articles*, and in the 2. Bookes of Homilies" (202–3). "This great cure" will be attacked by the Puritans.

While current literary history remembers Donne's sermons, William Haller's earlier history (like Clarendon's) noted the steady growth and immense influence of Puritan preaching, including the remarkable program of "puritan feoffees, that group of preachers, lawyers, and rich citizens who had been buying impropriations for the support of preaching."[110] In Samuel Hieron's 1616 tract, we see an already established political-stylistic position: "there is no certainty of any particular mans salvation, without ministeriall Teaching. . . . he who thinks to be saved without preaching, shal be damned. . . . Honour and esteeme is the due of preaching."[111]

But there is contempt for a "reading Ministry," (36) presumably one which reads the Homilies that Donne recommends above. Behind the sermon is the Word, "the substantial Word of God, the second Person in the Trinity . . . the written and sounding Word . . . the working and effectual Word"; the ardor climaxes in "The Word is a Love-Letter from God."[112] That Word is the soul of preaching. Lord Falkland will accuse the Bishops of having "brought in catechizing onely to thrust out preaching" (*Episcopacy*, 5). A later anonymous commentator will oppose an able and praying ministry to "the reading of a publique liturgie . . . the cold and powerles use of homilies, they being both of them an alike, uncouth, and *Bab[ylon]ish* publike mysteriall serving of God and his church."[113]

Hieron nicely reflects Baconian influence, too, when he attacks "[too] much exactnesse: as when men strive to have everie word in print . . . and do affect termes more then matter": "It is the pithie plainnesse, which is the beautie of preaching. A text well opened, handsomely divided, instructions familiarly raised, substantially proved by Scripture, powerfully pressed upon the hidden man of the heart, faithfully applied to the soule and conscience of the hearer" (*Dignity*, 31, 40). Hieron counsels the righteous: "Woe to the servant, that wrappeth his talent in a napkin, and encreaseth not his Masters gaine. God grant such idle and slothfull Ministers grace to know their office, and to do it: If not, God give the people grace to know them, & to shun them, and to flie from them" (*Dignity*, 50).

That talent which is death to hide meant many things to Milton and to his contemporaries; certainly he did not view it as restricted to his study.

When John Preston followed John Donne as Lecturer at Lincoln's Inn, the chapel had to be enlarged to house those who came to hear him preach there.[114] One of Emanuel

College's most illustrious sons, he was a major influence on the preachers and writers of the Puritan persuasion. In the last years of James's reign, Preston offered the Puritans some hope of influence over Prince Charles. Hugh Trevor-Roper notes Preston's reputation as "the greatest pulpit-monger in England," one whom Buckingham at one time nominated as Lord Keeper.[115] Preston died in 1628, but his reputation and his prescriptions for powerful preaching remained alive for decades. His sermons were published posthumously, having been carefully preserved and circulated in manuscript. The powerful "Pattern of Wholesome Words. Or Pauls charge to Timothy, in A Treatise on 2 *Tim.* 1.13" is printed in 1658 with *The Riches Of Mercy To Men in Misery.* Preston is antiacademic, antiornamental, anticomplex. The words of a minister must be wholesome, he says,

> not onely pleasing to the pallat, and delightful to the taste, as some Sermons that are neatly made which like music tickles the ears for the present, but leave no fruit behinde them . . . they must be pure words, no *Heterogenea* must be mixed . . . [avoid] squinty-eyed words that speak not plainly, but border on errour . . . [let] their termes be not too high, so that the people understand them not . . . it is the fault of some to preach University Sermons to the people, which they have made for a more learned auditory . . . what racking is there of wits to please the people, and what choise of phrases, when plain preaching profits more . . . the Word is not to be interpreted but by the Word; to say this is the sense, because *Augustine, Calvin,* and other Writers say so, it is not reason enough; if we must give a sence it must be because the litteral sence is so . . . [a minister] is a Minister of the Gospel not of humane learning.[116]

Preston gives specific cautions on adornment, for example, against light or metrical speechifying, "that it stand not upon paranomasias and verbal conceits, that it do tickle the ears and move laughter, or poetical allusions, as the *hire of a whore* might not be brought into the temple though it was silver" (312). Latin is not to be used even if translated afterward (313). The eloquence "that adorns a speech" may not agree with "the gravity of the Word" (313). "Why do we go into the wide waste to gather flowers, when the Scripture is the garden of Eden?" (326).

Preston is a *locus classicus* for construing the Puritan debate on sermons. The cautions he emphasizes toward the display of learning or style are picked up by his successors and become sharply anti-intellectual in the 1630s and 1640s. In the first of the series of monthly Fast sermons, Cornelius Burges makes preaching an exclusively Puritan virtue: "our blind guides and Idol Shepherds" are against preaching, so that "it is made a matter of scorne, and become the odious Character of a *Puritan* to be an assiduous Preacher!" Assiduous preaching is not like the preaching of the prelatical church which is "onely a frigid, toothlesse discourse, never piercing deeper than the eare."[117] John Fenwick writes:

> They set up a new Kinde of reading-preaching, and suppresse sound preaching, silence and suspend the orthodox Preachers, and fill their places with Metaphysicall, cloudy-brain'd Humanists, Arminian and Popish fellowes, who usually stuffe their Sermons out of *Aristotles* Ethicks, and the Fryars Postills.[118]

Elizabeth Warren will later speak simply and with assurance: "How do they then mistake themselves, who (soaring aloft in fruitlesse speculations) do think it incompatible with the calling of Ministers, to stoop to the capacities of the simple and untrained."[119] Six years later, Robert Harris will praise John Bradford for being "resolved, with a good orator, to speak beneath himself rather than above his auditory"; and he identifies other aspects of good Puritan preaching that will shape discourse for some years: "his eloquence was confessedly great, that is native, masculine, modest, in one, heavenly."[120]

Lord Brooke attacks the Bishops for their "Criticall, Cabalisticall, Scepticall, Scholasticall Learning: which fills the head with empty, aeriall, notions; but gives no sound food to the Reasonable part of man" (*Discourse*, 10). Thomas Case attacks the polished sermon as spoon-feeding: "oyled Sermons, plausible discourses that may not disquiet and perplex tender consciences."[121] "Why must [the Minister] have Hebrew, Greek and Latin? Cannot the truthes of the *Gospel* be spoken by *plain Englishmen?"* asks another unidentified writer.[122] John Cotton writes that "preaching in the wisedome of words, (or in carnall eloquence) is forbidden."[123] The 1645 *Directory For the Publique worship of God* assumes that ministers will have "skill in the Originall Languages" but urges the "abstaining also from an unprofitable use of unknowne Tongues, strange phrases, and cadences of sounds and words, sparingly citing sentences of Ecclesiasticall, or other humane Writers, ancient or moderne, be they never so elegant."[124]

Prelatical pride in the learning and style of the Church of England was, in many ways, justified: "there are at this day more learned men in this Land, in this one kingdom; then are to bee found among all the Ministers of the Religion in . . . (to speake in a word) all *Europe* besides."[125] The underside of that reputation for elegant learning was evident in the charges of neglect of pastoral duties, neglect of preaching especially, multiple livings, the "will-worshiping" focus on a "learned auditory"—worldliness in the decorum of the preacher as against pious devotion to exposition of the Word. By 1642 that worldliness is explicitly labeled as political propaganda: "The world hath been long abus'd by *Court-Preachers* . . . first crying up the *sole Divinity* of *Monarchy* in generall, and then (what must follow) the *absolutenesse* of this in the *Kings sole Person*."[126]

On the other side, John Taylor, prolific "Water Poet," focuses on the tub preacher in Anglican terms, the logical opposite of the learned minister. His satire of Samuel Howe is effective and conventional:

> For when his speech lack'd either sence or weight,
> He made it up in measure and conceit.
> 'Gainst Schooles, and learning he exclaimed amain,
> Tongues, Science, Logick, Rhetorick, all are vain,
> And wisdome much unfitting for a Preacher,
> Because the Spirit is the only teacher.[127]

In the conceiving of his own last great poems, would Milton remember Taylor's arrogant attack on arrogance in *A Swarme?*

Some there have been, so malapertly mad,
To guesse what talk Christ with the Doctors had:
Where Eden's garden was, or paradise,
What God did before the world he fram'd,
And where hell stands (appointed for the damn'd)
These curious Constables would search and peepe
Through heaven, earth, sea, aire, and th' infernal deep.

(Swarme, 15)

In the caricature of Puritan preaching, intellectual over-reaching accompanies low birth. Vanity, hypocrisy, ignorance, acquisitiveness, above all, *verbosity*, became the hallmarks of the tub-preacher, a cartoon image long in the making (among eminent contributors were Shakespeare and Jonson). Bishop Hall gives his tub-preachers cartoonish low-brow names: "and for a Doctor, who, and where, and what? *John a Nokes,* and *John a Stiles,* the Elders; *Smug the Smith,* a Deacon; and whom, or what should these rule, but themselves, and their plough-shares?" (*Works,* 4:269). And one of Milton's college-mates, John Cleveland, parodies preacherly stances: "Such pious gagle at the Eye, such a melodious twange at the nose, such a splay mouth drawn dry, as it were, edifying the eare in private."[128]

But under the cartoonery is the essential class issue: "Mechanick persons, for the most part unlectured grooms, *Coachmen, Feltmakers, Coblers, Weavers, Glovers,* hauking *Ironmongers* walking after the imaginations of their owne hearts," with "wits as rusty as a peece of old Iron which has been broken and throwne on the dunghill."[129] Christ chose "mechanics" to show his power, but now there are educated men available, no need for those "in the forenoone making a hat, or rubbing a horse, in the after-noone preaching a Sermon."[130] In 1645, Martin Mar-Priest (thought to be Richard Overton) will sneer at that attitude: "our *Presbyters* are *University-men,* not like the mechanick Primitive *Presbyters,* like *Fishermen, Tent-makers,* or such inferiour fellowes as *Paul,* the *scumme or offscouring of the World.*"[131]

Along with the contempt there is recognition of the power, the danger of the Puritan preacher: "all order, and decent comelynesse is thrust out of the Church . . . and in the place thereof is most nasty filthy, Loathsome slovenry and beastlinesse, our Doctrines being vented in long and tedious Sermons, to move and stirre the people to Rebellion."[132] As for these "raging Ministers": "*Machiavell* is their Master, whose doctrine was *Leonine assuere vulpinum* to peece out the Lyons skinne with the Foxes; like Satan that roaring Lyon, they thirst for bloud, and like Butchers dogges they yelpe for it" (Symmons, 74). Anglican condescension had turned into an experienced political alarm. The political and ecclesiastical communities, of the 1630s and 1640s especially, produced some extraordinary conformities: amongst the Anglicans an appetite for an elaborate and perhaps suspiciously traditional ritual, along with a contempt for extempore garrulity; amongst the Puritans, a stunning capacity for sermons. Certainly the silencing of those preachers addressing what Donne called "great and curious Auditories" (Donne, *Sermons*, 4:205) contributed importantly to the collapse of Archbishop Laud and ultimately to the fall of Charles.

The best-known attack on the nonpreaching ministry and, by implication, on the suppression of preaching, is, of course, "Lycidas." Much has been done to examine the context of Milton's great poem, from the early work of William Haller and the useful collections by Scott Elledge and C. A. Patrides to the more recent work of David Norbrook (see esp. Norbrook, *Poetry and Politics*, 264–85). I would like now to look at how one detail of this poetic text is specifically influenced by the matters I have just examined.

Haller describes Laud's restrictions on lecturers in 1629 and his dissolution of the Puritan feoffees in 1633; but Puritan preaching was far from eradicated by such measures. The 1630s were a time when "the Puritanism of conventicle and tub, in a word, of populistic Puritanism began to flourish" (*Rise*, 262). This is the age when the trials and punishment of Bastwick, Burton, and Prynne—those three loud proclaimers shorn of their ears on June 30, 1637—became great signifying events of the decade. The "*three eminent persons of the three* most noble Professions in the Kingdom, Divinity, Law, Physick"[133] were

surely the most celebrated martyrs of the 1630s.[134] This is the
age when Bishop Matthew Wren was accused of silencing 50
or 60 preaching ministers and bringing in "idle drones, dumb
curres";[135] this is the age of the suppression of the kerygma,
the preaching voice, by what Milton will brilliantly label "the
strangle of silence" (*CPW,* 1:669). That silencing becomes a
critical center of the debate on the prelacy.

Blind guides and *dumb dogs* were almost ubiquitous, and
often paired, as terms for the venal clergy. It is Milton who
fused the images in the passage from "Lycidas":

> Blind mouths! That scarce themselves know how to hold
> A Sheep-hook, or have learn'd aught else the least
> That to the faithful Herdman's art belongs!   (119–21)

The synergy of the two contemptuous epithets was widely
recognized from Scripture. Isaiah had written,

> His watchmen *are* blind: they are all ignorant. They *are* all dumb
> dogs, they cannot bark; sleeping, lying down, loving to slumber.
> Yea, *they are* greedy dogs *which* can never have enough, and they
> *are* shepherds *that* cannot understand: they all look to their own
> way, every one for his gain, from his quarter. (Isa. 56.10–11)

In Matthew, the blind guides are associated with mouths:

> Let them [the Pharisees] alone; they be blind leaders of the blind.
> (15:14)
> Do not ye yet understand, that whatsoever entereth in at the mouth
> goeth into the belly, and is cast out into the draught? But those
> things which proceed out of the mouth come forth from the heart;
> and they defile the man. (15.17–18)

The passage on eating explains the passage on seeing. An even
heavier emphasis on blindness appears in Matthew 23, the
generation of vipers chapter, which attacks specious, greedy,
guides as *typhlos*—blind—and relates that blindness to pride,
greed, and petty legalism (23.13–16).

The second image has a long pedigree from Isaiah and
Jeremiah to Spenser. The corrupted shepherd is described as

an unspeaking minister or dumb dog. The attacks on the *Book of Common Prayer*, and later on the *Directory for Public Worship*, regularly invoke this image of dumbness in ministers or congregation or both, a dumbness often equated with the mouthing of set prayers, with rote congregational responses. In Puritan polemic, in the Parliament, and in the streets, *dumbness* applies to those modes of set discourse opposed to inspired preaching; it applies, too, to the refusal to preach, and to the effect of multiple livings.

Making epithets stick (good and bad) was one of the main purposes of the tract wars, and "Blind Guides" and "Dumb Dogs" become the spearheads of much debate from 1633 to 1646 at least. Occasionally an epithet is seized by the opposition; for Laud "Blind guides" are the "Sects" and "Separatists" (*Jesuite*, sig.*v). Most often the two terms are applied to the prelates and their church officers, as a few quotations will show. Though these postdate "Lycidas," they all share the same zealous and bitter tonality that characterizes the digression in Milton's poem.

In the speech cited above, Lord Falkland writes: "Bishops are the dogges in the manger, to have neither preached themselves, nor employ those that should, nor sufferd those that would." (*Episcopacy*, 5) In an anonymous tract of 1640 attacking Laud, bishops are accused of making

> bare reading Ministers [that is, users of prayerbooks and books of homilies] . . . they heare out of *Gods* word, that they are blind and dumb dogs (*Esay*, 56). . . . In tollerating them to be so . . . the people are as Sheep without a Shepherd Mat. 9, Mat. 15.14.[136]

In *The Humble Petition* of 1640 there is resentment against *"Idol-Shepherds, Dumb-Dogges, No Ministers and such like"* (15). And Henry Burton speaks of "false or unprofitable or idle Teachers, Non Residents dumbe dogs."[137] Occasionally the two epithets almost fuse. The anonymous *Canterburies Pilgrimage* (Oct. 1641) condemns "blind unpreaching Prelates, & Ministers" (A2v). The Fast Sermon by Simon Ash speaks of "Blind Seers, who know not Heaven-way, dumb dogs which cannot barke. . . . Idle drones who either preach not at all, or very seldome. . . . Mis-guiding Guides."[138]

The images, though separately identifiable, cannot be isolated from the whole panoply of Christian pastoral images: *shepherd, flock, nourishment, devouring, wolf*—the whole moral scenario of blessed feeding and guidance and damned gorging and neglect. In this savage competition for the swords, pockets, and souls of men and women, the most malign image conceivable is that of the hypocritical and maimed provider, the blind mouth of an authority who consumes but is incapable of (or uninclined toward) providing, who yet blocks others from that office. "They are all ignorant. . . . Dumb-Dogs; They cannot barke. They are greedy dogs that can never have enough."[139]

Milton's Puritan readers would have read his "Blind Mouths" with double pleasure: surprise at the initial illogicality and, after consideration, satisfaction at the appropriateness. Milton took two stock epithets for the corrupted clergy and put them together: he intruded his politics into his poetry; and he intruded his poetry into his politics with this act of fusion. (After lo! these many years and dismissals, John Ruskin's treatment of the "audacity and pithiness" of this "broken metaphor" is still an example of intuitive and responsible criticism.)[140]

Some eight years into the future, Laud will be mourned in a poem by another of the contributors to *Obsequies to the Memory of Mr. Edward King,* the volume that gave us "Lycidas." John Cleveland's "On the Archbishop of Cantebury" is the first political poem I know to make reference to Milton's political poem, criticizing it for its political digression, its insincerity, its ambition:

> I need no Muse to give my passion vent,
> He brews his teares that studies to lament.
> Verse chymically weeps; that pious raine
> Distill'd with Art, is but the sweat o'the braine.
> Who ever sob'd in numbers? can a groan
> Be quaver'd out by soft division?
> 'Tis true, for common formal Elegies,

> Not *Bushels* Wells can match a Poets eyes:
> In wanton water-works hee'l tune his tears
> From a *Geneva* Jig up to the sphears.   (*Poems*, 38)

Is it possible that Cleveland, who mourned Edward King in the best late fantastical manner yet disliked "tears in tune" (*Poems*, 1), is here remembering the poem and the poet, a "Geneva Jigger," who earned the position of honor, in the memorial volume? A small example of the interchange of poetry and politics, of the uses of vanity, and, to return us to our subject, of the debates on language and its public uses.

A POSTULATE

Milton lived and intellectually thrived in an historical period and a national environment of linguistic and cultural adventuring. Language, and the cultural attitudes which created and responded to that language, strenuously tested the boundaries of tradition, of conformity, of respectability. There has never, Douglas Bush once suggested, been a time that was not "transitional."[141] Has there ever been a period of human history that was not in some way revolutionary, an era that did not explore, as part of its maturation, the efficacy and the "proper" uses of language? Probably not. Yet print culture matures in this earlier part of the seventeenth century precisely because it undergoes a remarkably "immature," even a bratty, adolescence. Milton uses language with a *deliberate* indecorum vis à vis the past, and with a creative decorum for an indefinite but lambent Christian future. The seeker of the permanent, the monumental, the unified, adopts the provisional, the incomplete, the processive. And yet the expectation of arrival, of a resolved potentiality, never disappears from Milton's page; we expect him to rest in a standing position. "They also serve . . ."—the sonnet is a powerful emblem of Milton's expectations of arrival and of his embrace of process.[142]

Tradition was for Milton both beloved and expendable. *Mere* tradition aroused his contempt, a contempt licensed by the rhetoric of zeal that had permeated the theological, and to a lesser extent, the political, debates of the period. Zeal gave Milton (and Burton and Bastwick and Prynne and Preston and Lilburne and Lord Brooke) the warrant for a rhetoric that subverted the traditional and historical hierarchies of education, class, and profession. Empowered by an Angel/Christ who vomited out the lukewarm—in a sense the too easily "appropriate"—Milton could slander the prelates and even the prelate-martyrs, challenge the learned doctors, condemn the quodlibets and commonplace books of the conveniently educated. He could, and he would, substitute the flaming rhetoric of personal inspiration, a language of demand and of dismissed boundaries. That rhetoric would include a large quota of unpleasantness, the gutter language of ungracious and intolerant righteousness, a language particularly offensive to our modern sensibilities and our traditional professions of letters—still either *belle* or *correct* after all. Separated by time, by changes in custom and creed, perhaps rather by creedlessness, we have lost the common religious rhetorics in use by the polemicists of Milton's period. Until quite recently, and for some three hundred years past, these changes have conspired with Milton's earlier reputation as "divorcer," "regicide," and egotist to keep his prose in a more or less dusty isolation, with the notable exception of the grand and still useful *Areopagitica*. In 1940, William Riley Parker could write with assurance that Milton

> had a genuine talent (God-given, he sincerely believed) for the vigorous, vituperative give-and-take of controversy. His bad manners in debate were, of course, not unique; they were his heritage as a child of his age; but he took his heritage, unsheathed it, sharpened it, and wielded it so enthusiastically that his own contem-poraries found his language unusual, and today his more squeamish admirers avert their eyes from the unpleasant spectacle.[143]

The magnificent retrievals of David Masson, William Haller, and Arthur Barker were not exactly ignored, but they were certainly minimized until Don M. Wolfe and his fellow editors gave us the Yale edition of the prose. The current surges of interest in the prose must in part be due to the availability of this edition; its very weightiness and the thoroughness of the background information invite scholarly attention, while something like its stolidity challenges the critical faculties. In 1968 Joan Webber's *The Eloquent "I"*[144] brought a new level of engagement, followed by the collection *Achievements of the Left Hand*[145] (edited by John T. Shawcross and Michael Lieb), and the work of Christopher Hill,[146] Stanley Fish, and William Hunter, among others. Now the field flourishes, with a significant group of writers who are providing both a rich context for, and stimulating theoretical approaches to, the study of this once-neglected subject.[147] This younger group of scholars is treating the prose with an historical and linguistic precision that is remarkable and perhaps unequaled in the study of Milton since the eighteenth century.

My study remains within the boundaries of an historicism that values texts over critical or theoretical positions. For the methodology I have tried to maintain, I borrow the words, but not the breadth, of the foremost scholar of the field, Thomas N. Corns:

> The emphasis is not on illuminating obscurities through the explanation of historical or biographical allusion. Rather, it is the exploration of the complex ways in which the text engages other texts, addresses the reader, and participates in the political struggles which it is intended to shape and influence.[148]

Not "simply contextualizing," and with the addition of some neglected ecclesiological issues, this brief history of the rhetoric of zeal will, I hope, help to illuminate the thought and art of the writers of the period, particularly that of Milton during a critical, indeed seminal, phase of his career. "The Author John Milton," writes J. Martin Evans, "took a long time to be born";[149] the period I am examining is a critical segment of that long labor.

Like Annabel Patterson in her *Early Modern Liberalism*, I am seeking "to recuperate a cultural history," one that is "inseparable from both its historical conditions and its forms of expression."[150] Without an overt theoretical framework, my inquiry has operated like the process Sharon Achinstein has described: "Rather than seeking for consistent philosophies, [I have tried to] become more attentive to the nuances, inconsistencies, and literary qualities of texts," (*Revolutionary Reader*, 8). In some sense then this study of zeal leads nowhere and everywhere, dying into a tradition of being satirized rather than satirizing, yet renewing itself, despite the repeated alarms of inconsistency, with demonstrations of enormous, conflicted energy. It has a profound influence on radical politics of the left and of the right. In many of its manifestations zeal is vehemently opposed to liberalism. Yet in the earlier seventeenth century (and, I would argue, in the 1960s), it contributed to the creation of a subversive discourse of individual freedom which helped to establish a new political base enfranchised by a moral indignation that was, to a significant degree, benevolent and democratic. It is difficult, but it should not be impossible, to recognize this contribution while remembering the self-righteous suspension of reason, the ultimately intolerant assumption of authority. Long after September 11, 2001, I continue to think that the main point of this study is the astounding energy of zeal.

I turn now to analyzing Milton's individual texts as works of literature, not always successful but almost always interesting in and of themselves, and as representative texts of a thrilling era. I read these tracts as a student of language, with a more or less innocent, and certainly old-fashioned, reverence for literary texts, texts located within a period of English history that took huge intellectual risks. Throughout the following chapters I try to remember that Milton wrote as a poet, one committed to religious, social, and psychological performance, performance as kerygma, God's truth proclaimed in duty and with a remarkable degree of passion. These commitments released extraordinary energies in a poet supremely gifted and brilliantly educated, energies which continuously evolved in response to political and ecclesiological realities. In the first several years of the 1640s, these energies were channeled into a rhetoric of zeal, widely recognized, widely attacked, which was a dominating factor in Milton's English prose, especially in the antiprelatical tracts. The readings which now follow should at once demonstrate this influence, while arguing for a larger value to these five polemical documents. In each of the following chapters I have chosen to emphasize a particular aspect of these energies. In the chapter on *Of Reformation*, I especially note the dazzling visionary qualities; in chapter 3, on *Of Prelatical Episcopacy*, I note the emphasis on methodology. Chapter 4 emphasizes the claims of authorial rectitude in *Animadversions*; chapter 5 shows especially the satirical vituperation that *A Modest Confutation* elicits in *An Apology*. In chapter 6, I emphasize the Miltonic attempt to represent his arrival at a sure kerygmatic authority, one which serves as a transition to the exalted poetic career which the autobiographical digression announces. Often shrill, often redundant, sometimes coarse, Milton's antiprelatical tracts are, nevertheless, major proclamations of the English Reformation. They are complex, inventive, witty, and often beautiful pieces by a major writer of English prose.

Two

Of Reformation

The Politics of Vision

In the carefully nurtured Puritan view of providential history, the year 1640–1641 joined 1588 and 1605 as another *annus mirabilis*.[1] Like the defeat of the Spanish Armada and the discovery of the Gunpowder Plot, the falls of Lord Protector Strafford and Archbishop William Laud were seen as direct interventions by a God who really did take sides. The old calendar made it possible to include the "miraculous" deliverance of the Five Members of Parliament[2] whom Charles had personally come to take into custody on 4 January 1642. Added to that was the triumphant return of the three Puritan martyrs, Bastwick, Burton, and Prynne, in November and December of 1640. However bizarrely constructed as history, this "evidence" of divine intervention was useful to those calling for swift and decisive action. Procrastination in God's own cause was sin for those who would "[be] clad with zeal as a cloak" (Isaiah 59.17). Surely this political ferment contributed to the validation of the rhetoric of zeal; and surely it had a powerful and urgent appeal for Milton, drawing him away from his sober, ambitious career itinerary, including the Grand Tour and the intentional sequestration at Horton and Hammersmith. Between late May (or early June) of 1641 and April of 1642 he produced five pamphlets on topics he would earlier have considered, if not beneath him, at least out of the immediate range of his interests and plans. He must have devoted virtually full attention to the case against prelacy for an entire year, a year that had an immense influence on his life and on the great poetic future for which he was preparing.

Yet the ambiguities abound. How urgently did he feel the call to participate in the pamphlet wars? How long did he deliberate over the delaying of his literary plans? The internal struggle must have been intense; yet the report of that struggle in the *Second Defense* seems disingenuous. The anonymous publication of the first three tracts is puzzling, and the purported curtailment of the longed-for Grand Tour in favor of impulsive patriotism seems improbable: "Although I desired also to cross to Sicily and Greece, the sad tidings of civil war from England summoned me back. For I thought it base that I should travel abroad at my ease for the cultivation of my mind, while my fellow-citizens at home were fighting for liberty" (*CPW*, 4, pt. 1:618–19).

By his own account the return took six months, a leisurely pace even in those days. Presumably he took some time to consider the personal costs before plunging into a controversial milieu whose call was urgent but obviously disruptive of his literary plans.[3]

Milton's first polemical prose was the "Postscript" to the widely circulated Smectymnuan pamphlet, *An Answer to a Booke entituled, An Humble Remonstrance.*[4] This vehement scholarly addendum to the arguments of the five Puritan clergymen against Bishop Joseph Hall has been attributed to Milton since at least Masson's time; Don M. Wolfe summarizes the evidence for authorship as "formidable" and "compelling" (*CPW*, 1:961–65, 977–79).[5] Milton's own later statements about participating in the struggle against the prelates suggest specific contribution to a powerful polemical work. His relationship with Thomas Young, his leanings at that time

toward the Presbyterian party, the very tone and attitude of
the argument suggest that the addendum to the Smectymnuan
Answer is the "participation" to which those later comments
refer. This "Postscript" is well worth a brief look as an
apprentice work of suggestive vigor.

The piece exudes a kind of leashed power, an implication,
almost a threat, of resources and talents held back: "Though
we might have added . . ."; "yet unwilling to break the thread
of our discourse . . ."; "wee have chosen rather . . ."; "we wil
bound ourselves . . . ." These locutions suggest a decision,
made from strength, to limit the attack strictly to rebuttal of
the historical claims made for prelacy by Bishop Hall, claims
to which Milton refers with some condescension, as "severall
occasions given us in the *Remonstrance*" (*CPW*, 1:966). But
there is also a familiar vehemence in the tone, the pounding
lists to which the reader becomes accustomed in the tracts:
"those bitter fruits, *Pride, Rebellion, Treason, Unthankefulnes,
&c* which have issued from *Episcopacy*." There is, Don Wolfe
suggests, "an acid antagonism unlike the Smectymnuan tone
of moderation" (*CPW*, 1:80).

The underlying assurance is that of the professional
propagandist rather than the apprentice zealot. Anglican icons
are treated with sardonic pseudo-respect: "their Founder
Austin the *Monk*"; or "those poore laborious Monks of
Bangor," or "*Dunstan* the Sainted Prelate" or Anselm who,
for his "good service received great honour from the Pope, by
being seated at his right *foot* [my italics] in a Synod" (*CPW*,
1:966–67). The briskness is journalistic, the data common; the
indignation we will learn to identify as Miltonic. The Anglican
hero is the Puritan villain: "*Beckets* pride and outragious
treasons are too manifest"; the "noble" Henry II was
"disciplin'd by the Bishops and Monks, first with a bare foot
penance, that drew blood from his feet, and lastly, with
fourescore lashes on his anointed body with rods" (968–69).
The history warms up as the author imagines, not "without
mirth" (970), the contests for precedence, including the well-
known story of the Archbishop of York, who, protesting the
order of seating, "squatts him down on [the Archbishop of

Canterbury's] lap" (969). Comic contempt mingles with disgust at the treachery of those prelates who would have betrayed the kings Richard II and Henry IV (equally treated in this history), Henry V, and Edward IV. When it addresses more recent history, the attack is harsher. Wolsey serves as the model of the low-born and prideful usurper of kingly powers; Edward the VI is emphatically morally superior to his bishops.

The "Postscript" is an effective piece of the attack on prelacy, convincingly circumstantial and rhetorically effective in its mixing of humor, contempt, and indignation. The powerful imagistic contrasts of specious outsides and authentic insides are only hinted at here. But the prelates are already those whose "great designe" is "to beate downe the Preaching of the Word, to silence the faithfull Preachers of it, to oppose and [persecute] the most zealous professours, to silence the faithfull Preachers of it, and to turne all Religion into a pompous outside" (*CPW*, 1:975). Already the author notes "The deficiencie of zeale and courage even in those Bishops who afterwards proved Martyrs," a prelude to the notorious attack on Cranmer, Latimer, and Ridley in *Of Reformation*. As the work of an apprentice propagandist, this appendix to one of the important documents in the Wars of Truth is remarkable for its assurance, for its suggestion of burgeoning power deliberately held in check, and for its moralistic aggressiveness. It is an early example of Milton's mastery of decorum, with its rhetoric consciously appropriate to place, time, subject and prospective reader. That decorum, stretched to the point of rupture in the pamphlets that follow, includes a note of *fairness* that has too often been ignored. The "Archbishop of *York* was, *though perhaps unwillingly* [my italics] . . . the unhappy instrument of pulling the young Duke of *Yorke* out of Sanctuary, into his cruel Unckles [Richard III's] hands" (*CPW*, 1:972). This modest example contests the view that Milton in his early prose is a mere abuser of his opponents. It shows an element of fairness which will remain a concern, and not a negligible one, for John Milton in the midst of the temptations to political reductionism that beckon him.

The young poet's involvement in the controversy with the prestigious Bishop of Ely probably stemmed from his relation with his ex-tutor Thomas Young, generally considered the "convener" of the Smectymnuan group.[6] This would account for the tone of respectful autonomy, not quite deference, which the younger man exhibits in his part of the piece. He identifies with the main body of the tract, but makes no attempt to claim equal billing, as it were. His style differs noticeably from that of the Smectymnuans, yet there is a claim to continuity and at least some curtailment of the energies of expansion and emphasis that will operate a few months later.

Milton never refers directly to the "Postscript"; but one deduces that he felt, even in this first sortie into the tract wars, that he was adding something to the Puritan arsenal. In the *Second Defence,* he is blunt in his claims: "I brought succor to the ministers, who were, as it was said, scarcely able to withstand the eloquence of this bishop" *(CPW,* 4:623; see also *Colasterion, CPW,* 2:753; of course, the claims are most obviously for the *Animadversions* and the *Apology).* The gradual dissipation of this posture of deference to his elder colleagues will proceed throughout the antiprelatical and divorce tracts, as the "scarcely able" of the above quote suggests, one of the measures of Milton's deep ambiguities over supervision, over his disappearing youth, and his delayed fulfillment of great promise. That concern produces some irritable rationalizing about his age, and underlies his claim to the vulnerability of youth. Milton is 32; he has traveled widely, published successfully, been praised by important people both in England and abroad. Still the mismatch between his great expectations and his real accomplishments is considerable. Coupled with this is a smolderingly scornful sense of being monitored and criticized by elders whom he barely accepts as his superiors. His nervous awareness of the judgment of these others, usually older others, affects much of his early prose.

One of the reasons for the power of Milton's first independent tract[7] is that the speaker seldom looks over his shoulder; he confidently states his right to speak the truth. The deference in *Of Reformation* is not projected toward a tutor, but toward a courtly—here a parliamentary—auditor, one who is instructed as well as petitioned. The move is under the aegis of a kerygmatic empowerment that Milton is deliberately seeking, and beginning to find. The search gives off that "earlier brilliance," which Thomas Corns suggests comes "from the friction of genius and genre as Milton the poet redirected his energies in the limiting medium of prose."[8] Beneath that friction lies Milton's assurance of hermeneutic and moral security.

Of Reformation begins with the speaker emerging from a rich meditative retirement into the controversial arena of church government. The first part of the first sentence enacts that acceptance of a new responsibility:

> Amidst those deepe and retired thoughts, which with every man Christianly instructed, ought to be most frequent, of *God*, and of our *Religion* and *Worship*, to be perform'd to him; I do not know of any thing more worthy to take up the whole passion of pitty, on the one side, and joy on the other: then to consider first the foule and sudden corruption, and then after many a tedious age, the long-deferr'd, but much more wonderfull and happy reformation of the *Church* in these latter dayes. (*CPW*, 1:519)

Religion and *Worship* are the subjects of retired contemplation, but the naming and italicizing of them brings them, and the speaker, out of the study, into the heart of contemporary controversy. The movement imitates the motions outward from *God* to his *ways* and *works*, horizontally outward (creating) not downward (contemplating).

God creates, and poet emerges to his prose vocation. But there is a second, a vertical, movement: God descends in incarnation to save man, suffers, dies and rises again. The Church too descends from Christ, suffers, dies and rises again, and again, and again. In this paragraph the vertical is better traveled than the horizontal. Christ descends to "the lowest bent of weakness, in the *Flesh*," and triumphs "to the highest pitch of *glory*, in the *Spirit* till we in both be united in the

Revelation of his Kingdome" (*CPW*, 1:519). The structural principle of the piece is plain. The horizontal movement of history is initiated by the speaker's emergence from retirement, and in imitation of God's movement of Creation. The vertical movement is defined by the Incarnation and Resurrection of Christ, and repeated by His Church, and the speaker as member of that Church, in the search for union. In his poetic vocation the speaker identifies with the Son through this repetition as well as through creation. The two movements, horizontal and vertical, intersect historically, theologically, and emotionally at the figure of Christ, not crucified but triumphant.

The repetitions of Christ's descents and ascents place the vertical movement outside of time, and yet there is an envisioned final return, a final, but not static, resting, or rather settling, in God. The final pages of the tract will present the *sealing in love* promised in Revelation and anticipated throughout this text in the recurring imagery of the last days. The horizontal moves toward another aspect of the same end, the *judgment* of Apocalypse. The structure then is not a simple perpendicular; there is a pull between the end points of the two journeys; individual *"settling"* in love and the political "solution" that is judgment are at the same point. We are simultaneously aware of a perpendicular, the Crucifix, and of a closing angle, the Apocalypse: Christ with outspread arms in both images, at once embracing in mercy and rejecting in judgment.

As orator, polemicist, and recorder, the speaker will give an historical survey, and he will reason. He will pause to attend to an ephemeral irritant, the speech by Lord Digby. On this axis, he will finally arrive at the scene of God's judgment of men and communities for their acts. As private and poetical visionary, the speaker will ascend the vertical axis defined by the Father's sacrifice, imitating the movement of the Son of God, and of the members of Christ's body the Church, the parts and the whole. He too ascends and descends with the insistently rising and falling imagery of moral journey: *corruption, refin'd, height, drag so downwards, backslide, high soaring*. This motion of Christ, of His Church, and of the speaker as a member of that Church will not end until "we in both [spirit and body] be united to him in the Revelation of his Kingdome" (*CPW*, 1:519). The Church of Christ will arrive at "Divine intercours, betwixt *God*, and the Soule" (520), a spiritual sealing that is the chief aspect of the final day. Both justice and mercy are assumed in these opening paragraphs.

There are psychological tensions and releases at the points where history and vision cross. Milton exploits these stresses and makes us aware of the speaker at the junction of body and spirit, feeling the demands of both. But the larger excitement of this tract comes from its positioning in that closing angle of Apocalypse. The real time of *Of Reformation* is the present, but it is also the passionately awaited "last days," and the sense of urgency and of the imminence of final grandeur is that of Revelation. We are not only at the crossroads of time and eternity, the point at which we are to choose body or spirit. We are also approaching the end, the terminal fusion of the historical journey and the journey of the individual soul.

The polarities are everywhere, opposing movements along both planes. Prelatical usurpation for carnal reasons is the principal instance of pride; it imitates but opposes, like Satan throughout *Paradise Lost*, the righteous soul's powerful motions—"triumphing to the highest" (*CPW*, 1:519–22). On the horizontal plane the great arc of salvation history—stately, swift, assured—is contrasted to the tinkling and parochial repetitions of Anglican ceremony, devastatingly imitated and ridiculed:

> they hallow'd it, they fum'd it, they sprincl'd it, they be deck't it, not in robes of pure innocency, but of pure Linnen, with other deformed, and fantastick dresses in Palls, and Miters, gold, and guegaw's fetcht from *Arons* old wardrope, or the *Flamins vestry:* then was the *Priest* set to *con his motions*, and his *Postures* his *Liturgies*, and his *Lurries*. (*CPW*, 1:521–22)

The prelates drudge in the "Trade of outward conformity"; the attack on Laudian decorum is specific: "they knew not how to hide their Slavish approach to *Gods* behests by them not understood . . . but by their Servile crouching to all *Religious* Presentments, somtimes lawfull, sometimes Idolatrous, under the name of *humility*, and terming the Pybald frippery, and ostentation of Ceremony's, decency" (*CPW*, 1:522). Milton moves easily between vision and politics.

The simplest purpose of the text is to expound the deplorable carnality of the Church of England and the need for acceptance of a new (that is, a renewed) presbyterial discipline. But the argument must be referred to ultimate issues of salvation history and salvation psychology, the journeys of soul, of body, of church, and of state. So before he begins his historical survey, Milton must inundate us with images of communal and personal destiny. The personal emergence of the speaker is paralleled with images of a powerfully emergent English Reformation. The *"embers of forgotten tongues"* which were raked out in the service of Reformation may have been temporarily stifled by popes and prelates, but the English Reformation is being reborn, *emerging* out of that danger (perhaps with a touch of Donne's usage in the *Devotions*). These images of *coming out* dominate these passages. Milton's inquiry into Reformation is worthwhile "(at this time especially) when the *Kingdome* is in good *propensity* thereto" (524–27). The arrival of Reformation is sensuous as well as dramatic:

> when I recall to mind at last . . . how the bright and blissfull *Reformation* (by Divine Power) strook through the black and settled Night of *Ignorance* and *Antichristian Tyranny*, me thinks a soveraigne and reviving joy must needs rush into the bosome of him that reades or heares; and the sweet Odour of the returning *Gospell* imbath his Soule with the fragrancy of Heaven. (*CPW*, 1:524)

Not only the *now* but the *here* is celebrated in these proud images of England: "(having had this *grace* and *honour* from GOD to bee the first that should set up a Standard for the recovery of *lost Truth*, and blow the first *Evangelick Trumpet* to the *Nations*, holding up, as from a Hill, the Lampe of *saving light* to all *Christendome*)" (525).

In the face of these ardors it is difficult to accept David Loewenstein's view, that *Of Reformation* is a piece of "extraordinary uneasiness," in which Milton has "emplotted history . . . as a tragic process of degeneracy beginning with the age of Constantine," a text in which "he laments his nation in mourning."[9] Surely "Milton's dark view of history since the rise of the bishops"—also noted by David Norbrook[10]—is subsumed in the enthusiasm of the vision of a presently reforming church under "the assistance of *God* as neer now to us as ever" (*CPW*, 1:568), not only here and not only in the last great prayer. The "pitty" and "joy" of the first paragraph arise from considering first "the foule and sudden corruption, and then after many a tedious age, the long-deferr'd, but *much more wonderfull and happy reformation of the Church in these latter days*" (my italics, *CPW*, 1:519). The progressive decay of ecclesiastical tradition is now reversed in the "light that we enjoy"; and God is *available* to all. "The very essence of Truth is plainesse and brightnesse; the darknes and crookednesse is our own." The main point is elation at the plainness, the brightness, the comprehensiveness *now:*

> If we will but purge with sovrain eyesalve that intellectual ray which *God* hath planted in us, then we would beleeve the Scriptures protesting their own plainnes, and perspicuity, calling to them to be instructed, not only the *wise*, and *learned*, but the *simple*, the *poor*, the *babes*, foretelling an extraordinary effusion of *Gods* Spirit upon every age, and sex. (566)

The optimism of the tract arises from this elation at the roles that England, in the form of a broadly construed commonwealth, and the speaker himself, are about to play in a remarkably inclusive reformation.

Milton's view of this period in history is one of momentous and positive change, as the opening of the *Second Defence* will later claim:

> I was born at a time in the history of my country when her citizens, with pre-eminent virtue and a nobility and steadfastness surpassing all the glory of their ancestors, invoked the Lord, followed his manifest guidance, and after accomplishing the most heroic and exemplary achievements since the foundation of the world,

freed the state from grievous tyranny and the church from unworthy servitude. (*CPW*, 4, pt. 1:548–49)

Post facto propaganda? Perhaps. But it is equally possible that Milton remembers this period as one of enormous potential for glory, one in which celebration and denunciation were both animated by expectations of imminent reform and illumination for masses of people. Reform is in progress, and Milton's present writing is a part of that reform.

The energy of his conviction will produce powerful rhythmic effects, as in this description of those who pursue a specious tradition:

> they feare the plain field of the Scriptures, the chase is too hot; they seek the dark, the bushie, the tangled Forrest, they would imbosk: they feel themselvs strook in the transparent streams of divine Truth, they would plunge, and tumble, and thinke to ly hid in the foul weeds, and muddy waters, where no plummet can reach the bottome. (*CPW*, 1:569)

Against a confused and almost prurient darkness, "the Gospel . . . like a mirror of Diamond,"[11] dazzles with "the honour of its absolute sufficiency, and supremacy inviolable" (569–70). Even at the end of the long disquisition on the decay of the Church in book 1, celebration of *this time of Reformation* still governs the tone.

After stating England's claims to leadership of Reformation and lamenting its loss, Milton interjects his intended organization: "to declare those Causes that hinder the forwarding of *true Discipline*. . . . Orderly proceeding will divide our inquirie into our *Fore-Fathers dayes*, and into *our Times*" (528). And the argument unfolds, logically and chronologically, but certainly not with the proportional emphases the outline suggests. Images with a directional force all their own have poured into the introduction of the argument, from salvation history and from personal vision. The "orderly proceeding" is distracted by these groups of images, whose effect is to pull the argument, the whole language of the piece, toward the high psycho-theological magnet of Apocalypse.

The substantial argument for separation of Church and State is not merely orthodox anti-popery; it counters the powerful argument of the prelates that has as its motto King James's famous declaration at Hampton Court in January 1604, "No Bishop, No King."[12] The Donation of Constantine (that gross and convenient forgery which gave the Bishop of Rome temporal dominion over "the provinces, places and *civitates* of the western regions") becomes here one of the darkest pages in the history of the Church; She, it is argued, is not a vine that needs to clasp "the Elme of worldly strength, and felicity, as if the heavenly City could not support it selfe without the props and buttresses of secular Authoritie" (*CPW*, 1:554). In book 2 this argument is still more focused. Citing "The ancient Republick of the Jews," Milton proposes that: "If . . . the Constitution of the Church be already set down by divine prescript, as all sides confesse, then can she not be a handmaid to wait on civil commodities, and respects" (574–75).

In the private man, carnal and spiritual values are in delicate and necessary symbiosis. In institutions, the risks are too great; fusion of Church and State would be ruinous.

Milton is a monarchist still, but the signs of an evolving willingness to question the King's authority are here. "A Commonwealth ought to be but as one huge Christian personage," but England is instead "the floating carcas of a crazie, and diseased Monarchy." Janel Mueller's argument is powerful; working from *Of Reformation*, she points out the need to "rethink and redate Milton's embrace of parliamentary supremacy in government," and the "need to redraw our picture of the political Milton and ascribe to him more features of a vanguard revolutionary at a considerably earlier point than we have been inclined to recognize."[13] Milton's "radicalism" and his "elitism" are still under debate; I will address some of those debates below. For now, one notes Milton's firm statement: "that which is good, and agreeable to monarchy, will appear soonest to be so, by being good, and agreeable to the true welfare of every Christian" (*CPW*, 1:572).

In refuting James's long-lived argument that monarchy needs Prelacy in order to survive, Milton must demythologize the

martyrological tradition of the English Bishops, continuing
an established process of separating out the "good" Protestant
martyr, the true speaking witness, from the "bad" Catholic
martyr, who is mere victim, testifying through physical
suffering. "The hooly blisful martir," Becket himself, had
already been used as a wedge against Catholicism and against
Prelacy, transformed by the Puritans into an officious meddler
who got what he deserved. Alexander Leighton called him
"that proud Popeling . . . [whose] pride and rebellion was
transubstantiated by the Pope . . . unto an Idolatrous and
blasphemous *saint-ship.*"[14] Puritans favored versions of King
John as an antipapal hero, including the play by John Bale.[15] In
the evolving history of a reformed England, Cardinal Wolsey
was the classic example of prelatical hubris. Now Laud joined
him, and the two were castigated for disastrous interventions
in matters of state, members of the line of overreaching
meddlers and villains.[16]

Yet, apart from Laud, these were all examples of Roman
Catholic interference. For the Church of England, the Bishops
Latimer and Ridley and Archbishop Cranmer were different:
they died for God and Reformation, burned at the stake by
the papist "Bloody Mary"; they were "the prelate martyrs."
Milton is attacking a still-powerful icon when he coolly
deflates the political careers which preceded their deaths:

> But it will be said, These men were *Martyrs:* What then? Though
> every true Christian will be a *Martyr* when he is called to it; not
> presently does it follow that every one suffering for Religion, is
> without exception. Saint *Paul* writes, that *A man may give his
> Body to be burnt,* (meaning for Religion) *and yet not have Charitie:*
> He is not therfore above all possibility of erring, because hee burnes
> for some Points of Truth. (*CPW,* 1:533)

Milton shares passion and common sense with St. Paul,
along with the deliberate facing of difficult issues and the
unflinching judgmental stance—even when the judge is aware
of, even emphasizes, his vulnerability to the charge of harshness. The citation, after all, is from the most celebrated passage
on love in all of Christian literature:

> though I speak with the tongues of men and of angels . . . though I
> have the gift of prophecy, and understand all mysteries, all
> knowledge; and though I have all faith, so that I could remove
> mountains, and have not charity, I am nothing . . . and though I
> give my body to be burned, and have not charity, it profiteth me
> nothing. (1 Cor. 13.1–5)

This is an extraordinary passage from which to choose a
text to disparage martyrdom! Certainly Milton was aware that
the Pauline context here was risky, as it was when he flaunted
faith, hope and *chastity* in "A Maske."[17]

"Thus the prices of Martyrs ashes rise and fall in Smith-
field market," wrote Thomas Fuller, sadly.[18] Yet Milton's
unsentimental history of the political involvement of the
prelate martyrs is impressive, as is his stoutly allusive summoning of a text which could be used against him to show his
lack of Christian charity: *"sounding brass, tinkling cymbal,
puffed up, unseemly, self-seeking, easily provoked, rejoicing
in iniquity, nothing"* (1 Cor. 13.1, 5, 6, 2). The words are like
search lights on the dangers of self-righteousness and pompous
judgmentalism.

But one uses polemic to win an argument, not to
demonstrate tolerance, and the speaker summons all possible
assistance. Milton cites Cyprian in support of that Gospel
supremacy which is the foundation of his strength and
direction. Thus, the issue of unseemliness, now specifically
addressed, is put in the context of the revealed truth of
Scripture:

> and heerewithall I invoke the *Immortall* DEITIE *Reveler* and *Judge*
> of Secrets. That wherever I have in this BOOKE plainely and
> roundly (though worthily and truly) laid open the faults and
> blemishes of *Fathers, Martyrs,* or Christian *Emperors;* or have
> otherwise inveighed against Error and Superstition with vehement
> Expressions: I have done it, neither out of malice, nor list to speak
> evill, nor any vaineglory; but of meere necessity, to vindicate the
> spotlesse *Truth* from an ignominious bondage, whose native worth
> is now become of such a low esteeme, that shee is like to finde
> small credit with us for what she can say, unlesse shee bring a
> Ticket from *Cranmer, Latimer,* and *Ridley;* or prove her selfe a
> retainer to *Constantine,* and weare his *badge.* (*CPW,* 1:535)

Milton knows the uses and abuses of poetic authority, and of the will itself. The use of "vehement expressions" is conscious and necessary for the vindication of truth. The possibilities of malice and vainglory are recognized in the list of disavowals, an awareness that coexists with the sense of rectitude and with severe judgment, as the blazoned reference to Paul has established. In immediate political terms, the dispatching of the Prelate Martyrs and of the Donation of Constantine is effected by "vehement expressions"; and the need for that rhetoric of zeal—the "ignominious bondage" of Truth—is a part of the argument.

Fuller's shock at Milton's harshness loses some of its effect if one remembers that Puritans of the period often questioned the prelate martyrology. Lord Brooke criticizes Cranmer and Ridley on the same grounds as Milton does, and suggests "some *Good* men were *Bad* Bishops, and the *Evill* were intolerable."[19] Lilburne's strong statement comes four years later, but it is relevant here: "And what if *Latimer*, and the rest of the martyrs had communion with the Church of England, is that of a sufficient ground, that therefore wee must not separate away from it? I hope not, for what if God winked at their blindnes, darknes, and ignorance."[20] The martyred bishops had at best checkered spiritual careers; they suffered a martyrdom that was separate from their office: "It was not *Episcopacie* that wrought in them the Heavenly Fortitude of *Martyrdome*; as little is it that *Martyrdome* can make good *Episcopacie*" (*CPW*, 1:536).

Denied of its "credit" for the prelate martyrs, Episcopacy is now impugned in terms that fuse Puritan impatience with lukewarmness to the images of gross and corrupted spirituality. I have already cited the striking passage in which Milton describes the process of corruption of prelatical discipline; I repeat the powerful and ugly close: "their *devotion* most commonly comes to that queazy temper of luke-warmnesse, that gives a Vomit to GOD himselfe" (536–37). Images of corruption, excrescence, and illness accumulate: "Misshapen and enormous *Prelatisme*," "deformities," "gross corruption," "universal rottennes, and gangrene," "a meere aguecake coagulated of a certaine Fever they have," "Tympany" (537, 538, 582, 587). In the fable of the Wen that claimed precedence after the head, the political violence climaxes: "Lourdan, quoth the Philosopher, thy folly is as great as thy filth; . . . thou containst no good thing in thee, but a heape of hard and loathsome uncleanes, and art to the head a foul disfigurment and burden, when I have cut thee off, and open'd thee, as by the help of these implements I will doe, all men shall see" (584).

The violence comes out of the anger building throughout the tract, a violence validated by a long tradition in Christian and especially Puritan rhetoric. Richard Sibbes, whose sermons became "something like classics of popular edification"[21] echoes Scripture and states as doctrine that *"The violent and only the violent, and all the violent, doe at length certainly obtaine what they strive for, the King-dome of Heaven."*[22] The major message that Milton's fable carries is that Archbishop Laud is, like Haman, "hois[t]ed up (like some excrementitious vapour into the place of great dignity and power, by the sole beames and warmth of his Princes favour."[23] That "Sty of all Pestilential Filth" (Grimstone, cited in *CPW*, 1:64), and the advisor now closest to the crowned head, should be taken from the Tower and beheaded.[24]

The image of the ship of state and church sailing through "all the gusts and tides of the World's mutability" signals a closing cadence, one now deflected by the "Here I might have ended, but . . ." of the answer to Digby's claims against "sudden extream" (*CPW*, 1:601). George W. Whiting has shown this repetitive and relatively unsatisfying section to be a direct answer to Digby's *Third Speech* of 8 February 1641 (see *CPW*, 1:601, n. 112). The section begins sarcastically, "We must not run into sudden extreams. This is a fallacious rule" (601), and it exhibits that contempt which Thomas Corns finds to be Milton's most original contribution to the rhetoric of Puritan controversy at this stage.[25] I would suggest that Bastwick's *Letany* (cited in chapter 1) may have been a model for a passage like the following, where the "unctuous, and epicurean paunches" of the prelates are here contrasted with the needs of "the lame, the impotent, the aged, the orfan, the widow"; "they would request us to indure still the russling of their Silken Cassocks, and that we would burst our *midriffes* rather then laugh to see them under Sayl in all their Lawn" (*CPW*, 1:601–2). This interlude of contempt delays the concluding prayer, which would more appropriately follow the image of the virtuous ship of state sailing into peaceful port.

As terminus of the historical argument, that prayer synthesizes the tumultuous image patterns of the tract, a convergence of horizontal and vertical metaphorics. It complements the opening paragraph as the speaker reasserts himself. The "O Sir" reintroduces a down-to-earth, minimally deferential, speaker "wrapt on the sodaine into those mazes and *Labyrinths* of dreadfull and hideous thoughts" (*CPW*, 1:613). The only way out is up: to lift his eyes and hands in prayer. All the strained rationality of the piece to this point, the assiduous sorting out of true from false on a human level, has led the speaker to a point from which he must look up for guidance. For Milton, reason can take one up to the emblem of God's Judgment; it is the strenuous proem to the moment of enlightenment, when reason must buckle to Faith. The author of "Lycidas" knew this; so did the author of *De Doctrina*, and of *Paradise Lost*. Samson's rousing motions do not invalidate the experience of his careful self-examination in *Samson Agonistes*. To see the surrender of reason at a certain point as an ironical disparagement of reason is an error;[26] Milton carries human judgment *into* the emblem of Apocalypse.

The speaker raises his eyes and hands and voice to the Trinity—"*Parent* . . . King, Redeemer . . . *Love* . . . *illumining Spirit* . . . joy and solace . . . one Tri-personall GODHEAD"; his plea is for succor of "this thy poore and almost spent, and expiring *Church*" (*CPW*, 1:613–14); her enemies are described in images drawn from Revelation, and they provide the usual sharp rhythms of description of evil masses:

> leave her not thus a prey to these importunate *Wolves* . . .
> these wilde Boares that have broke into thy *Vineyard*. . . .
> O let them not bring about their damned *designes* that stand now

> at the entrance of the bottomless pit expecting the Watch-word to
> open and let out those dreadfull *Locusts* and *Scorpions,* to *re-
> involve* us in that pitchy *Cloud* of infernall darknes, where we
> shall never more see the *Sunne* of thy *Truth* againe, never hope for
> the cheerfull dawne, never more heare the *Bird* of *Morning* sing.
> (*CPW,* 1:614)

This grim proem must be seen within the context of the
Book of Revelation, as the dark before the firmly expected,
the *emerging,* dawn. Those who are trying to destroy the Saints
cannot. The locusts and scorpions verse in Revelation is
followed immediately by the command that "they should not
hurt the grass of the earth, neither any green thing, neither
any tree; but only those men which have not the seal of God
in their foreheads" (Rev. 9.4).

God's threat is also his promise that he will be "mov'd with
pity at the afflicted state of this our shaken *Monarchy.*" The
headlong pace of the prayer-peroration does not slacken: "the
impetuous rage of five bloody Inundations . . . soaking the Land
in her owne gore . . . the sad and ceasles revolution of our
swift and thick-comming sorrowes when wee were quite
breathlesse" (*CPW,* 1:614).

The rhythm of this passage suggests disorientation of
"our halfe Obedience and will-Worship" and introduces
the image that is in transition from Spenser's monstrous Error
into Milton's horrifying Sin: "that *Viper* of *Sedition,* that . . .
hath been breeding to eat through the entrals of our *Peace;*
but let her cast her Abortive Spawne without the danger of
this travailling & throbbing *Kingdome*" (614–15).[27]

Milton continues to refine his uses of change of pace with
considerable effect. The sustained organicism demonstrates
that Milton's ideas work in, and as, images, that their
intellectual effect is always something more than logical. This
is very different from saying that the prose is illogical, or from
saying that the prose is most effective rhetorically when least
effective politically.[28] The fervency is based on the Puritan
view of English history, from Roman invasion to Spanish
Armada and up to the present, the Laudian, "corruption."
Prayer and exhortation fuse with the celebration of Christian

"Fact," and the prayer crescendoes into the future:

> O how much more glorious will those former Deliverances ap-
> peare, when we shall know them not onely to have sav'd us from
> greatest miseries past, but to have reserv'd us for greatest
> happinesse to come . . . now unite us intirely, and appropriate us
> to thy selfe, tie us everlastingly in willing Homage to the
> *Prerogative* of thy eternall *Throne*. (*CPW*, 1:615)

In this last rush to Apocalypse, Milton gathers together
God's, and England's, worst enemies, "the *great Whore*" and "that
sad Intelligencing Tyrant . . . thirsting to revenge his Navall
ruines that have larded our Seas." The last stage of human
history will be the destruction of the Papacy and of Spain:
"let them embattell themselves and bee broken, let them
imbattell, and bee broken, for thou art with us." (616)

The responsible poet has emerged from "those deepe and
retired thoughts" of the opening sentence to become the
celebrant at the last day. As in "Lycidas," the process of
emergence has earned a new song, a new style: "Then amidst
the *Hymns*, and *Halleluiahs* of *Saints* some one may perhaps
bee heard offering at high *strains* in new and lofty *Measures*
to sing and celebrate thy divine *Mercies*, and *marvelous
Judgements* in this Land throughout all AGES" (*CPW*, 1:616).
From the grating discord of controversy, the jingle of ceremony,
and the specious rhythms of corruption, we are arrived at the
great polyphony of Apocalypse—and it is polyphony, a solo
voice over a grand communal complex—where, immodestly
but thrillingly, the voice of John Milton is imagined as offering
a song in high strains and new and lofty Measures. The voice
of the soloist is presented "amidst" and "perhaps," a soloist,
but a member of the Choir, not up front and "starring"; there
is a difference in the ways solo voices are heard in choral
singing. I think both Stanley Fish and Hugh Trevor-Roper are
wrong in their reading of this passage. Yes, it is, to some extent,
arrogant; it is also breathtakingly vulnerable. And it is
communal, choral. Milton is "in his garland and singing robes"
(Trevor-Roper, *Catholics*, 276), but he is not center stage. And
he is not "at once seek[ing] and resist[ing] dissolution" (Fish,

HMW, 253). He is a member of the choir of the Church, of the Body of Christ—self and member—singing, both aspects performative. What will that song be? We taste its style, and yet it is yet to come. Its themes are Mercies and Judgments, divine and marvelous, salvation more than damnation. The emphasis is also national and hence immediately political: "[T]his great and Warlike Nation instructed and inur'd to the fervent and continuall practice of *Truth* and *righteousnesse . . .* may presse on hard to that *high* and *happy* emulation to be found the *soberest, wisest,* and *most Christian People* at that day" (*CPW,* 1:616). Of course Milton sees himself as one of the instructors of the nation. And his instruction is not trivial "tutoring." From the beginning of his prose career, he has valued the *celebration* of Christian leadership as second only to that leadership itself in value to the commonwealth. "To govern a Nation piously, and justly . . . is for a spirit of the greatest size, and divinest mettle . . . of no lesse a mind, nor of lesse excellence in another way, were they who by writing layd the solid, and true foundations of this Science" (*CPW,* 1:571).

Of Reformation has already been instructing us on God's divine Mercies, His Protestant benevolence toward the growth of a new elect nation. It has been celebrating a democratic and nationalistic reform of education that starts with Scripture and now will end in visionary community.

It has also argued the prelatical threat to England's "manhood" posed by Episcopal effeminization of "this Warlike Nation" by "Mother Church," a topic of considerable subtlety, one which I have treated in chapter 1 and to which I will return in chapters 4 and 5. Its author has argued the need for clear and fervent language and simplified Church discipline and the "casting farre from her the *rags* of her old vices," a rejection of the vestments, real and metaphoric, of prelacy. England is to emerge as *high, happy, sober, wise, most Christian.* And she is to be rewarded at that day when

> the eternall and shortly-expected King shalt open the Clouds to judge the severall Kingdomes of the World, and distributing

> *National Honours and Rewards* to Religious and just Common-
> *wealths*, shall put an end to all Earthly *Tyrannies*, proclaiming
> thy universal and milde *Monarchy* through Heaven and Earth.
> (*CPW*, 1:616)

Notable in the fervor is the strain of mildness which
accompanies God's judgment. The day of doom is a day of
judgment *and* a day of rewards and honors. Most certainly to
be honored is that Parliament, the implied "Sir" of the address:
"they undoubtedly that by their *Labours, Counsels,* and
Prayers have been earnest for the *Common good* of *Religion*
and their *Countrey*" (616).

Almost certainly the singer here distances himself from
these rewards, standing off to one side, but critical to the
occasion, as celebrant in the great tableau of Revelation. The
good men, especially those public men, "shall receive, above
the inferiour *Orders* of the *Blessed,* the *Regall* addition of
Principalities, *Legions,* and *Thrones* into their glorious Titles."
And the ecstasy reaches its peak "in supereminence of
beatifick Vision progressing the *datelesse* and *irrevoluble*
Circle of eternity shall clasp inseparable Hands with *joy* and
blisse in over measure for ever" (616).

The blissful vision is a summary of Christian images for
perfection: harmony, hierarchy, the moving circle, hands
clasped with joy, eternity, recognition, mercy and activity.

But God's order must be maintained. The elimination of
the prelatical hierarchy is no threat to public discipline, as
Milton has argued, and as the final vision now confirms.
Hierarchy and the system of rewards and punishments
for public service will be proclaimed at and by the last trumpet.
God is merciful, and He is just. His justice will also condemn.
In 2 Thessalonians 1.4–12, St. Paul provides a model for the
celebratory judgmental tone Milton uses here:

> And to you who are troubled rest with us, when the Lord Jesus
> shall be revealed from heaven with his mighty angels. In flaming
> fire taking vengeance on them that know not God, and that obey
> not the gospel of our Lord Jesus Christ: Who shall be punished
> with everlasting destruction from the presence of the Lord, and
> from the glory of his power.

The last harsh scene of this tract is the condemnation and punishment of those whom God, with Milton's aid, has adjudged corrupt:

> But they contrary that by the impairing and diminution of the true *Faith*, the distresses and servitude of their *Countrey* aspire to high *Dignity, Rule* and *Promotion* here, after a shamefull end in this *Life* (which *God* grant them) shall be thrown downe eternally into the *darkest* and *deepest Gulfe* of HELL, where under the *despightfull controule*, the trample and spurne of all the other *Damned*, that in the anguish of their *Torture* shall have no other ease then to exercise a *Raving* and *Bestiall Tyranny* over them as their *Slaves* and *Negro's*, they shall remaine in that plight for ever, the *basest*, the *lowermost*, the *most dejected*, most *underfoot* and *downe-trodden Vassals of Perdition.* (CPW, 1:616–17)

The vision of the Anglican Bishops, pompous and hypocritical, humbled at the bottom of Hell, is one that continues to offend. Surely there is too much zest to the condemnation, a kind of zest that is the malignant edge of zeal in triumph (I have just seen on television the celebrations in Palestine of the destruction of the World Trade Center). But I would disagree with the editors of the Yale edition—whose erudition and tolerance I have learned to admire—when they note that "in his pamphleteering zeal, Milton, like many other Puritans, applied such abuse indiscriminately" (617, n. 179). One might ask whether Michelangelo was indiscriminate in the bottom half of his Last Judgment. The terrific rhetoric is essential to the vision of the last, great judgment. The horror is the shadow of the bliss, not an inhuman rejection of humanity, but an emblematic reassurance that life has consequence.

The Apocalypse is a mediating emblem between the concept of election and the moral law. Like Michelangelo, Milton is clearly telling us that those who do evil on this earth shall be punished. The blessed in Milton's passage have "earned" their election—what else is the praise of those who have been "earnest for the *Common good* of *Religion* and their countrey"? The damned have "earned" their punishment "by the impairing and diminution of the true *Faith*." Milton's vision is both a Judgment and a Sealing of the elect and the damned. The very clarity of the demarcation, the clear use of antithesis, argues this. Throughout the first of his tracts, the rational mind has sought to establish praise and blame, to urge the reader on to judgment in the final great vision of a judging and merciful God revealed at the last day as rational beyond our comprehension.

This rhetorical vision of the Apocalypse as both cause and effect recurs throughout John Milton's career. It is the end, at first shortly-expected, in later works in a distant future, the hope of which is preserved in the Ark of *Paradise Lost*. It is also the cause propelling Milton's readers by its promise and by its threat of judgment, to an emulation that will lead us "progressing the *datelesse* and *irrevoluable* Circle of *Eternity*" to "clasp inseparable Hands with *joy*, and *blisse* in over measure for ever" (*CPW*, 1:616). Under the extraordinary passion of this close there subsists an assurance, a vision, of a triumphantly virtuous England overcoming the errors and temptations of a vicious history. Through a zeal that empowered the elect with a language that identified corruption and enabled reform, England would confidently march toward Apocalypse, propelled by Providence, yet boldly defining its own route. *Of Reformation* firmly proclaims the end of a history of endured suffering and the imminent triumph of a resplendent English Reformation.

THREE

Words, Words, Words
and the Word

Of Prelatical Episcopacy

O f Prelatical Episcopacy[1] is the shortest of the anti-prelatical tracts, the most subdued in rhetorical spirit and, on the surface at least, in intellectual ambition. Yet even here there are passages of power and (more rarely) of beauty, usually in the condemnation of spurious authority or in the praise of Scripture. And there is an impression of success, of Milton's having used the piece as he intended.

The tract is essentially devoted to discrediting, with some sophistication the authority of the ancient Fathers, especially as they are cited by Bishop Hall in *Episcopacie by Divine Right*, by the pseudonymous Peloni Almoni in *A Compendious Discourse*, and by James Ussher, Archbishop of Armagh, in *The Judgement of Doctor Reignolds*.[2] The subtitle provides a scheme for the piece: a challenge of "those Testimonies which are alledg'd to that purpose in some late Treatises." Ussher, a scholar and theologian whom the Puritans had once considered one of their own and were now rather nervously denouncing, is the most important antagonist. Milton puts Ussher's name on the title page and concentrates on his "alledg'd" argument. Hall, though not mentioned by name, appears to be directly answered in at least one passage, and the still unidentified Almoni receives no specified attention. Milton is himself anonymous but by no means characterless. The fervent dedication of the fledgling poet-prophet is muted here—in respite after *Of Reformation*. But the assurance has grown; perhaps Milton feels that the opposition is simply not that formidable.

He appears to be fighting with one hand tied behind his back—a different restriction from that of writing with the left hand. Milton is fully committed to his argument, but the task at hand does not engage all his faculties; as in the "Postscript" to the Smectymnuan *Answer*, he seems consciously to be holding back: "it came into my thoughts . . . that I could do Religion, and my Country no better service . . . then . . . to recall the people of GOD from this vaine forraging after straw . . . by making appeare to them, first the insufficiency, next the inconvenience, and lastly the impiety of these gay testimonies, that their great Doctors would bring them to dote on" (*CPW*, 1:627).

Despite his "utmost endeavour," the tone is almost patronizing; the speaker puts aside "nice respects" and "for the time" devotes himself to an argument in which his intellectual energies seem circumscribed, "no more exact in Methode" than necessary. The speaker of the earlier and of the later tracts is also unwilling, but he is seldom so casual about his opponents, or about the magnitude of the task. In the other four antiprelatical tracts, even the magisterial *Reason of Church-Government*, the personal stakes are higher, the language far more passionate. Here the speaker is a proud Englishman, "borne free, and in the Mistresse Iland of the *British*" (624), but the nationalism, the sense of English moment and momentum, is not so strong as in the other tracts. Concern shrinks to the problem at hand: "gay testimonies." The speaker needs to dispatch—logically, briskly, really quite easily—"the broken reed of *tradition,*" "that undigested heap, and frie of Authors, which they call Antiquity" (*CPW,* 1:624–26).

The battle over prelacy is reported as won in the first 20 lines; and in fact Milton thinks that his thesis is absolutely clearly and distinctly true.[3] Episcopacy is either of divine constitution or of human. If only of human, we can take it or leave it. If of divine, the only authority is Scripture, but nowhere in Scripture, "either by plaine Text, or solid reasoning" is there found "any difference betweene a Bishop, and a Presbyter" (*CPW,* 1:623). Ergo, we can leave it.

The tract does not discredit the great doctors, but their evidence. Milton would "recall the people of GOD" and "reduce them," lead them back, "to their firme stations under the standard of the Gospell." The promise of a systematic traversal of the subject is not fulfilled, and the emphases, as in *Of Reformation* are disproportionate. The tract restates Milton's hostility to a tradition that prides itself on age and volume, unexamined sanctities and repetitions, "fragments of old *Martyrologies,* and *legends*" (626–27)—the contempt is obvious. Throughout his career, Milton hates the use of compendia of borrowed knowledge: "*quodlibets,*" "alphabetical servility," commonplace books (yes, he keeps one), the yellowing notes of dormant educations. This persistent charge against his scholarly foes implies his own strenuous rethinking of controversial positions, his insistence on the continuous activism of mind and will on earth, in paradise, in heaven.

The details and context of the historical arguments are most conveniently discussed in W. R. Parker's biography, in J. Max Patrick's notes to the Yale edition of Milton's prose, and especially in the general introduction to the same volume.[4] I should like here to comment briefly on what Milton finds spurious or disturbing in the evidence summoned by Hall and Ussher, and then to examine what programmatic use he makes of this occasion. In opposing their uses of evidence, Milton employs common sense and a pose of naive suspicion. The one just man is admirable in action, the oral witness to truth in the hostile arena, but the single witness in history is not enough; the evidence of "an obscure, and single witnesse" is "this bare Testimony" (*CPW*, 1: 627, 628). Faith in titles is disparaged; "Councells" are suspect, as are present day "Convocations" for containing "some bad and slippery men" (628). Written records have been falsified "both anciently by other *Heretiks*, and modernly by Papists . . . whence Canons, Acts, and whole spurious Councels are thrust upon us" (628–29), a point made earlier in *Of Reformation* (553). Spurious, fabricated tradition joins the accidental in this extraordinary image of the Fathers: "Whatsoever time, or the heedless hand of blind chance, hath drawne down from of old to this present, in her huge dragnet whether Fish, or Sea-weed, Shells, or Shrubbs, unpickt, unchosen, those are the Fathers" (626).

Those who aspire *plunge:* "ungodly Prelatisme . . . so farre plung'd into worldly ambition" (*CPW*, 1:629) leaps into a threatening and debris-filled sea of "authorities" to seek endorsement, to hide, to feed away from the light. Keep in mind the richer statement on carnal enmeshment in *Of Reformation*, discussed in chapter 2; the fervency is indeed muted. In *Of Reformation*, the prelates had at once hid and sought reassurance, in "the foul weeds and Muddy waters" (*CPW*, 1:569); now these "blind Judges of things before their eyes" (629) operate as often as not "from reason of State." A council "beginning in the Spirit, ended thus in the flesh," gives us little hope even if the records of it are authentic (630).

Antiquity itself—at least the better part of it—"turn'd over the controversie to that sovran Book which we had fondly straggl'd from" (631); *Of Reformation* had already separated out those who correctly used the past from the venal "votarists of Antiquity": "the best of them that then wrote, disclaim that any man should repose on them, and send all to the Scriptures" (*CPW*, 1:541; compare 553). Eusebius of Caesarea, a famous writer, finds it difficult to establish what individuals were appointed bishops by the Apostles; Leontius, "an obscure Bishop speaking beyond his own Diocesse," is therefore to be doubted (*CPW*, 1:631). Extrascriptural evidence, no matter how early, should be viewed with care, and a rigorous common sense ministers to that care—a rule of evidence to be observed throughout Milton's writings on church history and doctrine. The end of this tract will give us a quite startling statement on the uses of theological writing.

The sufficiency of Scripture is complemented and confirmed by its simplicity as *Of Reformation* had eloquently argued in the passage cited above (chapter 2); and the inadequacy of antiquity is confirmed by its complexity, for example, the creation of "a new Lexicon to name themselves by "προεϛὼς (. . . or *Antistes* . . . Gnostick . . . Sacerdos" (632). Again, Scripture is the original, the simple, the sufficient. Tradition is, paradoxically, "newfangled" "innovation." Invented words and titles, like logic-chopping and obscurity, are in Milton's eyes characteristic of the authority cited by the prelatical party, authority often carelessly or selectively cited. Photius, for example, upon whose testimony the tradition of Timothy's martyrdom is based, follows that topic with the Martyrdom of the Seven Sleepers of Ephesus (633). Milton's contempt is not explicit because the main point of the tract is not mere contempt; it is the examination of standards of evidence, a methodological treatise on Christian polemic.

To this point the opposition has suffered little of the lavish abuse deployed in *Of Reformation*. Perhaps the figure of the Archbishop of Armagh temporarily blunts the Puritan invective. Milton will again address himself to Ussher in *The Reason of Church-Government*, and there too one will note a "comparative mildness." In his editorial preface, Ralph Haug suggests that "Ussher was an old man, with a European reputation for integrity and learning. Moreover, Ussher was not particularly high church in his doctrines; his compromise of the summer of 1641 was notably tolerant" (*CPW*, 1:739). But Bishop Hall was a moderate too, and, if not so learned, at least "literary"; he would soon be vehemently attacked, in spite of such considerations. Ussher, though Archbishop and a pleader for the hated Strafford's life, was a special problem for the Puritans, not only as a moderate but as a former Puritan sympathizer; and he was a truly distinguished scholar and public figure, as Hugh Trevor-Roper has shown;[5] ultimately, under Cromwell's directions, he would be interred in

Westminster Abbey with honors. Bishop Hall's earlier career will be impugned in the debates with Milton; Ussher's will not.

There is a small piece of Puritan legendry about Ussher, including a moderately "Puritanical" sermon falsely attributed to him in December of 1641.[6] As late as July 1645, an anonymous writer singles him out because he has "formerly given to the truly Godly and Religious party in these Kingdoms (both by your life and doctrine) that you are one of them."[7] In another tract issued that year, Ussher was said to have "Ebb'd so far from his *Archiepiscopal* dignity, as to turn *Lecturer,* and so brought himselfe into a possibility of *Heaven,* till the old man began to dote upon the *World* again."[8] At the false news of his death in December 1645, there appeared a series of announcements about the once honorable, lately defected, great scholar:

> That unhappy and unholy *Neuter* or *Ambo-dexter,* Dr. *Usher Arch-prelate of Armagh,* resident at *Oxford,* a man once, I confess, of good, yea of great esteem . . .; but at length, whose last days (hitherto) have proved his worst days.[9]

> Hee was much admired and reverenced for his learning and parts, and honoured for a shew of Pietie and Devotion but his adhering unto the Popish partie lost his repute, and will eclipse that glorie which would have otherwise been ascribed unto him by this Age.[10]

> Surely many excellent parts died with him, (the best before him) for he was a brave Scholar and an excellent Preacher; had he not been poysoned with the Office of a Bishop, and sullyed by the vices of a Courtier, he had beene one of ten thousand: but ambition and timeritie lost his Nobilitie, and his good name went to the Grave before him; it is my sorrow, that such a man should staine his vertues, and in so great oblivion goe into the chambers of death.[11]

I cite these statements not only as possible explanations for Milton's modest deference (the news accounts *are* dated 1645), but also as indications that the Puritans did not apply "such abuse indiscriminately" (*CPW,* 1:617). Neither did Milton in particular look upon all bishops, as Hugh Trevor-Roper has stunningly accused him of doing, "with the same hysterical, obscene hatred with which Hitler looked at his diabolical stereotype, the Jews."[12] Milton adjusted his decorum to the problem at hand. What he will do to Hall in *Animadversions*, published only a few weeks later, will be vastly different from what he does to Ussher in this tract. Here, Anglican methodology and the evidence derived from the Fathers are the real issues.

If, in sifting this evidence, Milton does not find logical imprecision, he does find "judaical," papist, or pagan taints (*CPW*, 1:634–38), betrayed by suspicious references that imply sacrifice. Nearness to a known corrupt passage makes a second passage suspect. In a brisk analysis of Ignatius's *To the Smyrnaeans*, he finds that "all those short Epistles must either be adulterat or else *Ignatius* was not *Ignatius*, nor a Martyr, but most adulterate, and corrupt himselfe" (639). After the scholarly analysis, Milton concludes with a roll of abuse, one of the characteristic modes of these tracts:

> Had *God* ever intended that we should have sought any part of usefull instruction fro[m] *Ignatius*, doubtles he would not have so ill provided for our knowledge, as to send him to our hands in this broken and disjoynted plight; and if he intended no such thing, we doe injuriously in thinking to tast better the pure Evangelick Manna by seasoning our mouths with the tainted scraps, and fragments of an unknown table; and searching among the verminous, and polluted rags dropt overworn from the toylng shoulders of Time, with these deformedly to quilt, and interlace the intire, the spotless, and undecaying robe of Truth. (639)

The records of history are part of God's plan for our education. Our analysis of those records, *over against* the standard of Scripture, is an essential part of the experience of revelation. The Word of God is food; "tainted scraps" are an injury to God. But not all the words of man are tainted and fragmented; reason must strive to identify the truth as it has come down to us through God's will. Reason and common sense are the necessary human elements.

The double metaphor of food and clothing is typical of Milton's continuous synthesizing. Both figures, the true

"Evangelick Manna" and Truth in her undecaying robe, are daughters "not of Time, but of Heaven"; yet, crucially, both are "bred up heer below in Christian hearts, between two grave & holy nurses the Doctrine, and Discipline of the Gospel." Faith and reason, revelation and study—we are not far from some passages of the *Christian Doctrine*, quoted below. Milton is hooting at the specious uses of human learning and analysis, but at the same time he insists on the necessity of their proper use. He is not being anti-rational; the "two grave & holy nurses" are earned knowledge—not revelation.

Though Milton tends to overstate his own youth, here he dismisses the testimony of Irenaeus, Bishop of Lyons, because it depended on memories from childhood. The problem is quite delicate, because the testimony criticized is embedded in a powerful passage of Eusebius, one which follows a touching injunction to "keep those truly saintly men of an earlier generation in mind, as a splendid example of meticulous accuracy."[13] Yet Milton denies that one could properly "conclude a distinct and superiour order from the young observation of *Irenaeus*" (640). This debunking of the Fathers was a regular part of these tracts from the beginning. *Of Reformation* had decried "the foul errors, the ridiculous wresting of Scripture, the Heresies, the vanities thick sown through the volumes" (*CPW*, 1:551) of the Fathers. In *Of Prelatical Episcopacy*, fallibility of the Fathers and their theological progeny becomes a major issue.

Milton expresses firm admiration for the primitive church. Anglicans and Puritans both celebrated that period, but for the latter it was of much briefer duration. For Milton, the golden age of Christianity endured scarcely a generation— through the mature days of the Messiah and the lives of his Apostles. Decay followed almost immediately: "They which came after these Apostolick men being lesse in merit, but bigger in ambition, strove to invade those priviledges by intrusion and pleas of right, which *Polycarpus*, and others like him possest from the voluntary surrender of men subdu'd by the excellencie of their heavenly gifts" (*CPW*, 1:640–41). The corruption of the church was the movement into carnality, a fall recorded in language which drops away from the truth of Scripture. Measuring the distance we have fallen is a primary purpose of theology.

In *Of Reformation*, the speaker defended zeal against the charges of Lord Digby; now he accuses Irenaeus of being "so rash as to take unexamin'd opinions from an Author [Papias] of so small capacity," and ascribes the spread of idle traditions to "the inconsiderate zeal of the next age, that heed more the person, then the Doctrine" (641). There is no contradiction here. Both Anglicans and Puritans knew St. Paul's distinction in Romans 10.2[14] and regularly cited Saul's persecution of the church as "inconsiderate zeal" (Philippians 3.6). This inconsiderate zeal is now linked to the anecdotal, the personal, perhaps even to what we now call the cult of personality, while true zeal has a strict observance to scriptural injunction and example. So, in a shrewd passage, Milton describes how

> the exercise of right instructing was chang'd into the curiosity of impertinent fabling . . . with less fervency was studied what Saint *Paul*, or Saint *John* had written then was listen'd to one that could say here hee taught, here he stood, this was his stature, and thus he went habited, and O happy this house that harbour'd him, and that cold stone whereon he rested, this Village wherein he wrought such a miracle, and that pavement bedew'd with the warme effusion of his last blood, that sprouted up into eternall Roses to crowne his Martyrdome. (641–42)

In an age that canonizes Princess "Di" and "John-John" Kennedy, the passage should be instructive; it is also important to remember it when contemplating Milton's conception of the hero, political and poetic, a hero to whom its author does not surrender in sentimental grief. Sarcasm was that face of zeal which ridiculed the vestments, gestures, and rituals of the prelates; now it is aimed directly at Irenaeus. Yet one is tempted to see a larger suspicion behind it: Milton had a distaste for the public exploitation of private emotions, as the moving but carefully intellectualized expositions on his blindness demonstrate. Part of his contempt for the *Eikon Basilike* is rooted in this distaste.

The polemical point is both more precise and more important. Sentimental concerns for personality obscure the essentiality of Scripture:

> Thus while all their thoughts were powr'd out upon circumstances, and the gazing after such men as had sate at table with the *Apostles* (many of which *Christ* hath profest, yea though they had cast out Divells in his name, he will not know at the last day) by this meanes they lost their time, and truanted in the fundamentall grounds of saving knowledge, as was seene shortly by their writings. (*CPW*, 1:642)

Milton's cardinal tenet: keep your eye on the word—and the Word. When the eye strays, when the mind falters, error creeps in. The need for intellectual rigor is perpetual. Irenaeus faltered so badly as to call Mary the advocate of Eve (642), a serious lapse toward Mariolatry, and its consequent supplanting of Christ as exclusive mediator.

With this tract Milton makes an important and rather surprising statement. The Logos speaks, but, having been spoken, the Word is written down and confirmed. Apart from that of Christ and the Apostles, oral tradition has been disparaged here. Consider the passage in *Of Reformation:* "doubtlesse that which led the good men into fraud and error was, that they attended more to the meer tradition of what they heard the Apostles sometimes did, then to what they had left written" (*CPW*, 1:550). For Milton now, Truth is printed, not spoken. His concern with these specious oral traditions is a sign of his increasing insistence on having the Word—and likewise the word—in hand, where it can be perused by the human reason. This emphasis would account for the increasing number of times Milton makes the printed word an autonomous body, as in the memorable passage in *Areopagitica:* "a good Booke is the pretious life-blood of a master spirit, imbalm'd and treasur'd up on purpose to a life beyond life" (*CPW*, 2:493). On the one hand, the spoken word is holy when it comes from Christ's lips, when it comes from one whose lips are touched and purified by God's seraphim "with the hallow'd fire of his Altar" (*CPW*, 1:821, and also the

Nativity ode); and when it is preached fervently, intelligently, from the pulpits of the nation. Inspired speech is the highest virtue of the godly preacher, silence the vice and sin of the "dumb dog," the ultimate villain of Puritan politics. But the Puritan revolutionary ministry is about to become the preaching establishment. And here are the signs that Milton is beginning, consciously or not, to describe an oral tradition that is not as responsible to the reason as the written word. (By 1649, the real villains of the *Tenure of Kings and Magistrates* will be the venal preachers, including Stephen Marshall himself.) The critique is already in process, and so is the recognition that zeal can move too easily into "inconsiderate zeal."

Rhetorical zeal is an energy essential to the early stages of a revolution. It moves monolithically, as with an overwhelming identity. Yet even in its first uses Milton knows that it has faces, subcategories and even weaknesses. Zeal's "substance is ethereal," an "invincible warrior" (*CPW*, 1:900). Yet it has two aspects, "resembling two of those four which *Ezechiel* and S. *John* saw, the one visag'd like a Lion to expresse power, high autority and indignation, the other of count'nance like a man to cast derision and scorn upon perverse and fraudulent seducers" (900). As the movement matures and assumes power, the possibilities of corruption of that zeal increase, and the need for rational control becomes greater. For Milton, the emblem and mode of rational truth are now the perused printed text read under the offices of the Holy Spirit. There is, of course, no hint of doubt of Scripture's simple and obvious veracity. But the holiness of the Word must be confirmed in every *dependent* instance. This may seem a contradiction to us; it is not to Milton. This is an early statement of the absolute veracity of Scripture and the absolute need to confirm that veracity, an argument which will dominate the opening of the *De Doctrina:*

> God has revealed the way of eternal salvation only to the individual faith of each man, and demands of us that any man who wishes to be saved should work out his beliefs for himself. So I made up my

mind to puzzle out a religious creed for myself by my own exertions. (*CPW*, 6:118)

God offers all his rewards not to those who are thoughtless and credulous, but to those who labor constantly and seek tirelessly after truth. (120)

I advise every reader, and set him an example by doing the same myself to withhold his consent from those opinions about which he does not feel fully convinced, until the evidence of the Bible convinces him and induces his reason to assent and to believe. (122)

In the antiprelatical tracts, Milton establishes the symbiotic relationship of reason and faith, but with no definition of thresholds. He sustains his belief in that relationship throughout his career—in the *Christian Doctrine* and in the three great last poems.

As part of his methodological inquiry, Milton now analyzes the creation of legends. In *Of Reformation*, the focus was on legends that grew into myths of considerable political power: the myth of Becket, the myth of the Prelate-Martyrs, the myth of "No Bishop, No King." These issues were treated as the dangerous political arguments that Anglican apologetic had made of them. Here the legends are more easily patronized, attacked rather for fostering habits of mind, and as representatives of methodologies and traditions dangerous to the exercise of reason and the pursuit of truth. Milton credits "the great honour, and affection" (*CPW*, 1:642) that the brethren bore Polycarpus, but the stories of his miraculous death must be coolly dismantled and dispatched. The Bishop had foretold his death by fire, but the fire would not consume him. He was stabbed, "and such abundance of bloud gusht forth as quencht the fire. By this relation it appeares not, how the fire was guilty of his death, and then how could the prophesie be fulfilled?" (643).

Indignation has given way to sophisticated dryness. "We grant them Bishops, we grant them worthy men"; we do not grant that the Apostles "alterd their owne decree set downe by St. *Paul*, and made all the *Presbyters* underlings to one

Bishop" (*CPW*, 1:644–45). Heresy and foolish legends contributed to making "the tradition of the Church . . . ridiculous . . . disconsenting from the Doctrine of the *Apostles*" (645–46). The "cloud" or "petty-fog of witnesses, with which Episcopall men would cast a mist before us" (648), has been dispatched. But the war is not over, for "it be the wonted shift of errour, and fond Opinion, when they find themselves outlaw'd by the Bible, and forsaken of sound reason, to betake them with all speed to their old starting hole of tradition, and that wild and overgrowne Covert antiquity" (648). That Covert is like the rubbish "drawne down from of old to this present" (626) and "the dark, the bushie, the tangled Forrest" (569), an emblem of error in tradition, disordered and congested. Almost throughout the canon, Milton insists that tradition is suspect; at the very least he argues that the good Christian should maintain a defensive alertness when evaluating theological materials outside of Scripture.

There is a correct use of the Fathers, in whose volumes all good scholars should of course have read: full recognition that the Fathers are a measure of distance from truth! We should read them, "not hereby to controule, and new fangle the Scripture, *God* forbid, but to marke how corruption, and *Apostacy* crept in by degrees" (*CPW*, 1:650). We must "take the good which wee light on in the Fathers, and set it to oppose the evil which other men seek from them." We must not "turne this our discreet, and wary usage of them into a blind devotion towards them"; we must "hold to the Scriptures against all antiquity" (650). Few would have disagreed with this last statement. Fewer still would have insisted on the Fathers as a text from which to learn how error has crept into the Christian tradition. The iconoclast John Bastwick was one who had preceded Milton in the attack. In 1637, defending himself, he had praised the "majesty and simplicity of the languages [the Scriptures] are writ in," and had attacked those who "do as it were lend luster unto the Sun from a smoaking snuffe, that from the mist of the Fathers would bring light unto the Scriptures."[15] It is not, therefore, enough to say that Milton calls for the proper uses of patriarchal tradition and decries the wrong ones. His suspicions and hostility are too pronounced. And they are sustained; throughout the early tracts one of Milton's major strategies is "to free ingenuous minds from that over-awfull esteeme of those more ancient then trusty fathers whom custome and fond opinion . . . hath exalted so high" (*CPW*, 1:698). The whole, elsewhere nearly sacred, corpus of traditional writings on the doctrine and discipline of Christianity is to be approached with the conviction that much of it is spurious, superficial, or just plain wrong: even the best among them see but through a glass, darkly.

There is little of Milton's customary spaciousness in *Of Prelatical Episcopacy*. The confident debater moves briskly through his self-appointed tasks, and the tract closes quickly and simply. It issues one last warning, that the acceptance of episcopacy logically implies the acceptance of Roman Catholicism. The admission of one nonscriptural tenet opens "a broad passage for a multitude of Doctrines that have no ground in Scripture, to break in upon us." The Gospel mentions only two ecclesiastical orders, bishops (presbyters) and deacons. To deny this is to oppose "the offals, and sweepings of antiquity" to "the sacred verity of Saint *Paul*":

> And this shall bee our *righteousnes*, our ample warrant, and strong assurance both now, and at the last day never to be asham'd of, against all the heaped names of Angells, and Martyrs, Counsells, and Fathers urg'd upon us, if we have given our selves up to be taught by the pure, and living precept of Gods word onely, which without more additions, nay with a forbidding of them hath within it selfe the promise of eternall life, the end of all our wearisome labours, and all our sustaining hopes. (*CPW*, 1:651–52)

Christ's Word is not to be denied or altered, nor is it to be appropriated to the mere service of self or institution. In a final dismissal of authorities invoked by the prelatical party, Milton celebrates the Word against words, words, words: "But if any shall strive to set up his *Ephod*, and *Teraphim* of Antiquity against the brightness, and perfection of the *Gospell*, let him feare lest he and his *Baal* be turn'd into

Bosheth. And thus much may suffice to shew that the pretended *Episcopacy* cannot be deduc't from the *Apostolicall* TIMES" (*CPW*, 1:652). Thus the tract ends, its salient polemical point restated simply in the last sentence.

The statement has some power. Theology is a measure of our distance from Scripture. All right doctrine and discipline should return us to Scripture, where we confront the exemplary life and teaching of Jesus Christ. Nothing hindering that return is acceptable. Man's role as a thinking, acting creature is to examine, forcefully and unsentimentally, the records of our decay in order to return to the health of Scripture, to repair the ruins of our first parents. There is no substitute for the process, no mystical or mediated way outside Christ. The process itself is not to be distorted into an idolatrous view of the materials or the actors in that process, turning his *Baal* into *Bosheth*. As J. Max Patrick reminded us, "the Hebrew *Baal* (Lord) in the names of Saul's family was superseded by the contemptuous *bosheth* (shame)" (*CPW*, 1:652, n. 93). Behind that lordship is the idolatry of the Old Testament, perhaps most obviously the Baal of Jezebel. Again the passage has contemporary significance. Archbishop Laud is sitting in the Tower; his Lordship's "idolatry" has been turned to shame, and he, like Strafford, will die on the block. The threat is very real. More subtle is the glancing reference to Queen Henrietta Maria, who is at this time coming under increasing attack as the "strange woman," the Jezebel who brings false gods in to the very palace of the king. The metamorphosis of *Baal* into *Bosheth* is a final demonstration of the vitality, and danger, of language. One word literally changes into another; *Esh-baal* becomes *Ishbosheth* (652, n. 93).[16] Lordship based on idolatry becomes shame, archbishops fall, and queens—perhaps—face threats for importing false gods. Under the etymological bluster is an ominous density.

Yet in much of this early prose, there is a present joy at Milton's apprehension of an imminent return to scriptural truth. The aspiring motion upward crosses, braces and reinforces the strong horizontal thrust toward Apocalypse. The overall movement in *Of Reformation* is toward the emblem of revelation in the final paragraphs. In Milton's second tract, the forward and upward movements are muted; the major motion is of localized search for method, specifically the demythologizing of parascriptural evidence, the challenging of authorities that "Tradition" had virtually sanctified. *Of Prelatical Episcopacy* offers a demonstration of ordinary, but rigorous, rational humanity—the epistemological search for the way back to Scriptural truth. Neither frivolous contention nor the contemplation of blood-roses is useful to the good Christian. Mere testimonial, however prestigious or antique, is not enough. The encrustations of tradition must submit to a rigorous analysis. Our reason, which *is* our God-given humanity, is properly engaged in the study of God's word, the rigorous study of our fall from that Word, and the ways of our return.

FOUR

Style and Rectitude

Hall, Smectymnuus and Milton's *Animadversions*[1]

M ilton's first plunge into controversy must have been effective. The "Postscript" to the Smectymnuan *Answer* elicited pointed remarks from Bishop Hall in *A Defence of the Humble Remonstrance,* including accusation of plagiarizing the well-known Puritan pamphlet *Sions Plea.* Did Milton contribute to the second Smectymnuan pamphlet, *A Vindication of the Answer to the Humble Remonstrance?* I find it probable that he had a hand in the final pages (*Vindication*, 216–19), subtitled "To all the Postscripts."[2] Here the text speaks, with Miltonic assurance, of "our sincerity . . . prodigiously wounded. . . . Why should we be thought to have borrowed from him [that is, Alexander Leighton, author of *Sions Plea*] . . . rather than from the Chronicles themselves?" And the bishop's foot is remembered from Hall's text, to reappear, unfortunately, in Milton's next contribution. The

Vindication was published in June of 1641, *Animadversions upon the Remonstrants Defence against Smectymnuus* in July, continuations of the intense and prolonged Smectymnuan engagement with Bishop Joseph Hall.[3] That engagement included two substantial texts by the five nonconformist clergymen, three by Hall, and *A Modest Confutation*, written by an anonymous champion of the Bishop.[4] Milton's two pamphlets, like the "Postscript" (and perhaps "To all the Postscripts") must be viewed as part of this larger group. Though the publication of *The Reason of Church-Government* intervenes between the first and second anti-Hall pieces, I will treat *An Apology* following *Animadversions*. Later I will suggest why *Reason* seems to me to have been planned originally as Milton's final statement on the prelatical matter.

Despite the complexity of the issues debated, much, if not most, of the energy of these writers goes into establishing their own authority and reliability, not only in their skill and comprehensiveness in presenting evidence, but in the actual presentation of self as truth-teller. Bishop Hall labors to put himself forward as a superior and gentle being—a Bishop (though not aggressively presented as such), a learned man, a man of letters, one privy to rare scholarly documents and rare scholarly friendships (like Ussher's), a man secure enough to be humble, to scold and to condescend. The Hall persona was famous, thanks to his supple controversial style. But he was more than "the English Seneca"; he had triumphed at the Synod of Dort and recently had been singled out by Laud as his foremost publicist.[5] Hall's image as authoritative peace-maker is carefully cultivated, a classic of self-presentation:

> As one whose heart (amongst many thousands) bleeds with the sad thoughts of the wofull *Divisions* of our deare Fellow-Subjects; and unfainedly pitties the misguidance of those poore soules amongst them.[6]

> I confesse my charity led me into an error; . . . how apt I am to be overtaken with these better deceits of an over kinde credulity.[7]

Or he can complain a little less sweetly:

> It is no easie matter for a man so far to mortifie his self-love, as to neglect himselfe for the publique good; & to vaile his private ingagements (though with some seeming disadvantage) to the peace of the Church. (*Reconciler*, 37)

Yet, Hall can write as roughly as Milton when he chooses; of a Jesuit opponent he had written in 1643:

> a fouler mouth hath seldome ever wiped it selfe upon cleane Paper. . . . babbling vagaries . . . ugly, inhumane, loathsome ribaldry . . . His unmanly unnatural Stile belcheth this . . . *Thus* [citing his opponent] Luther *of* Katherine Bore, *his Sow had sixe Piges.* Away nasty *C. E.* transformed by *Circe!* Hay! Backe to her Styes, yea thine, where thou maist freely *Grunnire in septiis cum faedo hoc agmine clausus.*[8]

The man who wrote these passages against Rome could and did write similar ones against the Puritans.

Yet during his earlier career in the Church, Hall was considered to have Puritan leanings. Sir Edward Dering could say of him (in a speech of 22 November, 1641), "The B. of *Exeter* (however mistaken in the Divinity of Episcopacy) hath ever had the repute both of a good man, and a good Bishop. He hath not only held and maintained his station, but advanced also, and made good impressions upon the Idolaters of Rome."[9] Professor Frank Huntley eloquently treats him as proponent of "the liberal Puritanism, the Anglican order and peace which James I made central to his policy."[10] Hall did get into trouble with James and Laud over his "liberal" sympathies, or at least for his excessive hostility to the Arminians (Huntley, 88, 102, 111–12), but by 1630 generally, and by 1639 eagerly, he was assisting Laud in his attacks on the Puritans. Hall had the experience, and by now the politics, of the Established Church. He could have written or helped to write *A Modest Confutation.*[11] And he was a formidable opponent.

At his best Hall could reconcile an acute polemical tone with one of conciliatory moderation, reluctant to give offence. At his worst, he was the Establishment Style incarnate: "let

us reason together and I will tell you what to think." One
necessary caution: the attack on Hall is not merely an attack
on "fine writing," though that is part of the Puritan argument.
That traditional hostility toward literary display can, for
example, slip easily into pure anti-intellectualism (as in most
hortatory rhetorics). Henry Burton early (1628) demonstrated
his suspicion of the Bishop's fine style: "it is a matter not to
be maintained by finenesse of wit, or quaint rhetoricall
discourse, but upon sound ground and substantiall demonstration."[12] This complaint is quoted and met head-on by
Robert Butterfield in a passage of unusual interest to students
of seventeenth century prose:

> Mr. Butron [*sic*] least the Bishop by his divine Eloquence, and
> accurate speech should prevaile too farre with his Readers, strikes
> first at that, by disgrace tearming it finenesse of wit, and quaint
> Rhetoricke; a little hurting his adversarie thereby, but singularly,
> dishonouring Almightie God. For whose are the arts? Whose is
> Eloquence, and utterance? who gave man the wit and braine?

> But who sees not whereunto this tendeth? Those irreproveable
> labours which the present age admireth, and posteritie shall rather
> envie than equall, That admirable facultie wherewithall the Author
> of every good gift hath blessed our most heavenly Prelate above all
> the sonnes of men, all is blowne away with a puffe, as if it were
> nothing but froth: and to what end, but to elevate his [i.e., Burton's]
> authorite by bringing his person into disesteeme, to enervate his
> writings . . . to presume to write Divinitie without eloquence, is
> impudencie, and if it be purposely done, madness.[13]

The critical history of the controversy on style between
Hall's "moderation" and Milton's vehemence shows these
curious trajectories, some of them personal. David Masson,
for example, had an uncanny feel for Milton's dislike of Hall:
"he regarded Hall . . . as, to a great extent, a literary impostor,
a man of an essentially coarse and mean order of talent, who
had been rated far above his deserts, and whom it would be a
service to literature, as well as to sound Church-polity, to blast
and show up" (*Life,* 2:257); another nineteenth century editor
who shares this view is J. A. St. John.[14] By comparison, the
editors of the *Complete Prose Works* appear to bend over

backwards not to appear partisan, rather sympathizing with Hall over Milton.[15]

These debates are about style, yet they emphasize political and theological issues over matters of "fine writing," tradition, the vernacular, Ciceronianism, Senecanism, over Baconian analysis of word and thing. Participants search for the style of truth-from-Scripture, of words from the Word, of what I will now call *kerygmatic authority,* with a new emphasis on the relation between speaker and audience. Decorum *kata ton akroaten,* with regard to the audience, is the issue, now more problematic, and more central, as printed texts proliferate, reaching a wider and more varied audience, and as individual interpretation threatens the mediatorial role of the Church. For the author the increasing number of printing presses, licensed and unlicensed, combines with the new Reformational freedom to interpret. The call is to forge a new decorum to fill all those blank pages, to win all those souls.

Newspaper style has not yet been established;[16] in transition, the ephemeral tract, one could argue, becomes the essential genre of the 1640s in England. The range of possible expressions must have been intoxicating to young radical reformers like Milton and Lilburne, who make the righteousness, and hence the authority, of the speaker a critical element of the genre. The tract wars become wars between the rectitudes of the speakers. Styles express those rectitudes. Style becomes a major subject of the debates, as this debate supremely shows.

Bishop Hall represents the standard edition of Truth, elegant, fully annotated, well-bound, essentially the Established Text. Milton's response is a living text, and his book is conceived as an organism, experiencing, testing, translating, subverting, feeding on the ideas of the past and present and metabolizing them before our eyes into print, his anti-Establishment act something like a performance event. The organic images for books and for Truth—(the good writer "ought him selfe to bee a true Poem"; "a good Booke is the pretious life-blood of a master spirit")—are for Milton drawn *from the experience of virulent controversy,* not, as Stanley Fish argues, from a cool and disengaged analysis (*HMW,* 190–92).

Milton's timeliness was the opposite of "fashion," for which he had as much contempt as for canned knowledge. He valued the monuments of Western literature, but not as mere monuments. Instead he treated the literary past rather as T. S. Eliot did in "Tradition and the Individual Talent," as an articulated and continuously shifting progression. No perfection. No absoluteness or absolutism on earth. Even his later images of Eden and of Heaven are present progressive, not past perfect. Consider the "authorized excess" of the Garden[17] and the perfect bliss of Adam and Eve, "not in the least without tension and trial" (Lewalski, "Innocence," 117).[18] The cosmic dance of *Paradise Lost* is related to this present-imperfect sense of "perfection":

> Mystical dance, which yonder starry sphere
> Of planets and fixt in all her Wheels
> Resemble nearest, mazes intricate
> Eccentric, intervolv'd, yet regular
> Then most, when most irregular they seem.   (5.620–24)

Process is Milton's certainty, as the passage in *Areopagitica* eloquently argues. We must recover the scattered limbs of Truth "hewd . . . into a thousand pieces. . . . We have not yet found them all, Lords and Commons, nor ever shall doe, till her Masters second comming; he shall bring together every joynt and member, and shall mould them into an immortall feature of lovelines and perfection" (*CPW*, 2:549). No Miltonic version of the beautiful or the virtuous is static; we can infer that nowhere is his rectitude "perfect."

The demonstration of righteousness in these pieces is related to the ethical proof of classical oration, as numerous scholars have argued. But it is not identical with that proof, since this righteousness often usurps the very role of invention, virtually cannibalizing the other parts, as in the great digressions on career. Thus an emphasis on "ethical proof" as terminology ultimately misreads the real structure of pieces primarily advertising rectitude and, in the process, subverting the rules of classical rhetoric. All decorum is provisional. One can accept the existence of potent genres, of sophisticated Renaissance critical theory, of Milton's vast preparation in rhetoric, and still insist that decorum—the rhetorical moment—must be positioned historically, with as much political and theological, as well as literary, detail as possible. Within the Smectymnuan controversy, one must first evaluate Bishop Hall's range of style, his authority real and imagined, his complex attempt to control the discourse, in short his initiatory and initiating decorum. In order to understand Milton in this context, we must understand the Humble Remonstrant.

I

Between 1625 and 1638, there were six editions in at least eight printings of Bishop Hall's collected *Works*. These *Works* included a number of controversial pieces,[19] some of which Hall revised and enlarged over a period of years. By 1641, after *Episcopacie by Divine Right, Asserted* had been commissioned by Laud,[20] and after *An Humble Remonstrance*,[21] he was quite regularly attacked. His old enemy Henry Burton can mention almost casually, "Dr. *Hals* sweatie discourses."[22] Before the Smectymnuans responded to the *Remonstrance*, an anonymous writer issued *An Anti-Remonstrance*. This tract begins with a parody of Hall's style:

> These few Leaves of Paper breake on through, after the humble remonstrance, with less noyse, because of lesse bulke; and not stuffed with the huskes of a bare pleasing speech, but presented to your view with more substance than Rethorique, and with more things than words, and such as I hope will plucke off the vizard of dutifull Sonne from the Authour of the Remonstrance, or make his Mother [the Church] little beholding to him for his advice.[23]

This ironic Baconian sounds very like Milton, and he anticipates SMECTYMNUUS and Milton as well with these charges against Hall's style as famous, empty, and posturing. Other comments on Hall during this period are similar, often initially respectful, then critical, like those of John Vicars, who writes in 1642: "one of their most *moderate, wise men of peace,* since his being in prison in the *Tower,* hath not been asham'd with his accustom'd *rhetorically-glorious* and *smoothly painted phrases* to daub over his great guilt of conscience."[24] In *The Anatomy of the Service Book* (1641), "Dwalphintramis" sneers at the famous Bishop: "the Doctor his Charging upon Gods people with passionate reproaches, recoyles enough upon himselfe; though Tully telleth us that bad Orators instead of Reason use Declamations, we could not have expected it from so great an Orator as the Doctor."[25] Hall is shifty and hypocritical in the view of the influential Robert Baillie, who saw him as one of "the reserved squadron of Knights of [the Devil's] reconcilers, by whose pretences of friendship and peaceable mediations, he is [more]confident to overthrow the Protestant cause than by the heads and hands of all his former souldiers" (*Parallel,* A2–A2v). Elsewhere, Hall is accused of pride, "as having too long lorded it over his brethren" and of "uttering words of high disdain."[26] Milton and the Smectymnuans are not alone in finding Hall often flashy, proud, self-dramatizing, and ultimately hypocritical. Hall's rectitude *is* theatrical. At the beginning of *An Humble Remonstrance,* he presents himself as courageous and modest in the face of the libelous mob; he sustains the figure throughout the controversy:

> Lest the world should think the Presse had of late forgot to speake any language other then Libellous, this honest paper hath broken through the throng, and prostrates it selfe before you: How meanly soever, and unattended, it presents it selfe to your view. . . . how many furious and malignant spirits every where have burst forth into sclanderous libels, bitter Pasquines, railing Pamphlets . . . lewd boldnesse . . . daring, and misgrounded insolence . . . malicious, or ignorant presumption. (1–7)

This pose of beleaguered superiority stands at the head of the entire debate. The pose, and Hall's considerable reputation for successful self-righteousness, governs the style and much of the argument of the Smectymnuan *Answer,* which immediately addresses Hall's persona and his famous style.

Though the author's identity was widely known, the conventional fiction of anonymity was scrupulously maintained; the adversary of SMECTYMNUUS was Bishop Joseph Hall under the quite transparent mask of the Humble Remonstrant. The bishop's persona is immediately attacked as "neither *Humble* nor a *Remonstrance*," that of a writer who wastes one's time with "too large a *preface*," "so many passionate Rhetorications" and "Episcopall Bravado" (1–3); the writers deplore his "Rhetoricall Encomium" and "the Embroideries of his silken Language" (9–15), his "large praises of Persons," "His Encomiasticks" and his "Rhetorical insinuation" (65–66). The Remonstrant is dangerous largely *because* he is a skilled rhetorician, one who persuasively misuses the language. SMECTYMNUUS end their first tract with an important caution:

> Wee finde that the late innovations which have so much disturbed the peace & purity of our Church, did first beginne with the alteration of words. . . . And the Apostle exhorts us, 2 Tim. 1.13. *To hold fast the forme of sound words:* and 1 Tim. 6.20. *To avoide the prophane novelties of words.* (*An Answer*, 82)

Marshall, Calamy, Young, Newcomen, and Spurstowe point steadily to the possible corruptions in language and especially to the seductiveness of Hall's rhetoric: it is false but "passionate," "unparalell'd"; it "declaims," "flows," "insinuates" (65–66). All these terms are used pejoratively, but all attest to the skill, "the learning and fame" (62) of their opponent. The *de facto* identification of the Bishop coexists with the fiction of his anonymity.

When Hall responds, he responds very quickly. Both *A Defence of the Humble Remonstrance against the Frivolous and False Exceptions of SMECTYMNUUS* (1641) and *A Short Answer To the Tedious Vindications of SMECTYMNUUS*[27] appear one month after the pamphlets they are answering. In *Defence* Hall turns immediately to his opponents and their style:

> The quarrell is insolently managed by many unknowne hands [there would appear to be two kinds of anonymity: known and

unknown] . . . the riot of these impotent Assailants . . . their confident ostentation and proud carriage in this affray, hath won them some (how undeserved soever) opinion of skill, with their credulous Abettors . . . my daring Answerers; whose Abilities I taxe not. (A3v–A4)

This last quotation is a good example of Hall's technique of insulting while denying the insult—quite different from Milton, who would be unlikely to print so hypocritical a line as: "The good God of heaven be mercifull to such a miszealous obstinacy" (*Humble*, 21). There is also the citing of evidence not available to the callow upstarts: "the *Seder Tephilloth* of the Jews of Portugall," just published, and the Tecla manuscript, gift of Cyrill "the late Patriarch of Constantinople" (*Defence*, 16, 115). I am not criticizing Hall for having access to good libraries; I am only suggesting that the tone is a little unbrethrenly. Hall goes on to speak of SMECTYMNUUS' "trifling cavils," "light froth," and "this overflowing of your gall" (3–8). He chides them on their translations (13, 14); accuses them of garrulity, "over-comprehensive recapitulation"; of "frivolous waste"; and mocks "the battery of their Paper-pellets" (22–45); "you beat the ayre very furiously, and fight pitifully with your selves" he notes (73); and accuses the writers of a "dull and tedious hand" (98); of "mere Declamation, not worthy of any answere, but contempt and silence" (144); "ill-bred sonns" who "spit in the face of your mother" (145); making "your bold and unjust demands . . . those vain cavills" (158). Hall's epithets almost always express presumption in his opponents.

When the Smectymnuans reply, in *A Vindication of the Answer to the Humble Remonstrance from the Unjust Imputations of Frivolousnesse and Falsehood* (June 1641), they concede his legitimate raising of four issues; then they concentrate on his pride as revealed in his style. Hall's book is "full fraught with bitter invectives, false aspersions, hyperbolicall confidence, selfe contradictions, and such like extravagancies" (A4); "never man since *Mountagues Appeale* a notoriously aggressive prelatical pamphlet] wrote with more scorne and contempt" (a); "Sarcasmes and vaine

Rhetorications . . . confidence and Thrasonicall boasting" (a3). "As if all learning and acutenesse were lockt up in his breast (*Narcissus* like in love with his owne shadow)" (132). They protest their own sincerity: "We have written nothing out of a spirit of contention and faction, but onely as lovers of the Truth, and the peace of the Church" (46–47). They present themselves as underdogs: "poor men cannot have their Presse waited on, as your greatness may" (111). They skillfully emphasize Hall's schoolmasterliness: "Why should wee use him as a Father, that does not use us as Brethren? Makes sport with our wit, triumphs over it (184). . . . this great Corrector of Translations (189) . . . our Remonstrant is so busie with his *Ferula*, that no sooner can he thinke we trip, but he is presently upon us, *Corrigit Magnificat*" (190). Hall's "whole Remonstrance" was "but a *declamation* . . . [his] *Defence* but a Satyre" (196). The second Smectymnuan tract spends most of its energy in this kind of rhetorical parrying. This is confirmed in the last fifteen pages of the tract itself, with its sharp shift into tough, brisk analysis of the doctrine and discipline of the Church of England.

Milton's *Animadversions* appeared before Hall's *Short Answer*, but Hall did not see it—or at least did not refer to it— so I will briefly discuss his tract first. Hall appears to have his back to the wall. The Smectymnuans had opened their second tract with a list of the abusive terms that Hall had used against them; Hall now follows suit with his own list. Claiming for himself brevity and moderation, Hall attacks the Smectymnuans: "inraged with a moderate opposition, they heat their furnace seven times more, and break forth into a not more voluminous, then vehement Invective" (A3v). In a skillful "Preface to the Reader" he lays claim again to rational and disinterested analysis: "It matters not the person: let it please you to look at the cause" (A3v). But the matter proceeds to personal stylistics: "[they] present you with a whole bundle of such strange flowers of Rhetorick, as truly, I wondred should ever grow in my Garden" (A4). The attitudes I have emphasized in the *Defence* are if anything more marked in *A Short Answer*—superiority, "shy" boasting, and the veneer of charity.

If anything, the tension of the debate has weakened Hall's ability to maintain his studied humility. He is clearly offended and threatened by the Smectymnuans, their "strange insolence," (A4v) "the scornful, girding, and unmannerly passages of this their angry vindication" (Sig. a). He labels them presumptuous and unprepared, "Let them first . . . Answer . . . the Divine Right of Episcopacie [before] I should trouble my self with sweeping away these loose scraps of their exceptions" (av); and he mocks their "insolent wisdome," "your crowing insultation," . . . "I see the chief pride of your *Vindication* lies in this passage of Jewish skill" (34–47). Throughout, his famous benign tolerance is severely strained , and indeed it cracks, contending with "these deepe heads" (5) and their "strange project" at which he asks "leave to smile a little" at their "weary loquacitie" "overswolne, and unwieldie bulk," "so high insolence." (86–101)

Hall boasts of his privileged access to rare texts, with considerable pomposity:

> To prove that the Jews had a form of Liturgy even from *Moses* his time, I produced a monument above the reach of your either knowledge, or censure; [the] Samaritan Chronicle, now in the hands of our most learned and famous Primate of Ireland; written in Arabick, translated into that tongue, and of the Hebrew; as *Jos: Scaliger* (whose it once was) testifies; fetching down the story from *Moses* to *Adrians* time, and somewhat below it. (37–38)

This is not particularly brethrenly, nor is the final can't-be-bothered gesture of dismissal:

> You may perhaps expect to meet with fitter matches, that have more leasure. . . . I have determined to take off my hand from this remayning Controversie of *Episcopacy* . . . to turne off my combined opposites to matches more meet for their age and quality. (101–2)

These snappish claims of superiority in both the Remonstrant's tracts were long overlooked, or at least neglected. In fact, Hall's label as underdog in the Smectymnuan controversy is one of the small fallacies of literary history, despite the comments of Masson and St. John, and despite the sensible warning from William Riley Parker:

> Bishop Hall was a more experienced writer than the five Presbyterian ministers who had ventured to attack him, and in defending himself he used 'no common arts.' He was skilled as a satirist and a controversialist; there was no denying his 'voluble and smart fluence of tongue.' The Smectymnuans were in danger, therefore, of being talked down by sheer glibness and wit. (Parker, *Milton*, 1:205)

Hall's career was brilliant, sophisticated, and, to a point, independent. As late as 1640, his *Christian Moderation* speaks with authenticity of the need "to draw as neere as wee may to Christian adversaries."[28] But from at least 1628 onward, and certainly after Laud's instructions to be about his Archbishop's business, Hall's tone toward the Puritans changes, and his rational moderation turns tart and self-protective.[29]

Milton was right, and so were the Smectymnuans, to doubt the sincerity of the reiterated "Brethren"—over 50 times as a noun of address in *Defence* alone: "your use is, call brother and smite; call brother and smite" (*CPW*, 1:694). Rejected too are the exclamations of shocked righteousness, the "bewildered" exhortations to God and reason. For Bishop Hall engaged in a hard-core polemic under the pietistic proclamations of charity, a rhetoric of labels, impugning rather than illuminating. The Puritan five, and Milton, forged a style in response to that style and to the hitherto politically effective persona who spoke it. The fame, or notoriety, of the Smectymnuans during the better part of the next twenty years suggests that they did in fact "win," and not merely because they were attached to the side that won the war. Hall bungled this pamphlet battle, seriously miscalculated the decorum of the situation, and underestimated the complexity of his audience, adversaries, and topic. Hall's data and his forms of argument were perhaps no more vulnerable to criticism than Milton's; the war Hall lost was the war of styles. In the clash between The Establishment Bishop and A Young Puritan Divine (both figures abstracted into pseudo-anonymity), style and even personality were more important than logical demonstration. The chief appeal was not "Believe *this*" but rather "Believe *me.*" Hall failed at just the kind of performance for which he had earlier achieved fame. But in the midst of these powerful disagreements, he was still a most dangerous opponent. It is at this point, when Hall's persona and decorum have been established as prime concerns, that Milton enters the debate on his own.[30]

II

For the fourth time within a few months Milton attacks the institution of Prelacy. Neither the raptures of *Of Reformation* nor the ponderous concisions of the "Postscript" and *Of Prelatical Episcopacy* had solved the problem. *Animadversions Upon the Remonstrants Defence Against SMEC-TYMNUUS* (July 1641) is another circling round, another try at what must at first have seemed like a brief digression to straighten things out for his friends. Milton always seems surprised when the world doesn't accept his solutions. This accounts for an engaging, half sad, half humorous, quality to his bemused returns to a controversial topic.

For Milton, this new tract must be different from the others because (1) the others didn't work as expected, and (2) the others didn't focus on personalities (despite Ussher's name on the title page of the second tract). Here the persona of the adversary is more fully experienced, by author and by reader. Hall had attacked Milton's section of the Smectymnuuan *Answer,* calling the Postscript "a goodly Pasquin," "a rhapsody of histories," "tedious," "full of these hatefull instances," "miserably uncharitable." He had accused this section of the tract of bad taste and of plagiarism. Second, and much more important, Hall was saliently a figure in his own tracts; and that figure was a true goad to Milton, as it had been to the Smectymnuans.

Animadversions opens with the claim that the Remonstrant—an unidentified but recognizable Bishop Joseph

Hall[31]—is a clear and present danger to the English Reformation. Against such a danger, a special style is necessary. That style may be shocking, and it may need to be explained beforehand, even when the apologist is above normal rhetorical constraints:

> Although it be a certaine truth that they who undertake a Religious Cause need not care to be Men-pleasers; yet because the satisfaction of tender and mild consciences is far different from that which is call'd Men-pleasing, to satisfie such, I shall adresse my selfe in few words to give notice before hand of something in this booke, which to some men perhaps, may seeme offensive, that when I have render'd a lawfull reason of what is done, I may trust to have sav'd the labour of defending or excusing hereafter. (*CPW*, 1:662; I have normalized italics)

This is careful preparation for the defense of style which follows. His decorum, while emphasizing "tender and mild consciences," must reflect his heterogeneous audience. Characteristically, Milton cites the strongest evidence he must contravene: Christ teaches us "not to answer the reviler in his language though never so much provok't." Only the most pressing need can go against this injunction: "any notorious enimie to truth and his Countries peace, especially that is conceited to have a voluble and smart fluence of tongue." Bishop Hall "stands up for all the rest" because of his "vaine confidence" in his rhetorical skills and "out of a more tenacious cling to worldly respects." Hall is "such a one" who must be handled "in a rougher accent" (662). The constraints of Christian charity are dissolved; vehemence becomes the appropriate mode for this encounter.

Hall is far from being treated as "an ultra-stupid mouse"[32] by Cat Milton. This Bishop corrupts "by subtle dissimulation" and "wily Strategem"; he "creeps," "hovering"; he "traines on the easie Christian insensibly within the close ambushment of worst errors, and with a slye shuffle of counterfeit principles chopping and changing till hee have glean'd all the good ones out of their minds" (*CPW*, 1:663). Hall practices "collusion," "grand imposture"; he is "a false Prophet," "the cheat of soules" (663–64). He is Comus:

I under fair pretence of friendly ends
And well-plac't words of glozing courtesie
Baited with reasons not unplausible,
Wind me into the easy-hearted man,
And hugg him into snares. (*A Mask*, 160–64, in *Riverside Milton*,
131)

Milton justifies the style of his tract by showing his adversary as dangerously facile with language and learning. "Who a more dangerous deceiver then he who defending a traditionall corruption uses no common Arts[?]" (*CPW*, 1:663) The major purport of the tract—an animadversion—is to expose and eliminate that danger. It is necessary to return to that portrait of a dangerous Hall—not only wrong-minded , or foolish, but dangerous—again and again. In the middle of the piece Milton suggests that even the Smectymnuans "have too credulously thought him if not an over-logicall, yet a well-meaning man; but now we find him either grossly deficient in his principles of *Logick*, or else purposely bent to delude the *Parliament* with equivocall Sophistry" (694).

With an extraordinary intuition of the modern uses of propaganda, he accuses Hall of "scattering among his periods ambiguous words, whose interpretations he will afterwards dispence according to his pleasure" (694). Near the end, just preceding his description of "the messenger, and Herald of heavenly truth from God to man" (721) comes this portrait of the English Seneca: "[The learned Hypocrite] is still using his sophisticated arts and bending all his studies how to make his insatiate avarice, & ambition seem pious, and orthodoxall by painting his lewd and deceitfull principles with a smooth, and glossy varnish in a doctrinall way to bring about his wickedest purposes" (720).

This is Bishop Joseph Hall, spokesman for Archbishop Laud, come upon the stage at a time when "God and man are now ready to explode and hisse [Pseudepiscopy] out of the land." "It will be nothing disagreeing from Christian meeknesse . . . to send home his haughtinesse well bespurted with his owne holy-water." Solomon allowed these "vehemencies," and so did Christ, "as nothing could be more killingly spoken." "The noblest jealousie" transports "with the zeale of truth to a well heated fervencie." "They that love the soules of men" must undertake, "not without a sad and unwilling anger" "the serious uncasing of a grand imposture" "with a grim laughter . . . in an austere visage." "This veine of laughing . . . hath oft-times a strong and sinewy force in teaching and confuting." For this, "two most rationall faculties of humane intellect anger and laughter were first seated in the brest of man" (*CPW*, 1:662–64). Anger and laughter become the vehicles for delivering Milton's demythologizing message.

The Preface to *Animadversions* is one of the most explicit rhetorical programs for a single text in English Renaissance literature. Milton has defined his adversary and identified the vehemencies—grim laughter and anger—that he will use against him. He identifies his scriptural models and rejects "menpleasing," presumably the easy decorum of speaking softly; and yet, precisely for "the softer spirited Christians," he has written this detailed and committed preface.

To the general reader he gives explanations of his structure: the setting of a passage from Hall followed by Milton's comment on it. He has chosen this format, "this close and succinct way of dealing with the Adversary," in order to simplify, to eliminate the "labyrinth of controversall antiquity" and in order to cut into the Bishop's royalties (664). Less than a year later he would confirm his description and give further rationale for his writing:

> in that manner neglecting the maine bulk of all that specious antiquity, which might stunne children, but not men, I chose rather to observe some kinde of military advantages to await him at his forragings, at his watrings, and when ever he felt himselfe secure to solace his veine inderision of his more serious opponents. (*CPW*, 1:872)

The structure may have been chosen by Milton for the wrong reasons, (as Rudolf Kirk suggests in his Preface to the Yale edition of *Animadversions* [*CPW*, 1:654–55]), but I doubt it. Hugh Cholmley used the same model in defending Hall against Henry Burton;[33] Laud used it against Fisher.[34] So in

fact did Hall himself, and Marprelate and Sir Thomas More—
and Socrates. The device is not only common, it is rational,
since a major purpose of the debate was to show the opponent,
point by point, in an unfavorable light. The title, again, is
Animadversions.[35]

Milton was not guilty of any unusual wrenching out
of context (as many who have commented on this tract have
suggested). He is scrupulous in page citations in his margins,
including clear distinctions between the *Remonstrance* and
the *Defence*. Quotations and paraphrases are unusually
accurate for the period, and the quotations (with one exception)
are in the right order.[36] Elisions do not alter the basic meanings
of the sentences. By comparison with other polemicists,
including Hall in this controversy, Milton treats the text of
his opponent with more accuracy, if more vehemence. Despite
his own claim that he was trying to provide enough of his
opponent's text for his reader to make judgment, Milton
proceeds as though he imagined a different situation: a reader
with Hall's two texts and *Animadversions* before him. I have
said in chapter 3 that Milton's conception of the Word was at
this time of a printed text that could be perused. *Animadversions* proceeds on the assumption of a *present* printed text;
otherwise the punctilious citations and the accuracy of report
are, in contemporary terms, unusual. The argument
is *ad hominem*—of course; it *has* been, from the beginning
of the debate. Yet Milton's response is a fair as well as
an appropriate one. The rectitude of the speaker and the
hypocrisy of the adversary are in fact critical to these debates.

Section I provides some good examples of Milton's procedure. He begins by attacking Hall's position through ridicule,
an irreverence that transports individual words from one
context to another:

> *Remonstrant*
> My single *Remonstrance* is encountred with a plurall *Adversary*.
>
> Answere
> Did not your single Remonstrance bring along with it a hot sent of

> your more then singular affection to spirituall pluralities, your
> singlenesse would be lesse suspected with all good Christians then
> it is. (*CPW*, 1:664–65)

Milton's response is not quite a nonsequitur, since the
argument remains within the larger context of the debate over
prelacy. It is arguable that Hall's image of himself as the one
just man is less relevant than Milton's image of him as spiritual
pluralist. We are witnessing a debate from one point of view,
not a logical demonstration.

Milton derides and denies Hall's stance, sometimes by
flooding the persona with a larger context, as above. He attacks
the image of beleagueredness and emphasizes, instead, Hall's
self-righteousness—"My cause, you Gods" (665). Here, and
here only, Milton distorts the bishop's language by repeating
the phrase three times. He challenges Hall's claim to being
David. He ridicules his quibble on *Areopagi*, accusing him of
itching with "parlous Criticism," of citing the Smectymnuans
"to appear for certaine *Paragogicall* contempts before a
capricious *Paedantie* of hot liver'd Grammarians" (666). This
is typically Martinist, and, as in Marprelate, the ridiculing of
pedantry is followed by a "functional" pedantry, a demonstration of the ridiculer's knowledge: "they did not more then
the elegantest Authors among the *Greeks*, Romans, and at
this day the *Italians*" (667). Hall's knowledge is showy and
irrelevant in the eyes of the Animadverter, who presents his
own as solid and useful.

In the plea of the one Remonstrant against the plural
adversary Hall had written: "But could they say my name is
Legion; for wee are many." Milton takes the opportunity to
challenge one of Hall's major strengths as a polemicist, his
reputation for clarity: "Wherefore should you begin with the
Devils name descanting upon the number of your opponents?
Wherefore that conceit of *Legion* with a by-wipe? Was it
because you would have men take notice how you esteeme
them, whom through all your booke so bountifully you call
your brethren?" (665). The point is well taken, and the dry
"so bountifully" shows Milton's sharp eye for adversarial

detail. The Bishop's selective tolerance for libels is also cited (with Bacon's testimony as ballast) as proof of insincerity (668).

Now, Milton's first flight begins with his discussion of the "shameful number of libells," transformed into a substantive discussion of freedom of expression. The prelates complain of libel when they are the targets. But *now* is a special time for the free-born people of England:

> after all your Monkish prohibitions, and expurgatorious indexes, your gags and snaffles, your proud *Imprimaturs* not to be obtain'd without the shallow surview, but not shallow hand of some mercenary, narrow Soul'd, and illitterate Chaplain; when liberty of speaking then which nothing is more sweet to man, was girded, and straight lac't almost to a broken-winded tizzick, if now at a good time, our time of *Parliament*, the very jubily, and resurrection of the State, if now the conceal'd, the aggreev'd, and long persecuted Truth, could not be suffer'd speak, and though she burst out with some efficacy of words, could not be excus'd after such an injurious strangle of silence, nor avoyde the censure of Libelling, twere hard, twere something pinching in a Kingdome of free spirits. (*CPW*, 1:669)

The energy here is like that of *Areopagitica*, and so is the diction and the argument itself. Clearly *Animadversions* is the thematic and imagistic womb of Milton's greatest tract. The Areopagus is here, the virulent *Imprimatur*, the illiterate and venal censor. Most important is the heady celebration of "liberty of speaking," the exuberant embrace of all that controversy and its abrasive multiplicity. There is a physical sense of liberation *now*, liberation from "gags and snaffles," from "broken-winded tizzick[s]" from the "injurious strangle of silence." Read aloud, the congested sounds virtually enact the argument in the throat, become almost physically memorable. The strangle of silence remains in the memory of mind and throat. Speaking freely is the objective correlative of liberation; censorship is strangulation because life *is* being able to speak freely. Parliament bursts out as "jubily" and "resurrection."

There is information as well as exhilaration in free speaking. No longer need the prince, like the Duke in *Measure for*

Measure,[37] lurk in disguise "that they might hear every where the free utterances of privat brests" and "avoid that deceitfull and close coucht evil of flattery" (from Angelo, from Strafford, from Laud). "This permission of free writing . . . makes not only the whole Nation in many points the wiser, but also . . . carries home to Princes . . . such a full insight of every lurking evil, or restrained good" (*CPW,* 1:670). The exposure of these "libells" can lead to accurate political information. The surgery is radical, but the patient is beloved: "such an unripping, such an Anatomie of the shiest and tenderest particular truths" (670).[38]

The impressive paragraph ends with a pedantic quibble on genre, of the sort for which Milton had called Hall "hot-liver'd Grammarian": "You love toothlesse Satyrs; let me informe you a toothlesse Satyr is as improper as a toothed sleekstone, and as bullish." Out of context the comment is humorless and pedantic. In context it is at least modestly relevant; it seeks to demonstrate Hall's fear of the abrasiveness of truth—even his satires are toothless—and that fear is behind his much-reiterated fear and contempt for the multitude of libels: "But these [free-spoken, and plaine harted men] are the nettlers, these are the blabbing Bookes that tell, though not halfe your fellowes feats" (*CPW,* 1:670). In *A Modest Confutation* and in *An Apology,* Milton and his adversary will haggle over genre. Here Milton is more concerned with Hall's epistemology than with his orthodox use of literary genres. He continues to insist that controversy must be free, must be allowed its harshness.

Passionate vision and clever, sometimes vulgar, *ad hominem* are the most obvious of Milton's media, but he ranges over a number of other rhetorical procedures. There are demonstrations of Hall's logical inconsistency, citing Bishop Downam's Ramistic logic (*CPW,* 1:672, 674, 710); new historical evidence, as from Hayward's *Edward the Sixt* (678), or Beza (707); and straightforward debate on the scriptural texts (710–14 especially). The Modest Confuter will not prove a good reader of Milton's text, but he will be correct in accusing Milton of marginalizing the prelatical matter in *Animadversions*: "For that which you professedly disavow [private and personal spleen] is the greatest matter in your book; the other business [the authority of prelacy] being handled but by the by, or not at all" (*Confutation*, 5–6). However approached, the greatest matter in this text is the confrontation of the persona of the Humble Remonstrant, Bishop Joseph Hall. The controversy has moved steadily toward sharper and sharper focus on personalities, on discrediting the adversary and defending the speaker. The last two items in the antiprelatical series will contain Milton's most heavily autobiographical work.

At the tail of a tedious argument, Hall, the Smectymnuans and Milton must have assumed that the respective evidence for Prelacy and Presbyterianism had been sufficiently presented. They turn to *ad hominem* attacks and to a domineering "ethical proof." Hall presents himself as David against Goliath, a charitable superior against a host of insolent, badly educated rabble. The Smectymnuans and Milton present themselves as well-educated righteous underdogs, and they cite the usual Puritan topoi against the Bishop—venality, fearfulness of the truth, and pride. Hall's special claim for himself is *noblesse oblige*—"Brethren!"; against his opponents, he charges ignorant disrespect. Milton's special claim is, for Hall, hypocrisy; for himself, zeal. Claims and counterclaims come together in two figures in Milton's attack: "You are not arm'd *Remonstrant*, nor any of your band, nor are not dieted, nor your loynes girt for spirituall valour, and Christian warfare, the luggage is too great that followes your Camp" (*CPW*, 1:666). David has gone flabby, with one eye on the baggage. Or, perhaps, Hall is transformed into a figure from another part of Scripture, one which caps and fully defines the figure of "the false prophet . . . the cheat of soules" (664); the collector of the "damned *Simony* of *Trentals*" (702); "false *Prophets* . . . a lie in the sight of all the people" (705).

In the *Defence*, Hall had rather mildly belittled the Smectymnuans with this: "Brethren how you have with *Simon* fisht all night, and caught nothing" (*Defence*, 76).[39] Milton prints the line then exploits it: "If we fishing with *Simon* the Apostle can catch nothing; see what you can catch with *Simon Magus*;

for all his hooks, & fishing implements he bequeath's among you" (*CPW*, 1:710). The figure has lurked in the epithets of opprobrium with which Milton had been attacking the Bishop from the very beginning. Since the Simon quotation is the only one to be taken from the middle parts of Hall's piece, it seems possible that Milton salvaged that Hall quote in order to introduce the Simon Magus figure as a mechanism for unifying his abuse against the Bishop.

An extensive tradition had made of Simon Magus a partly ominous, partly pathetic figure. He was seen as a good man gone wrong, a partial Christian. Post-Apostolic commentary saw him as the father of heresy, and Justin Martyr saw him as the father of Gnosticism.[40] John Downame wrote of him: "he only had an historicall Faith . . . wrought in him by the admirable miracles."[41] Calvin discussed him in the *Institutes* (3:2:10; 4:1:26) and at some length in *Commentary Upon the Acts of the Apostles*, where he is described as deceiver of the Samarians: "for the minds of all of them were bewitched with Simon's jigglings. And this amazedness was grown to some strength by reason of long space of time" (1:331).[42] The magician had attempted to buy the power passed on by the laying on of hands. Since that power was the chief claim of Episcopacy *jure divino*, Milton's citation is apposite, and I think planned for, in this first half of the *Animadversions*. Hall has been made to look surprisingly like

> a certain man called Simon, which beforetime in the same city used sorcery, and bewitched the people of Samaria, giving out that himself was some great one.
>
> To whom they all gave heed, from the least to the greatest, saying, This man is the great power of God.
>
> And when Simon saw that through the laying on of the apostles' hands, the holy Ghost was given, he offered them money,
>
> Saying, Give me also this power, that on whomsoever I lay hands, he may receive the Holy ghost
>
> But Peter said unto him, Thy money perish with thee, because thou hast thought that the gift of God may be purchased with money. (Acts 8.9–10, 18–20)

The figure of Hall as "cheat of soules" has drawn on Milton's earlier practice—Comus and the bad shepherds of "Lycidas"—

and on a very active contemporary emphasis on venal deceivers, bad ministers. It also has specific reference to the figure with which Milton closes this, the more polished, half of his tract. The figure of Simon Magus pulls together the major criticisms of Hall. The allusion also allows for some small, implicit exercise of Miltonic pity; Simon's last verse (24) in Acts is his request to Peter, "Pray ye to the Lord for me."

III

Animadversions proclaims itself a careful and systematic analysis of the errors of the Smectymnuan adversary. Following a remarkable description of his own rhetorical strategy, Milton begins with a section by section dismantling of the arguments and language of the remonstrant. Yet throughout the tract, and long before the leap in treatment from section 5 to section 13 of Hall's text, this regularity becomes the victim of Milton's digressions, ballooning into passages of personal, vocational, and political plans and predictions which appear to elude the major forensic purpose of the piece. These digressions tend to be the most interesting sections. They start with the vision of God's England, the imminent triumphs of the Saints, and an extraordinary sense of the thrilling here and *now* noted above: "God and man are now ready (662). . . . if now at a good time, our time. . . . if now the conceal'd, the aggreev'd , and the long persecuted Truth (669) . . . whereas now this permission of free writing (670) . . . Open your eyes to the light of grace" (*CPW*, 1:702). No other English poet has approached Milton's vision of the exalted *English present:* "the present age, which is to us an age of ages wherein God is manifestly come downe among us, to doe some remarkable good to our Church or state. . . . in this Age, *Brittains* God hath reform'd his Church" (703–4). God had always had a special love for his island fortress, "this Sceptered isle," but, as I have suggested above, the three *anni mirabili*—1588, 1605, 1641—were seen by the Puritans as sharper concentrations of His care, a care lovingly and intimately present in this prose:

> [He] sent first to us a healing messenger to touch softly our sore, and carry a gentle hand over our wounds: he knockt once and twice and came againe, opening our drousie eye-lids leasurely . . . still taking off by degrees the inveterat scales from our nigh perisht sight, purg'd also our deaf eares. . . . the sudden assault of his reforming Spirit . . . we that have liv'd so long in abundant light, besides the sunny reflection of all the neighbouring Churches . . . the morning beam of *Reformation*. . . . O if we freeze at noone after their earely thaw, let us feare lest the Sunne for ever hide himselfe. . . . thou hast open'd our difficult and sad times, and given us an unexpected breathing after our long oppressions. (704–5)

The "unexpected breathing" is the release from "the strangle of silence."

For Milton the present opposition is the shadow of the glorious vision, a shadow described in images that had been early expressed in the Nativity ode and will later appear in the *Areopagitica* and, more memorably, in *Paradise Lost:*

> a vaine shadow of wisedome in a tongue nothing slow to utter guile . . . thou hast made our false Prophets to be found a lie in the sight of all the people, and chac'd them with sudden confusion and amazement before the redoubled brightnesse of thy descending cloud that now covers thy Tabernacle. . . . When thou hast settl'd peace in the Church and righteous judgement in the Kingdome, then shall thy Saints address their voyces of joy, and triumph to thee, standing on the shoare of that red Sea into which our enemies had almost driven us. (*CPW*, 1:705–6)

The reference is of course to Exodus 14 and the song of triumph of Moses and the Israelites. The more extended use of the allusion in *Paradise Lost*[43] gives an interesting contrast. Satan's fallen angels are compared to the corpses of that "*Memphian* Chivalry" drowned by an act of God

> While with perfidious hatred they pursu'd
> The Sojourners of *Goshen*, who beheld
> From the safe shore their floating Carkases. (*PL*, 1.307, 308–10)

The passage from the epic celebrates the destruction of the enemy; the earlier prose piece celebrates the promise of the future.

Paradise Lost is the promised crown and climax of Milton's great career, and yet there is missing the fervor of imminence, the absolute freshness of promise which now resonates into the most famous passage from *Animadversions:*

> And he that now for haste snatches up a plain ungarnish't present as a thanke-offering to thee, which could not bee deferr'd in regard of thy so many late deliverances wrought for us one upon another, may then perhaps take up a Harp, and sing thee an elaborate Song to Generations. . . . thy Kingdome is now at hand, and thou standing at the dore. Come forth out of thy Royall Chambers, O Prince of all the Kings of the earth, put on the visible roabes of thy imperiall Majesty, take up that unlimited Scepter which thy Almighty Father hath bequeath'd thee; for now the voice of thy Bride calls thee, and all creatures sigh to bee renew'd. (*CPW*, 1:706–7)

Milton exults in God's victory and in anticipation of his own future celebration of that victory. He promises continuity and the imminent coming of Christ in images that flood the senses with the presence of deity. Christ is heard knocking, he touches, gives breath, but most especially He bathes the elect in His light: "abundant light . . . sunny reflection . . . morning beam . . . Sunne . . . ever-begotten light, and perfect Image of the Father . . . redoubled brightnesse of thy descending cloud . . . beamy walke" (705). The climactic image of the new dawn is a fusion of light and speech, the vehicle of the passionate intercourse between Christ and His church, and it is based on Psalm 19:

> The heavens declare the glory of God and the firmament sheweth his handy worke.
> Day unto Day uttereth speech, and night unto night sheweth knowledge.
> There is no speech nor language where their voice is not heard.
> Their line is gone out through all earth, and their words to the end of the world: In them hath he set a tabernacle for the sun.
> Which is as a bridegroom coming out of his chamber, and rejoiceth as a strong man to run a race.
> His going forth is from the end of the heaven, and his circuit unto the end of it; and there is nothing hid from the heat thereof.

In the *Apology* (*CPW*, 1:930), Milton will admit, happily, that his prayer "consisted most of Scripture language"; the closing of this section 4 does use the same religious and sexual materials as the Psalm. But his episode ends not with the traversal of space but in the Bride's voice *calling* and all creatures *sighing*. As in the *Of Reformation,* so in *Animadversions;* the passionate expression of breath accompanies the emblems of a triumphant Christ. In both pieces Milton celebrates too the thrilling *Now* of Reformation England. To repeat a point: despite the grim history of a corrupted Church, the present reverberates with optimism in the antiprelatical tracts. This is "an age of ages wherein God is manifestly come downe among us"; "in this Age *Brittains* God hath reformed his Church . . .; in this Age hee hath freed us . . .; in this age he hath renewed our *Protestation* against all those dregs of superstition" (703–4). "Every one can say that now certainly thou hast visited this land" (706). Ears are opened; "inveterate scales" are removed from "drousie eyelids"; tongues are loosened and the noon freeze thaws (704–5). These are images of enfranchisement and empowerment. They are human and humane images which, had they been left undone by God, would have been "this whole worke so contrary to flesh and blood" (705). It is critical to recognize this element in Milton's thinking. If he attacks "humane principles, and carnall sense, the pride of flesh" in his opponents, he certainly does not elide the needs and uses of the ordinary human being. The sensuality of this prayer is an argument for Milton's concern for a human audience with the ordinary human weaknesses. The severe polarities of Stanley Fish's analysis underestimate these mediating elements.[44]

Present at the vision of blissful community is the singer of "high *strains* in new and lofty *Measures*" (*CPW,* 1:616), now, again, clearly the choral soloist in "an elaborate Song to Generations" (706). Also present is the image of a reprobate community, damned and descending in counterpoint to the ascending of the Saints.

In one sense these passages are "digressions," mere expansions and inflations of the ethical proof. In a more empirical sense they are not ethical proof at all, but the crown and substance of the whole argument. The speaker has overwhelmed the adversary's argument with a vision of consummating unity, and yet that overwhelming has been executed within the boundaries of the debate. Milton's Puritan response to the claims of Anglican decency shapes the decorum of this tract and turns it, at least in part, into an eschatological poem. Diction, rhythm, and range of allusion move toward higher and deeper. Arguments are polarized, Puritans and Prelatists become Israelites and Egyptians. Judgment becomes the Last Judgment. Enlightenment becomes the Bridegroom Himself.

The distance between poles widens, but intermediate examples proliferate, as in the treatment of "the learned ministry." *Being taught* is a recurring anxiety for Milton; here he identifies the free teacher and the "pupil teacher" (compare with *Of Education, CPW*, 2:533), who "cannot be trusted to pray in his own words without being chew'd to, and fescu'd to a formal injunction of his rote-lesson" (*CPW*, 1:682). Behind his analysis is Paul's injunction on the tutelage of the Law, from which we are free by Christ:

> But before faith came, we were kept under the law, shut up unto the faith, which should afterwards be revealed.
> Wherefore the law was our schoolmaster *to bring us* unto Christ that we might be justified by faith.
> But after that faith is come, we are no longer under a schoolmaster. (Galatians, 3.23–25)

"The gowned *Rabbies*, the incomparable Doctors" (*CPW*, 1:690) are conflated with those purveying the "unprofitable nonscence" of set prayer and Homilies (692) as enemies of Christ. Yet there is good teaching, of which Christ is the model (722). The good minister is a free man enfranchised by Christ, not a student teacher under supervision; he is an instructor and a guide, not a lawgiver like Moses. He is not venal, most especially not venal; and here Milton's harshness moves toward almost pure anti-intellectualism.

The bad preachers are "young mercenary striplings" with "Simoniacall fathers," who exude "stale-growne piety" and think that learning comes "from the den of *Plutus*, or the cave of *Mammon*" (718–19). Against the prelatical claim that their learned ministry was the envy of Christian Europe and critical to the perpetuation of religion, is Milton's remarkable statement: "A plaine unlearned man that lives well by that light which he has, is better, and wiser, and edifies others more toward a godly and happy life then [the learned foole, or learned Hypocrite]" (720). But that is an extreme statement; the real models are the Apostles, whose eminence

> consisted in their powerfull preaching, their unwearied labouring in the Word, their unquenchable charity, which above all earthly respects like a working flame, had spun up to such a height of pure desire, as might be thought next to that love which dwels in God to save soules . . . it is the inward calling of God that makes a Minister, and his own painfull study and diligence that manures and improves his ministeriall gifts. (715)

The good minister is self-made under God's inspiration. The emphasis is on individual inspiration and preparation, not on institutional disciplines. The Apostles were Architects and builders of the Church, but "this was but as Scaffolding of a new edifice" (715), a telling trope to which Milton will return in *Reason of Church-Government (CPW*, 1:791). Love of God is the seed, and powerful preaching and service is the flower; but the process needs the manuring of intellectual discipline, construed as private study.

The venal minister is opposed to the sincere one. Prelatical encouragement of studies is "the very garbage that drawes together all the fowles of prey and ravin in the land," but the proper education enlarges a soul "to the dimensions of spacious art and high knowledge." The bad cleric "mounts in contemplation meerly for money" (718–20). The good minister (or is it the good Christian poet?) is, like God, a creator:

> for certainly there is no imployment more honourable, more worthy to take up a great spirit, more requiring a generous and free nurture, then to be the messenger, and Herald of heavenly truth from God to man . . . to procreate a number of faithfull men, making a kind of creation like to Gods, by infusing his spirit and

likenesse into them.... as God did into him ... raising out of darksome barennesse a delicious, and fragrant Spring of saving knowledge, and good workes. (721)

Milton's *o altitudo* for the ministry echoes the earlier one for the Sun-Son in his ascension, in its generative power, its sensuousness of light and dark, of suspiration and inspiration. The distinctions between poet and preacher are yet to come. Here the Office of Evangelist, *kerygmatic authority*, includes quite functionally both categories; and it illuminates the negatives of each. Good and bad mouths in teaching and preaching are everywhere in these tracts, whose chief argument is the government, for Milton, the *presence*, of the Church. While almost fusing the offices of poet and preacher, Milton widens the distance between inspired and venal (here institutional) speakers.

"Mother Church" receives a careful proscription. Milton notes the figure as rhetorical ploy: "If any man be dispos'd to use a trope or figure, as Saint *Paul* once did in calling her the common Mother of us all, let him doe as his owne rethorick shall perswade him" (727). He specifically identifies the prelatical process:

> they endeavour to impresse deeply into weak, and superstitious fancies the awfull notion of a mother, that hereby they might cheat them into a blind and implicite obedience to whatsoever they shall decree, or think fit. And if we come to aske a reason of ought from our deare mother, she's invisible, under the lock and key of the Prelates her spirituall adulterers, they onely are the internuntio's. . . . So that we who by Gods speciall grace have shak'n off the servitude of a great male Tyrant, our pretended Father the Pope, should now, if we be not betimes aware of these wily teachers, sink under the slavery of a Female notion, the cloudy conception of a demy-Iland mother, and while we think to be obedient sonnes, should make ourselves rather the Bastards, or the Centaurs of their spirituall fornications. (*CPW*, 1:728)

It is a stinging passage of recognition and identification, one which recognizes the potency of "the awfull notion of a mother." Milton understands the power of custodial claims on that figure, but deflates the iconic appeal of the figure, with the sardonic "our deare mother, she's invisible." Specifically attacking Hall's rhetorical practice in *Apology*, he labels as "frigid affectation" Hall's creation of a "prosopopaea a certain rhetoriz'd woman whom he calls mother" and of Hall's complaint that "some had laid whoredome to her charge" (*CPW*, 1:877). Milton's focus here suggests that George Herbert's image of the British Church was still a potent icon, one which the Puritans had to work hard at negating. The Primitive Doctors, here resurrected to his purposes, "writ to Churches, speaking to them as to a number of faithfull brethren and sons, and not to make a cloudy transmigration of sexes" (877). He does not, like SMECTYMNUUS (above), contrast the figure of God the Father except by indirect use of the "pretended Father." Both "pretended Father" and "demy-Iland mother" are to be dispatched. The "slavery of a Female notion" is a danger Milton will apply in the future prose, especially *Eikonoklastes*, and in two of the great last poems. The passage shows Milton's abiding distrust of the *vehicles* for female authority and his shrewd, and early, recognition of the uses of propaganda.[45] As Sharon Achinstein has put it: "Milton, throughout his career, sought to provide readers not only with images, but also with strategies for reading and ways of seeing."[46] In *An Apology* the process of de-iconicizing Mother Church will continue.

Two less emphasized themes need to be noted because they contribute intensity and a kind of social intimacy to Milton's description of the authentic Evangelical voice. The first is "democracy," common people, here conceived of largely as the recipients of the good news. The bishops have "that old Pharisaicall fear that still dogs them, the fear of the people" (*CPW*, 1:683). There is praise for the hounded underground press, as yeomanly "honest men" (679); a defense of the signers of the Root and Branch Petition from the "great Clarks" who "think that these men, because they have a Trade (as *Christ himselfe*, and Saint *Paul* had) cannot therefore attaine to some good measure of knowledge, and to a reason of their actions" (677). Emphasizing the universal availability of God's inspiration, he finds "more savoury knowledge in one Lay-man, than in a dozen Cathedrall *Prelates*" (690). The major concern of the populist argument is that the hypocrites have neglected "the Gospell faithfully preach'd to the poore, the desolate parishes visited and duely fed, loyterers throwne out, wolves driven from the fold" (731). However much of this is Puritan party line, there is also protest at the neglect of the populace. Milton's sympathy for the rights of the people continues to be an unfocused but real issue in the antiprelatical tracts.

Closely related is the theme of decorum in the Word, God's decorum *kata ton akroaten*, an almost tender concern for the ordinary man, a concern which must be reflected in God's minister. The Preface had addressed the needs of "tender and mild consciences" and "the softer spirited Christian" (662, 664); now the argument for a rhetoric of salvation accommo-dated to the needs of man widens:

> For certainly, every rule, and instrument of necessary knowledge that God hath given us, ought to be so in proportion as may bee weilded and manag'd by the life of man without penning him up from the duties of humane society, and such an instrument of knowledge perfectly is the holy Bible. (*CPW*, 1:699)

For all the Miltonic vehemence, the grim laughter, the extraordinary demands on personal behavior, on personal commitment to religion, there is this strain of quite gentle practicality, a recognition of human limits. God would not, man ought not, pen man up "from the duties of humane society." The concern for the people becomes an eminent concern for an appropriate style with which to address them, as *An Apology* will further show (*CPW*, 1:899–903). God himself has given us the model in Scripture, "which hee hath left us as the just and adequate measure of truth, fitted, and proportion'd to the diligent study, memory, and use of every faithfull man" (700). And God's timing is part of His decorum: He is drenching His Englishmen with the light of Reformation *now* (704–5).

Set against this humankind-nourishing Scripture is the image of a sterile, inert and threatening antiquity, "this unactive and livelesse *Colossus,* that like a carved Gyant terribly menacing to children, and weaklings lifts up his club, and strikes not, and is subject to the muting of every Sparrow" (699). The use here is cunning. Milton has it three ways. He denounces antiquity, here construed as post-Apostolic times, as an idol like that of Nebuchadnezzar's image; he parodies prelatical respect for the time of the Fathers as an Age of Gold; and he recalls the use of wheat/chaff imagery in both the Hebrew and New Testaments.[47] Another set of discriminations become antitheses: Hall's "mighty *Polyphem* of Antiquity" is "*Nebuchadnezzar's* Image" which "we shall batter, and throw down . . . and crumble like the chaffe of the Summer threshing floores" (700).

A final note on Milton's defense of the "Postscript," his own section of the Smectymnuan *Answer.* Don M. Wolfe cites Masson and "later scholars" as finding "that the violent language of *Animadversions* becomes most fierce and personal in Milton's discussion of Hall's comments on "A Postscript." (*CPW,* 1:961) Milton was angered at the charge of plagiarism,[48] but not unduly. The rhythm of the prose gets brisker and the diction a little grittier, but not much more pronounced than in the preface, or section 1, or several of the other sections. The Modest Confuter will in fact confirm this: when he cites the most offensive terms in the *Animadversions,* the section on the "Postscript" provides relatively few of them.

Some of Milton's strategies in this section are quite effective, for example the comic stychomythia (732):

> *Remon.* No diligence in preaching?
> *Answ.* Scarce any preaching at all.
> *Remon.* No holinesse in living?
> *Answ.* No.

If the tired joke about the Bishop's foot in the broth had been eliminated, this section would appear very like the rest of the piece: some evidence, some abuse, some vision. Milton's sense of personal injury in these pages has been exaggerated.

The rhetorical accomplishments of this sometime unpleasant tract are considerable, most eminently in the complementary images of true and false speakers. Milton has drawn on rich traditional and contemporary models for Hall as "cheat of soules" and then has set these bad figures against their virtuous, Puritan, counterparts. Against Simon Magus, he sets Simon Peter; against the learned hypocrite, the unwearied laborer in the word; the cunningest and most dangerous mercenary gives way to the true pastor; Spenser's false Shepherd to the good Shepherd. Out of the squalling, multitudinous libelers of Hall's tracts, Milton fashions and opposes to Hall the true Evangelical voice singing at the marriage supper of the Lamb. He fulfills what had appeared a grim promise in the Preface: he has "bespurted" Hall "with his owne holy-water."

Animadversions is a celebration by inversion, discrediting Hall in order to celebrate the community of Saints. This ultimate purpose is present throughout the discourse, but most clearly in "the big-mouthed, astounding prayer" where an ecstatic community is ministered to by good men. Part of that ministry is the purging from the community's mystical body of the bad ministers—the blind greedy mouths—brilliantly represented by Milton's version of the false-speaking mercenary of carnal preferment: the figure who set his own person at the head of the controversy; the Humble Remonstrant, Simon Magus, Bishop Joseph Hall.

FIVE

"Sanctifi'd Bitterness"

A Modest Confutation and *An Apology Against a Pamphlet*

I have argued that the emphasis in these debates was largely on the rectitude of the writers involved. Milton's presence is assertive and almost palpable. Yet the argument against prelacy is the reason for his presence, and that presence must be both justified and ancillary to his purpose. Donne and Herbert had earlier recorded their perceptions, often anguished, of *performing* in God's service, and of the danger of performing for the wrong reasons—praise, comfort, self-satisfaction, redress.[1] The controversial writers of the English 1640s, specifically the participants in the Hall-Smectymnuan exchanges, did proclaim, loudly, the moral, ethical, and scholarly credentials that would entitle them to speak God's truth, but the ultimate purpose of their discourse was to convince and to convert the reader, not to establish professional or even "laureate"[2] status for the writer. Milton craved recognition, expected adulation; but he always recognized the difference between the authority to proclaim God's truth and the capacity for achieving Fame, the spur which Phoebus had begun to challenge in "Lycidas," a spur which Stanley Fish, perhaps too relentlessly, pursues to Milton's erasure from that poem in *How Milton Works* (256–80). Marvell puts the present problem movingly in "The Coronet," where self-consciousness of one's excellent performance corrupts the very praising of God:

> And now when I have summ'd up all my store,
> Thinking (so I my self deceive)
> So rich a Chaplet thence to weave
> As never yet the king of Glory wore:
> Alas I find the Serpent old
> That, twining in his speckled breast,
> About the flow'rs disguis'd does fold,
> With wreaths of Fame and Interest.[3]

Marvell's recognition allows him to achieve an exemplary equilibrium in the rest of the poem. Milton identifies the problem early, but it remains unsolved until the great poems.

Tracts of this period proclaim and justify a kerygmatic voice that struggles to maintain awareness of the traps of professional and technical pride. Pride in education, technique, even in natural abilities, is continuously brought forward so that it may be subordinated to the message of Scripture, working to define itself in relationship to deity without pride and without false modesty. "I" have the right to preach God's truth, which is the end of my preaching—and I have a right to be praised for that preaching.

The proclamation of self in Milton's antiprelatical tracts is earnestly bound to a formula of deference to Scripture, but a deference that does not elide the value and the resonance of the inspired proclaimer. The worst hypocrisy was false deference, with a submerged but implicit pride of personal interpretive or, more thornily, inherited authority, rhetorical humility. The interpreters of the great text, on both sides, sought acceptance as proclaimers of the Truth which was Scripture, was the Church, was Christ's body: God and his adherent Creation together—including the created author as creator endowed by Scripture.

Both parties proclaimed the Church as literally Christ's body, the tradition derived from 1 Corinthians 12.12–31: "For as the body is one, and hath many members, and all the members of that one body, being many, are one body; so also *is* Christ . . . Now ye are the body of Christ, and members in particular" (12, 27). Marprelate's *Hay Any Work for Cooper*, another reprint for the Wars of Truth, proclaimed the identity of Church with Christ: "No civill magistrate may lawfully either maime or deforme the body of Christ, which is the Church. . . . *if our Saviour Christ hath left behind him a perfect body: surely he hath left therein no place, or no use for members of the Magistrates own making and invention*" (*Hay*, 6–7). Bishop Hall describes the equation for his church and his time:

> I do not then conceive of this union as some imaginary thing . . . But know that this is a true, reall, essentiall substantiall union, whereby the person of the believer is indisolubly united to the Glorious person of the Son of God . . . now, that this union is not more mysticall then certain; . . . this union is true, and really existent, but yet spirituall.[4]

With that union in mind, Puritan charges of violation become powerful propaganda: "you [prelates] are not onely the wound, but the very Plague and pestilence of our Church. You are those who maime, deforme, vex, persecute, grieve, and wound the Church" (*Hay*, 19). In defending his Church, in defending himself, Milton is defending Christ.

Milton saw Bishop Hall's rhetoric as speciously humble and self-aggrandizing. Hall and now his new ally, the Modest Confuter, viewed Milton's rhetoric as arrogant and misguided fanaticism. The competing claims on truth did not negate the acknowledged singleness of that truth. Hall and Milton could recognize a hundred versions of the same Scriptural passage and yet view that passage itself as stable. There was no assumption of a constellation of equally "right" answers.

Within six months *Animadversions* had elicited the anonymous *A Modest Confutation of A Slanderous and Scurrilous Libell, Entituled, Animadversions Upon the Remonstrants Defense Against SMECTYMNUUS* (February or March, 1642). The chimerical title suggests the ways in which issues were distended and distorted, moving from doctrinal and public to individual and personal, a familiar movement in controversy. As Joan Webber put it, "The fact that the titles keep getting longer is part of the warfare, as each engulfs the one that precedes it" (*Eloquent "I,"* 200). Implicit in this title is the claim that personal and legal untruth—libel—will be doctrinally corrected—confutation. The Confuter would establish a false and immoral Milton incapable of proclaiming the truth, while affirming his own, but especially Bishop Hall's, authentic virtue and wisdom. The argument over Church discipline is quite neglected, and almost no new evidence is offered.

The Confuter reacts to Milton's *Animadversions* with the usual prelatical shock. The earlier stages of the debate, in which Hall "starred," are treated as "solemn Scenes (it were too ominous to say Tragicall)"; Milton's role is that of "scurrilous Mime." (Neither description is correct: the self-exculpating and the abrasive simply coexist throughout the controversy.) Briskly, the Confuter plunges into contumely: the Animadverter is "a grim, lowring, bitter fool" who has written an "immodest and injurious Libell": "it is like hee spent his youth, in loytering, bezelling, and harlotting. Thus being grown to an Impostume in the brest of the University, he was at length vomited out thence into a Suburbe sinke about London, which since his comming up, hath groaned under two ills, Him, and the Plague" (*Confutation,* A3–A3v).

This is a fairly hostile opening, even for the England of 1642. The venom includes the charge of betrayal—the disciple/son, at the breast of the teacher/mother, become malignancy; and the slur against the "suburb sink." Much of this caustic diction is indeed from the *Animadversions,* but it is here clustered into an appearance of pure abuse. In contrast, Milton seldom plunges directly into vehement accusation without an explanation (in three of these tracts consisting of quite elaborate defenses of an immediate theory of decorum), the confirmation of which comes, usually, from Scripture. His opponent strikes preemptively, with an immediate *argumentum ad hominem,* and the rationale for his confutational style is never fully presented. The last paragraph of his address to the reader imitates Hall in its gestures of Davidic righteousness and vulnerability. For both the Confuter and Milton, self-righteous erudition and vehemence jeopardize the claims of humility and of high moral capacity and range. Yet the differences are clear, among them the injunctions to violence. They are there in Milton's prose (the fable of the Wen, for example), but seldom as immediately inflammatory as the "Modest Confuter's" closing remarks "To the Reader": "Horrid blasphemy! You that love Christ, and know this miscreant wretch, stone him to death, lest your selves smart for his impunity" (*Confutation,* A4). In an age of common extremism, the words carry real injunctions to isolate and even to punish.

The Confuter's least challengeable point has already been noted (see chapter 4): Milton handles "the other businesse [that is, the legitimacy of prelacy] . . . but by the by, or not at all" (*Confutation,* 5–6). Recognizing that the competition is for interpretive authority, he proceeds against the "miscreant wretch" who dares oppose the great Bishop Hall. The claims for Hall are based largely on his ecclesiastical status. Milton's claims will start from scriptural authority, with an increasingly bold claim for the natural—that is, the God-given—rights of human beings.

Intelligent, conservative, and witty, the Confuter is less sensitive than Milton is to the complexities of linguistic authority. Sensing the threat to Bishop Hall's claims to erudition, the Confuter makes the comments on "toothless satires" even more pedantic than they are in Milton's text; and he magnifies the Areopagi quibble. He settles astutely on one of the vanities against which Milton wages a sometimes half-hearted war: "Yes, yes, anything, rather than acknowledge the least error" (13). Yet the *Modest Confutation* reads Milton's text less fairly than *Animadversions* does Hall's text, with more distortion of emphasis and more frequent misrepresentation. Milton's scurrilities are made to appear obsessive; the attack on liturgy is read as flattery and railing (22); the nascent populism is seen as wooing the "mutinous rabble" (23, 24, 30). After he "destroys" his antiprelatical opponent, the Confuter proceeds to defend, conventionally, the maintenance of clergy, the *Book of Common Prayer* (24–30), and, in his last section, the office of Bishop itself.

Professor Frank Huntley has made the ablest defense of the anonymous author, asking us to read the *Confutation* as carefully as we have read Milton's two tracts. He suggests that the author was Robert Durkin, "who angered Milton because he had his own words, not merely his arguments, thrown back at him by a man ten years his senior." There is justice in Professor Huntley's request, but I cannot share his admiration for the Confuter as "wittier and more deft" (Huntley, 129) than Milton. The Confuter is more scurrilous, at once more pretentious and more irritatingly "humble" (an attitude that seemed to anger all of the Smectymnuan group when practiced by the Bishop himself). The description of Milton as regurgitated imposthume and as a whore-monger is cruder than Milton's crude enough "Ha, ha, ha," and "Wipe your fat corpulencies out of our light" (*CPW*, 1:726, 732). And the Confuter fails to recognize inspiration, to separate rhetorical display from passion. On Milton's great celebratory invocation (705–7) he can only make an academic joke: "[It is] a long, tedious, theatricall, big-mouthed astounding Prayer . . . which infinite of honest and simple Christians would no more know how to understand, than they would a Scene out of Johnsons Cataline" (*Confutation*, 22, 27). But for Milton's passage concerning moral virtue and Christian piety (*CPW*, 1:719), there is a grudging praise: "were I not assured that other passions distracted you, I could easily be enclined to think that this volley of expressions proceeded from a love of goodenesse. . . . For were there no guile in them, as I do continually nourish such thoughts, so would I never desire to have them better cloathed" (*Confutation*, 37).

The Confuter's performance is the least convincing of the documents in the now two-year-old exchange between Hall and the Smectymnuans. It champions the cliches of decorum, rigid classifications of history, class and diction—the *rigor mortis* of time, place and person. There is a mix of contempt and fear toward the new, larger reading public that Milton is trying to reach. On the one hand, they are "honest and simple Christians" who would not understand Catiline, and Milton is accused of thinking "an inspired Cobler may judge of Appeles his workmanship" (23). On the other hand, the people are dangerous: "Go you then to your mutinous rabble, and if you can appease their furies, enthrone their sage wisedomes upon some stall or bench, and cite before them the Clerks of either University" (24).

Fear and distrust of the "rabble" are real issues. Mobs and demonstrations exerted considerable force during this period,[5] and nervousness about the "mob" appeared on both sides; but Anglicans used the danger as a propaganda tool more often than their opponents. The image of Archbishop Laud surrounded by the threatening rabble was a popular emblem for Parliamentary disorder, and Laud's own account of his removal to the Tower (26 February 1641) still has poignancy: "the shouting was exceeding great. And so they followed me with Clamour and Revilings, even beyond Barbarity it self" (quoted in *CPW*, 1:88). Prelatical and Royalist propaganda promulgated images of the Parliamentary party as a mobocracy. Puritan/Parliamentary defenses against these charges were quite selective: after all, as Marshall Knappen long ago taught, their propagandists had been in training since before Marprelate; they need not react monolithically.[6]

Proud of his Italianate humanism, Milton surely participates in that literary elitism; he must accordingly meet the charge of bowing to the mob, while maintaining certain clear and distinct motions toward participatory democracy. The issue has engaged a new generation of scholars, as in the volume *Milton and Republicanism*, as has the issue of Milton's elitist ego. The Italian journey and the ways it is recalled, the whole management of the *Poems* of 1645, the numerous instances in the prose of aesthetic and intellectual pride in his own training and talents, the proud (but rather clenched-teeth) assertion of a fit audience (though *few*)—these obviously argue for elitism. Yet Thomas Corns, the scholar who had earlier identified Milton's anxieties about being associated with a radical left, can write more recently: "Especially in the vernacular works, there emerges an eloquent rehearsal, not of republican argument, but of republican values, inscribed both in his demystification of monarchy and in his assertion of the dignity of the English citizen."[7] And Barbara Lewalski notes Milton's early "class inflected defense" in Prolusion 6, his challenge of "the cultural politics" of the masque genre; whatever the revisionist argument about his politics, she writes, "Milton clearly thought the revolution was about profound religious and political differences" (*Life*, 31, 62, 121).

I would add two strands of Miltonic performance roughly correspondent to Corns's two categories. The first is a persistent opposition to academicism, an academicism construed as pretentious intellectual elitism, with pride in the material trappings of academic privilege, titles, positions, styles. This is at base an opposition to authority, to hierarchy, to the trickle-down theory of values, and it is everywhere in Milton's writing, including in the Latin prose, and in the poetry. What contempt there is in the "hors load of citations" in *Reason of Church-Government* and in the portrait of Salmasius! What analogous insight in the "Not to know mee argues your selves unknown" of *Paradise Lost* (4.830)! The snobbish dismissal of the low-born cleric (like Archbishop Laud) who can never elude his humble origins (see below, chapter 6), is often a reaction to pride in prelatical erudition. Claims of superiority through institutional education are consistent targets of Milton's contempt.

Secondly, there is an enthusiasm for crowded confrontational scenes—what amounts to an intellectual agoraphilia, one which will climax in *Areopagitica*. This is a genuine relish in confronting crowds with ideas, crowds of ordinary people, an exhilaration in ministering to, in informing, in exchanging ideas with, a people whose capacities have been shamefully underestimated by the prelatical party: "And thus the people vilifi'd and rejected by them, give over the study of vertue, and godlinesse as a thing of greater purity then they need, and the search of divine knowledge as a mystery too high for their capacity's, and only for Churchmen to meddle with" (*CPW*, 1:548). Milton is at this period convinced of the individual values of ordinary men and women, and of their educability.

The fencing off of sacred precincts ritualizes the Anglican position toward priestliness; and it concretizes the conceptual offence of elitism for Milton and his colleagues. Laud's "Decency," as he described it, was a ceremonial "fencing *in*" of that which was holy. For the Puritans, Laud's altar rails were a "fencing *out*," an exclusion of the people from proximity to holy mysteries, from the communal Feast of Love.[8] Milton's decorum democratizes sacred space by demolishing elitist prelatical thresholds that had become barriers.

This Miltonic openness to the people is not an instinctive gregariousness, so much as an eagerness for, and a curious confidence in, broad intellectual exchange.[9] Attendant on this is Milton's naive habit of assuming that his demonstrations of the truth will be self-evident to all who but encounter his arguments. Consider the poignancy of the "one gentle stroking" in the first divorce tract, a stroking he assumes will be immediately accepted as a solution to a major domestic ill (*CPW*, 2:245). The posture is too transparent to be arrogance; in the early prose, it is an interlacing of this love of ministering with deep confidence in the clarity and brightness of Truth: "who ever knew Truth put to the wors, in a free and open encounter" (*CPW*, 2:561). Part of this demotic stance arises out of the need to distance himself from the other party, and "that old Pharisaicall fear that still dogs them, the fear of the people" (683), but whatever the polemical need, and despite future disappointment, at this point Milton believes that the people are genuinely educable. They are beginning to prove him wrong. Despite the *Animadversions*, and not to mention the earlier tracts, he had failed to destroy Hall's reputation as a purveyor of truth, let alone the message itself. Milton would soon recognize that his message could be understood and still rejected.

The author of *A Modest Confutation* identifies Milton's disruption of hierarchy, his faith in the people, and, to some extent, his religious and social passion. Yet he rejects the arguments with his own sense of shock at the indecorum, his own deference to authority, his fear of the populace, and his pose of humility. Milton now responds to these attacks with a remarkable self-defense.

An Apology Against a Pamphlet Call'd A Modest Confutation of the Animadversions upon the Remonstrant against SMECTYMNUUS (April 1642) is, with *Colasterion* and *Pro Se Defensio*, one of the three extreme examples of the Disappointment/Revision topos in Milton. This revision of vision recurs throughout the canon, in both his prose and his poetry, and includes the several texts of the Masque; the multiple versions of the antiprelatical argument; the two editions of the *Doctrine and Discipline of Divorce,* and the other three divorce tracts—plus the two sonnets on the divorce tracts; the two editions of *The Tenure of Kings and Magistrates* and *The Readie and Easie Way.* Each of the three *Defensios* addresses a separate phase of the argument, but they are nevertheless developments of an originally assured and discrete argument. A limited instance of this, but a striking one because of the gestation period of the poem, is the addition of headnotes in the second printing of *Paradise Lost;* and the restructuring of books in the second edition.

The Apology is powerful evidence of this recurrence in Milton's monumental projects, a process marked initially by powerful commitment and high expectations of successful and immediate communication. A disappointed surprise or even shock follows when he finds himself misunderstood by his intended readership, or attacked by misreaders and corrupters of his text. There follows another attempt to get his point across, more fully documented perhaps, slightly embittered, slightly more ironical, but nevertheless necessary, and after that another—and another. In the series of antiprelatical tracts, in the divorce tracts, and in the last Latin *Defense,* the escalating acerbity is obvious. It is a product of Milton's high moral energy, his lust to communicate that energy, and his frustration and disappointment at his failure. Arrogance is an almost necessary part of the process, but so is an innocent expectation of being read seriously.[10]

The *Apology* carries a double load of weariness. After the Confuter's personal attack, the conventional pose of aloofness is too difficult to maintain.[11] "I shall be put unwillingly to molest the publick view with the vindication of a private name; as if it were worth the while that the people should care whether such a one were thus, or thus" (*CPW*, 1:870). The Animadverter against the Humble Remonstrant now becomes the pseudo-anonymous Apologist for John Milton; the fictions of anonymity are being dissolved. Despite F. R. Leavis's perverse misreading,[12] Milton understood the operations of the ego better than most. He recognized the demands of the self and the problems and dangers of its intrusion into controversy, most especially into religious controversy. His initial reluctance to use his personal history as a counter in the Smectymnuan controversy is at once egotistical and self-defensive, and intellectually modest about the decorum of proclaiming. Now, in the *Apology*, some barriers collapse, but the discrimination between public and private voices is not totally surrendered. By the time of the Latin *Defences* the situation changes.

The second disappointment is with the failure of his earlier explanation: he will "beginne therefore," with "an Apology for those animadversions, . . . since the Preface, which was purposely set before them, is not thought apologeticall enough" (*CPW*, 1:871). Under pressure from the Modest Confuter, the earlier persona of *Animadversions* almost merges with the real author of the *Apology*.

Rhetorical masks tend to be held a few inches in front of the protected face, often allowing a glimpse of the identity beneath. In Plato's *Apology*, Socrates lets the self-interested suggestion of a modest fine slip out, slightly destabilizing his mask of ethically pure and selfless teacher. The pamphlets by Hall and SMECTYMNUUS maintain an elaborate, yet ironic, charade of asserting and accepting Hall's anonymity, despite general knowledge that Hall was the Humble Remonstrant. Any reasonably intelligent reader of the tract in question would recognize the clues. The Remonstrant, for example, makes reference to "certain and irrefragable evidence," echoing one of the Bishop's earlier titles, and in his address to the King at the head of *A Defence of the Humble Remonstrance*, Hall writes, "Your Majesty was pleased to cast a gracious eye upon a late *Humble Remonstrance*, made to the High Court of Parliament" (A3). In "An Advertisement to the Reader," prefaced to the *Determination of the Question Concerning the Divine Right of Episcopacy* by Abraham Scultetus, Hall names himself. Robert Baillie knows that Hall is the author of the *Remonstrance* and refers to Hall's *Defence* in a marginal note (*Parallel*, A2–A2v).

Why this sustained pretence of anonymity? Don M. Wolfe quotes from the Smectymnuan *Answer*—"We will not enter into the Lists with a man of that learning and fame that Bishop Hall is, yet we dare tell this Remonstrant"; then he suggests, "Though they dared not compete with Hall, they were not afraid of the Remonstrant" (*CPW*, 1:78). That conjecture is unsatisfying. Are the Smectymnuans ironical, fearfully deferential? In the face of their adversary, are they pretending a humility that they do not feel? The only clear point here is the conventional fiction of anonymity.

This convention causes problems for both the writer and the reader of the *Apology*. As part of the introductory section establishing his decorum for the piece, Milton had registered his "suspicion that in setting forth this pamphlet the Remonstrant was not unconsulted with," and the identification of Hall as the author of the *Remonstrant* pamphlets is argued in some detail (876–77). The separation of Remonstrant and Confuter is assumed through most, but not all, of the tract: "I step againe to this emblazoner of his Title page [of the *Modest Confutation*] (whether it be the same man or no I leave it in the midst)"; and there is the cloudy suggestion that the Confuter is "neere a kin" to Hall (877), or Hall himself.[13] Later, in addressing section 6 of the *Confutation*,

Milton announces that his treatment will be "tough and dangerous, the baiting of a Satir" (914). He initially separates the Remonstrant from The Modest Confuter, then identifies the Remonstrant as the author of *Virgidemiarum*, that is, Joseph Hall, and the Confuter as a separate "Champion from behind the Arras," an adversary more ludicrous than Polonius, "a lozell Bachelour of Arts," a "graduat" (914, 920, 931). But to whom does the pronoun refer in the attack on the one who "could neigh out the remembrance of his old conversation among the *Viraginian* trollops" (914)? This simultaneous suppression of one's knowledge of the identity of one's opponent and exploitation of that identity has rhetorical benefits and ethical dangers. It licenses slander and imprecision—as Milton himself recognizes when he complains of having always "to contend with those who are nameless" in the *Second Defence* (*CPW*, 4:560).

If this is a unique personal strategy, it must be seen as deliberately dishonest, especially as it presages three later instances of "confused" ascriptions of adversarial personae. In *Eikonoklastes*, Milton will attack Charles I for plagiarizing the Pamela prayer from Sidney's pagan *Arcadia* in the *Eikon Basilike*. In *Colasterion*, the adversarial "barbar surgeon" is occasionally conflated with an unidentified group of authoritative seniors. And in *Pro Se Defensio*, Milton will continue his attack on Alexander More even after he receives information that More is not the author of *The Cry of the Royal Blood*.[14] In these three instances at least, Milton constructs portraits of the opposition which are at the least confusing, and at worst, deceptive.

I think it arguable that this blurring of adversarial personae is a coy (even unscrupulous) but useful convention of the tract wars; and it helps to explain some of Milton's rhetorical behavior here. He lashes out at his anonymous attackers and would name them; he demands face to face confrontation. In a few months he will complain again and again of the refusal of his opponents to debate the divorce matter openly, but now he uses aggressively the convention of specious anonymity to throw out a spectrum of identifications with some confidence that his scatter-shots will hit the target. The figure of Bishop Hall is absolutely critical to Milton's strategy in these two pamphlets, and his beginning and end prove that. The identity of the confuter intervenes, a problem that he handles with a very large brush, one that can besmirch a "lozell bachelor of arts," a kinsman of the Bishop, or the Bishop himself.[15]

Milton's own anonymity is curious and unconvincing. A part of the problem is the timing of the Confuter's attack, coming just as Milton was summing up his arguments and proclaiming his decision to move on. I will argue that *The Reason of Church-Government* was planned as the final statement on the antiprelatical matter and as the formal debut of the author, John Milton. *An Apology* appeared in reaction to the Confuter's intrusive attack; it perpetuates the strategies of the Smectymnuan controversy, including these problematic and unstable attributions.

Like the construction of the speaker's moral, spiritual, and academic pedigree, these transformations of adversarial persona are strategies of self-representation, candidates for studies of self-hood like the ones brilliantly initiated by Webber's *Eloquent "I."* Most readers now agree with Stephen M. Fallon that "If any author is in his or her texts, Milton is in his."[16] Among the studies of Milton's presence, and of his attempts to avoid detection, in his texts are some of the major studies in the field. They go back to Masson's superb biography-in-context and include John Crowe Ransom's essay "A Poem Nearly Anonymous," an essay to which Stanley Fish returns, as part of his pursuit of Milton's "self," in order to make the poem "Finally Anonymous." John S. Diekhoff long ago presented most of the relevant passages of overt autobiography in his useful *Milton on Himself*.[17] Authoritative biographies include the two volumes of W. R. Parker, updated by Gordon Campbell,[18] and Barbara K. Lewalski's *Life*. William Kerrigan argues for the psychoanalytic approach in *"The Sacred Complex."*[19] And currently the field thrives: "Postmodern biographical critics" Albert C. Labriola argues, "have been at work to discern the presences of Milton in his writings in ways previously unremarked," Labriola singles out John T.

Shawcross's *John Milton: The Self and the World* as the work whose psychological emphasis and methodology "in many ways underlie the essays in the present volume."[20] Milton's "I" still confounds, eludes, and beckons.

In the *Apology*, Milton's "I" is one beleaguered by the Modest Confuter, whoever he is, an "I" that has antecedents in the texts of the earlier tracts and, elliptically, in *A Masque* and in "Lycidas," and in the narrative of the Italian journey. It is an "I" who has made prophetic and even apostolic claims in *Of Reformation*, epistemological claims in *Of Prelatical Episcopacy*, and dogmatic and polemical claims throughout the prose, but nowhere as relentlessly as in *Animadversions*. In that earlier attack on Hall, Milton claimed kerygmatic authority for his speaker, but only typically and polemically, as young against old, pure against corrupt, free against venal. At the beginning of the *Animadversions*, he is still rather consciously a "Postscript" apprentice to his Smectyumnuan friends and mentors, anonymous and supplemental to their work of instruction/destruction, the young champion of his intellectual sponsors, speaking, initially, by their leave. The Confuter's attack frees him from the last vestiges of the ancillary status he has held in the earlier tracts (and in the Masque, where Lawes was the tutelary figure). *An Apology* is the "Lycidas" of the prose: at the end of it, the Apologist is his own man. The distresses of adjustment to adulthood and the deference to maturity are over. Milton, Webber writes, "is now committed to his role in this controversy, and he can come immediately and in his own person to grips with the reader and the subject" (201). The strange exaggeration of his youthfulness and inexperience, the concern with being overpowered by "tutors," are considerably dampened down. Now it is his good "name, however of small repute" that must be "not unneedfully defended." The unnamed must himself defend his name, even though "I have oft with inward contentment perceav'd my friends congratulating themselves in my innocence" (*CPW*, 1:870). Milton drops his deferential stance toward the Smectymnuans and begins to break away from their increasingly centrist positions. They will soon respond with criticism of his style and of his ideas.

The sense of this urgently personal service to God increases as the mediators are eliminated, as Milton sees himself operating on his own, not within a structure of church government. (Perhaps, as John Spencer Hill has argued, Milton has only now given up his expectations of a life in the ministry;[21] see also Shawcross, *Self*, 93–107.) Puritan distaste for mediation has been noted above (see chapter 1); for Milton, that distaste becomes almost fearful, and remains a lifelong obsession, part of the demand for immediacy with God: "to know God aright, and out of that knowledge to love him, to imitate him, to be like him" (*CPW*, 2:367). All study of Milton must defer to his assurance of and reliance on that immediacy and intimacy.

The autobiography will be straightforward, the voice not totally new, but one of the modulations of the emerging kerygmatic voice. There is some weariness and disappointment here; but the Confuter has also goaded Milton into sharp rephrasings of some of his earlier positions: "I could not to my thinking honor a good cause more from the heart, then by defending it earnestly . . . [by means of a] truth whose force is best seene against the ablest resistance" (*CPW*, 1:869). (Does "ablest resistance" here refer to Bishop Hall? to Ussher?) There are careful adjustments to the demands of the present: "the intrapping authority of great names titl'd to false opinions"; and candid claims of competence, "guifts of Gods imparting, which I boast not, but thankfully acknowledge . . . it be[ing] but justice not to defraud of due esteeme the wearisome labours and studious watchings, wherein I have spent and tir'd out almost a whole youth" (869). There is unusual opennness about the difficulties, concessions, and regrets of a personal discipline. But the passage also adjusts the decorum with regard to a mixed audience of adversaries, friends, and even some who have not yet chosen sides. "One thing I beg of ye Readers . . . [that] ye would not be offended, though I rate this cloister'd Lubber according to his deserts" (920).

From the first sentence the tract ponders the uses of the implied talent, the knowing what one "ought to do." The young man must see his foe clearly and on his own, not "through the deceaving glasse of other mens great opinion of him [i.e., Hall]." He must respond "against the rancor of an evill tongue," after "the unfained and diligent inquiry of mine owne conscience at home . . . to give a more true account of my selfe abroad than this modest Confuter" has done (869–70). The *Apology* sets the record straight in order to defend the good cause earnestly. The two interests are subsumed in the body of Christ:

> But when I discern'd his intent was not so much to smite at me, as through me to render odious the truth which I had written . . . I conceav'd my selfe now not as mine own person, but as a member incorporate into that truth, whereof I was perswaded, and whereof I had declar'd openly to be a partaker. (871)

The truth of Milton's antiprelatical tracts becomes the truth of evangelical doctrine, then Truth, and lastly part of the body of Christ.

I have suggested earlier that corruption in the Church was felt as a real wound on the body of Christ. Here—the phrase "member incorporate" is the key—a taint on Milton's reputation is such a wound. Is this Milton's communion—reverse transubstantiation? Instead of ingesting the body of the Son of God—commemorative or real—the "partaker" of the exchange becomes "a member incorporate," of Truth and of Christ, one who ingests true doctrine and is digested into the body of Christ.

Milton shows little interest in here debating the Eucharist, like paedobaptism and the calendars of Revelation, one of the "hot" issues he ignores. Rather, this passage and its concerns with violations of the Church/Christ's body generally, is in a sense analogic to the rituals of the Eucharist, images of incorporation. Truth is the sound argument: the uncorrupted Church, the inviolate Word; and those who proclaim that Word are part of the body of Christ. To corrupt the Christian Truth is to recrucify Christ, to mangle His body, like the "wicked deceivers" in the analogous myth of Isis and Osiris. They will appear in *Areopagitica*, a pamphlet which defends just the kind of writing in which Milton is presently engaged. The book as living organism, the Word as Christ's body, the communion of believers as the body of Christ—felt commonplaces. Hall and the Confuter are manglers of the Word, like those in *Areopagitica* "who . . . took the virgin Truth, hewd her lovely form into a thousand peeces, and scatter'd them to the four winds" (*CPW*, 2:549). For the "sad friends of Truth," the proper end of inquiry is to imitate "the carefull search that Isis made for the mangl'd body of Osiris," by going "up and down gathering up limb by limb still as they could find them" (*CPW*, 2: 549). Milton's task is to make Truth as whole as possible, recover the Word through the word, to repair the ruins of our First Parents, to "return, / Father, to see thy face" (*PL*, 3:262–63). Isis's search will become an icon for the ecclesiological and personal inquiry-against-opposition, an inquiry which seeks to gather in Christian data, and Christians, and to be gathered, with a fervor that arises from a contemplation of the *sparagmos* and the promised regeneration simultaneously. Yet, Milton will shortly tell us that there can be no completion until the "Masters second comming" (*CPW*, 2:549).

That sense of imminent apocalypse adds one more tension. In these last uncounted days, accounts must be settled, talents accounted for. Like Calvin, like George Herbert, like Christ Himself, Milton worries about his spiritual balance sheet: he would not through his "default" be "counted small credit for their cause" (*CPW*, 1:871).

There is a note of slight disapproval of the Smectymnuans who will not respond to Hall's *Short Answer*. The main stage is now Milton's, and he can stop to vent his contempt for Hall's Senecanism, which tried,

> if he could not refute them, yet at least with quips and snapping adagies to vapour them out . . . I took it as my part the lesse to endure that my respected friends through their own unnecessary patience should thus lye at the mercy of a coy flurting stile: to be girded about with frumps and curtall gibes, by one who makes sentences by the Statute, as if all above three inches long were confiscat. (872–73)

The attack on Senecanism is not an attack on brevity, but a sneer at affectation, at the "Statute" rather than the sentence.

As a Smectymnuan colleague, Milton cites Gregory Nyssen's observation that when a man contemplates censure "in the cause of his brother . . . perhaps it is worthier pardon to be angry, then to be cooler" (873)—a fraternal corollary to Revelation 3.16. Again, the prelatical party has no monopoly on the language: "Can nothing then but Episcopacy teach men to speak good English?"[22] Hall's excesses are ridiculed as "canons and quaint Sermonings interlin'd with barbarous Latin to illumin a period, to wreath an Enthymema with maistrous dexterity" (873–74). The argument resurfaces that prelatical rhetoric is ostentatious and artificial; implicitly, Milton's is natural and unadorned. In *Of Reformation,* "The very essence of Truth is plainesse, and brightnes; the darknes and crookednesse is our own" (566). Amidst the range of styles from colloquial to splendid, this commonplace becomes slogan, to reappear in *Areopagitica,* where Truth "needs no policies, nor stratagems, nor licencings . . . to make her victorious, those are the shifts and the defences that error uses against her power" (*CPW,* 2:563).

Milton has been preparing his readers for the "true poem" passage. As preface, he emphasizes regenerate and regenerating nature: "that indeed according to art is most eloquent, which returnes and approaches neerest to nature from whence it came; and they expresse nature best, who in their lives least wander from her safe leading, which may be call'd regenerate reason. So that how he should be truly eloquent who is not withall a good man, I see not" (*CPW,* 1:874). Establishing oneself as a worthy champion of the Truth is prerequisite to the integrity of the argument.

The good man is commanded to speak frankly and simply, out of his good nature, but he is enfranchised to deal "with men who pride themselves on their supposed art, to leave them unexcusable" (874)—as in the "continuall vehemence" against the "proud, the obstinate, the false Doctors of mens devices" in the *Animadversions.* These Doctors cannot be taught, "but discover'd and laid open they must be" (874). The "laying open," a virtual anatomizing, can be quite witty, as in the ridicule of the Confuter's, and by implication Hall's, "modesty set there to sale in the frontispiece." This "emblazoner of his Title page" (877) (here airily conflated with Hall) seeks "unseasonably to prepossesse men of his modesty," not allowing others "to judge of [it] by reading" (876–77). The charge of contrived humility—not quite the same as false modesty—is easily substantiated. The Confuter "rub[s] the forehead of his title with this word modest" (876) and hangs it out "like a toling signe-post to call passengers, not simply a confutation, but a modest confutation, with a laudatory of it selfe obtruded in the very first word" (*CPW*, 1:875–76). By contrast, Milton adds no self-congratulatory adjectives to his titles.

Even the pedantic comments on genre and style are useful, rebutting the charge that *Animadversions* was a comedy, a "scurrilous Mime, a personated and (as himself thinks) a grim, lowring, bitter fool" (*Confutation*, A3). Mime becomes both text and author/persona, and Milton criticizes both misapplications. The Confuter, "by sycophanting and misnaming the worke of his adversary" has invoked a context that is dangerous to his own hero. By likening "those grave controversies" between Hall and SMECTYMNUUS to "Stagery, or Scene-worke" (879), he only emphasizes Hall's theatricality. With a flourish of classical allusion, Milton defines and then justifies the uses of "mimicall mockery, to rip up the saddest vices with a laughing countenance" (882). The clinching argument is from Plato, whose dialogues had also been called mimes. With obvious relish, Milton notes, "there is scarce one of them, especially wherein some notable Sophister lies sweating and turmoyling under the inevitable and mercilesse dilemma's of Socrates, but that hee who reads, were it Saturne himselfe, would be often rob'd of more then a smile" (880). Now the Confuter is Hall, "himself the loosest and most extravagant Mime, that hath been heard of"; the source of a "hoard of slanderous inventions" (881–82). There is coarse pleasure here in the victim's helplessness, in his deserved come-uppance, and in the crude comments that follow on Hall's *Mundus Alter et Idem*. The Confuter invokes Hall's reputation in order to demand decorum from Milton, but here it is a restricted decorum of genre, one less responsive to occasion and total purpose of discourse than is Milton's. Yet Milton can respond in kind to these restricted demands, another instance of that capacity in the rhetoric of zeal to display at once contempt for and mastery of the limited skills its opponents would claim to monopolize.

Autobiography is implicit in all discourse, here a proper response for one who has been the object of opprobrious personal attack and who now seizes the opportunity to re-present himself accurately. Immensely self-conscious, yet working hard to avoid the appearance of egoism, Milton spends a full page on the very decision to defend himself. The balance between private and public witnessing is precarious, and Milton shrewdly recognizes the tactical trap. The Confuter has,

> under a pretended ignorance . . . let drive at randome . . . perhaps not without some suttlety to cast me into envie, by bringing on me a necessity to enter into my own praises . . . the just vindication of myselfe, which I could yet deferre, it being more meet that to those other matters of publick debatement in this book I should give attendance first, but that I feare it would but harme the truth, for me to reason in her behalfe, so long as I should suffer my honest estimation to lye unpurg'd from these insolent suspicions. (882–83)

These concerns for the potential accusations, and the dangers, of egoism are important to consider in an author often accused of just such egoism, arrogance, pride, and ignorance of the operations of will (Trevor-Roper, *Catholics*, 235). "A short slander," as Milton knows, and as literary history confirms, "will oft times reach further than a long apology" (*CPW* 1:883). Equilibrium is not quite achieved; but one agrees with Joan Webber that here "the Christian warrior and the poet-to-be become conditions of one another, neither intelligible without the other's presence" (*Eloquent "I,"* 199).

To recall the Confuter's allegations: the Animadverter was an "unknown," a libeler, "frivolous, tedious, and false," who, "after an inordinate and riotous youth spent at the university," was "vomited out thence," and was now residing in a "suburb sink"; he was a frequenter of playhouses and bordellos, an unqualified man seeking academic preferment and a rich widow. He was a rhetorician courting the mob, a bad stylist, a grim lowering fool who wrote scurrilous mimes full of horrid blasphemy. He was capable of eloquence, but rarely achieved it.

Milton answers quite systematically. He confronts head-on the charge against his university career with an edge of bitterness. Formally, almost formulaically, he proclaims his own success at Christ's College. The Confuter's lies give him "apt occasion to acknowledge publickly with all gratefull minde, that more then ordinary favour and respect which I found above any of my equals at the hands of those curteous and learned men, the Fellowes of that Colledge wherein I spent some yeares" (884). How carefully neutral these praises are and how dry the last words. Milton remembers his teachers, and the "singular good affection" of "those ingenuous and friendly men who were ever the countenancers of virtuous and hopeful wits" (884). This impersonal language changes as Milton turns on the university itself. He cares not at all about "the common approbation or dislike of that place" which he "never greatly admir'd, so now much lesse" (884–85)—in *Animadversions* he had noted that the universities had been "poyson'd and choak'd under your [prelatical] governance" (718). The anger turns to ugly threat: "She vomits now out of sicknesse, but ere it be well with her, she must vomit by strong physick" (885) (Puritan purges are in fact just around the corner). His "suburb sinke" is a better environment than the queasy university. His mornings are now disciplined pastorals, rendering "lightsome, cleare, and not lumpish obedience to the minde, to the cause of religion, and our Countries liberty" (885–86). The pastoral is disciplined by classical echo into the military *Sans mens in sano corpore:* Milton's private school as New Model Academy.

He studies better on his own. The university is a corrupt institution, even in its college theatricals, where "so many of the young Divines, and those in next aptitude to Divinity have bin seene . . . writhing and unboning their Clergie limmes . . . prostituting the shame of that ministery . . . to the eyes of Courtiers and Court-Ladies, with their Groomes and Madamoisellaes" (887).[23]

What fascinated distaste in that "unboning,"[24] and what contempt for the clergy, both those who teach and those who are being taught! And how can one read that Frenchified courtly audience except as pretentious and indulgent? This portrayal of clerical impropriety validates the dissolving of prelatical stewardship of Christian education; and it prepares the reader for the depiction of the good private education.

Milton again pleads the originality of his apology, something more than traditional ethical proof: "I shall intreat to be born with though I digresse: & in a way not often trod acquaint ye with the summe of my thoughts in this matter through the course of my yeares and studies" (*CPW,* 1:888). Ignorance of the beautiful and envy cause his enemies to censure his books, his external texts. Now he must "change the compact order, and instead of outward actions to bring inmost thoughts into front." The garment is turned inside out, "especially if the lining be of the same, or as it is sometimes, much better. So if my name and outward demeanour be not evident enough to defend me, I must make tryall, if the discovery of my inmost thoughts can" (888–89).

"Name" here is still *mere* name, as it tends to be in this early prose. I cite but one pejorative use from each of the antiprelatical tracts (all found in *CPW,* 1):

- [The Bishops are] but a Tyrannical crew and Corporation of Impostors, that have blinded and abus'd the World so long under that Name. (537)
- [Post-Apostolic times] must make a new Lexicon to name themselves. (632)
- As if we could be put off with Calvins name, unlesse we be convinc't with Calvins reason. (707)
- And many on the Prelatick side like the Church of Sardis have a name to live, and yet are dead. (788–89, echoing Rev. 3.1)
- [A seeker for patronage] trick[s] up the name of some Esquire,

Gentleman or Lord Paramont at Common Law, to be his book patron. (877)

In *Paradise Lost,* Adam and Eve proclaim their power and their knowledge in naming the flora and fauna of Eden; and John Leonard has urged us to see that "Naming is integral to the poem and implicit in its subject."[25] Here, however, "name" is misnomer, masking a specious attempt at control; typically Milton recoils at such usurpation of power through "idolatrous" designations of places, of titles, of processes. Analogous is the Puritan horror of bowing at the name of Jesus (as in Burton's *Jesu-Worship Confuted*), of the very designations "altar" and "priest."

Public misnaming is a masking and misreading of the external. Milton's defense will now be of his interior life, an apology that will allow him to proclaim his identity, to establish a real name. He sees himself as a processive subject, at once his past reading, his present (this text), and his potential poems to come. He will boldly include his personal behavior, academic, political, and sexual. All is to be poured into a new text, the text of the expanded self. Milton would emulate his classical masters in thinking,

> my selfe by every instinct and presage of nature which is not wont to be false . . . that what judgement, wit, or elegance was my share, would herein best appeare, and best value it selfe, by how much more wisely, and with more love of vertue I should choose (let rude eares be absent) the object of not unlike praises. (889–90)

An essential part of Milton's definition of "self" is this self searching for an appropriate spouse, the "meet help" which will reappear significantly in the divorce tracts. "Let rude eares be absent"; the aside is truly innocent.

The author is text and reader, reading himself but eminently part of a larger order, "now not as mine own person, but as a member incorporate into that truth whereof I was perswaded, and whereof I had declar'd openly to be a partaker" (871). Narcissus does not see the waterlilies and the fish: Milton sees himself both as true poem, an authentic and single text, and as part of a general chorus of praise and testimony, in the midst of the hymns and hallelujahs of the saints. He also sees himself as married, a state essential to his meaningfulness. The concept of the self as "true poem" is embedded in a discussion of social responsibility, and especially of marriage-choice.

Dense citations of authority and unusual awareness of audience precede the discussion of the moral responsibility that enables ideal love: "not to be sensible, when good and faire in one person meet, argues both a grosse and shallow judgement, and withall [an] ungentle and swainish brest." Yet those who spoke unworthy or unchaste things of themselves or of their loves were to be "deplor'd" even if their art was "applauded," an interesting concession by the moralist poet. Predictably, "above them all, [he] preferr'd the two famous renowners of Beatrice and Laura . . . displaying sublime and pure thoughts, without transgression" (890).

For Milton, a critical virtue of the true poet is his sexual purity, "chastity" which is not only "that vertue which abhorres the society of Bordello's" (891), but also a refusal to be "defiled with women, which doubtlesse meanes fornication" (892–93). Milton has thought much (and somewhat boyishly) about what is illicit in sexuality; a more serious definition of "fornication" will soon be an important part of his argument in the divorce tracts, especially *Tetrachordon*. Here the argument is less complicated but still ardent; the search for virtue includes the search for the right woman. Marriage choice is on Milton's mind, not merely in response to the charges of his having frequented bordellos or of seeking out "a rich widow, or a lecture, or both" (929). The self-consciousness about the marriage subject is essential to the idealism of his program, now fully stated:

> And long it was not after, when I was confirm'd in this opinion, that he who would not be frustrate of his hope to write well hereafter in laudable things, ought him selfe to bee a true Poem, that is, a composition, and patterne of the best and honourablest things; not presuming to sing high praises of heroick men, or famous Cities, unlesse he have in himselfe the experience and the

practice of all that which is praise-worthy. These reasonings, together with a certaine nicenesse of nature, an honest haughtinesse, and self-esteem either of what I was, or what I might be (which let envie call pride) and lastly that modesty, whereof though not in the Title page yet here I may be excus'd to make some beseeming profession, all these uniting the supply of their naturall aide together, kept me still above those low descents of minde, beneath which he must deject and plunge himself, that can agree to salable and unlawfull prostitutions. (890)

This radically exposed passage confirms Milton's personal dedication to an institutional literary idealism. It also proclaims "an honest haughtinesse, and self-esteem" that commits the speaker to public—and hence vulnerable—responsibility and service. As the claims for moral rectitude become completely personal, become in fact the person, the voice becomes "enfranchised to sing the highest music," "an achievement of personal history"[26]—and a public commitment.

As in the close of *Of Reformation* and the Introduction to book 2 of *The Reason of Church-Government*, the promise for the future is kerygma itself. A synchronic surge and soaring of temporal and spatial images identify the promise: "a song to generations"; "something so written to aftertimes, as they should not willingly let it die"; "laudable things . . . high praises of heroick men, or famous Cities" (616, 810, 890). The inclusion of the personal and the sexual has raised the stakes.

A brief survey of literary love follows, tempering the pesonal ardor, and demonstrating how much the literary and the personal reinforced each other in Milton's life. Defense of "the weaknesse of any attempted chastity" becomes the main point of the reading of romance. It was the knightly defenders of chastity who taught Milton to abhorre "the society of Bordello's." "From the Laureat fraternity of Poets, riper yeares, and the ceaselesse round of study and reading" he climbs the Neoplatonic ladder "to the shady spaces of philosophy, but chiefly to the divine volumes of Plato, and his equall Xenophon" where he learned of chastity and love "whose

charming cup is only vertue" (891), a cup chosen over that of
Circe, "a certaine Sorceresse, the abuser of loves name," whose
cup contains "a thick intoxicating potion." Six months before
his first marriage (23 October 1642), Milton still has a virginal,
almost adolescent, perception of sexuality—deadly serious.
The distance between him and "empiric" carnality is literary:
the brothel madam is "the sage and rheumatick old Prelatesse
with all her young Corinthian Laity." The evils of prostitution
are presented metaphorically and skittishly; the vision of
chaste married love is in a diction most immediate to Milton
and his readers, ardent and selectively egalitarian: "the body
is for the Lord and the Lord for the body . . . if unchastity in a
woman whom Saint Paul termes the glory of man, be such a
scandall and dishonour, then certainly in a man who is both
the image and the glory of God, it must, though commonly
not so thought, be much more deflouring and dishonourable"
(892). From this position of sexually honourable manhood,
Milton envisions the "high rewards of ever accompanying the
Lambe, with those celestiall songs to others inapprehensible,
but not to those who were not defil'd with women, which
doubtlesse means fornication: For mariage must not be call'd
a defilement" (892–93). The passage on the self as a true poem
is compact of sexual and social apology, and insistent on the
relevance of that apology. The ethical proof Milton offers
is conventional in its attacks on the adversary, explicit in
the data of its self-presentation, and unconventional in its
emphasis on future promise over present competence. It is
also unusually aware of the potentially bored reader. Self-
consciously, with something of a shrug, he leaves the personal apology with "if I have been already successelesse
in perswading them [my readers], all that I can furder say
will be but vaine; and it will be better thrift to save two
tedious labours, mine of excusing, and theirs of needlesse
hearing" (893).

Milton's autobiographical prose rhythms carry us toward a
pedestal from which he proclaims abstracted sublimities. Even
in the midst of defending himself against "the adversary . . .
barking at the doore; or searching for me at the Burdellos,"

his body is the Lord's. His marriage, which he is obviously pondering, is contiguous to the marriage supper of the Lamb (Rev. 14.1–5), with "those celestiall songs to others inapprehensible" (892), but not to those who have waited, have thought long and carefully about the right choice. In *Of Reformation*, Milton had put the rigorous honoring of the marriage bed at the heart of his society (*CPW*, 1:588). Now, in his response to charges of widow-shopping and of bordello-haunting, he celebrates chastity as a preface to marriage. The whole long crescendo of self-defense, of self as true poem, ends here in that simple sentence, "For mariage must not be call'd a defilement" (893). The best part of the tract is over.

The phrase "Thus large I have purposely bin" marks the transition. Much of the text now repeats earlier arguments: the standard attack on academic and prelatical tradition; the defense of the vehement style from history and Scripture; the wars of citation; the abuse of the opponent, with sometimes clumsy attempts at humor; the idealistic vision of the elect nation and the poet-super-laureate. The Confuter is contemptible and violent, a maimer, a depraver, a mangler of words, "tormenter of semicolons . . . as good at dismembring and slitting sentences, as his grave Fathers the Prelates have bin at stigmatizing & slitting noses" (894). The beleaguered text is like the beleaguered human body, a comparison validated by experiences as contemporary as those of Alexander Leighton (*CPW*, 1:37) as well as those of Bastwick, Burton, and Prynne (compare to the "Barbar Surgery" of *Colasterion*, *CPW*, 2:736–37).

"Unsavory traditions," "barbarous Declamation," the "Trojan horse," "plaine bedlam stuffe," "Guisian" treasons (*CPW*, 1:895) merge in the Confuter. In another Miltonic appropriation and reversal the "young queasinesse" (894) becomes himself "the Demoniack legion . . . which the Remonstrant feard had been against him, and now he may see is for him." The "young" is almost conflated with the Remonstrant, at least he "come[s] out of his shop" (895); perhaps they are "both one person or as I am told, Father and Son" (897). The "cursing Shimei a hurler of stones" has invoked a level of violence against "one who in all his writing spake not, that any mans skin should be rais'd" (896), a claim that is, at least, disingenuous. But Milton argues that Bishop Hall is the source of the problem of attribution. "He hath begun the measure namelesse, and when he pleases we may all appeare as we are. And let him be then what he will, he shall be to me so as I finde him principl'd" (897).

Conscious again of the ruthless tone, Milton defends vehement laughter, citing Horace, Cicero, Seneca, Sophocles (904–5), with two relatively rare references to contemporaries—"Lysimachus Nicanor" (John Corbet), and *A Survey of . . . Protestation Protested* (1641),[27] which he, with some good evidence, attributes to Hall. The real justification comes from Christ himself, who scrupled not "to name the Dunghill and the Jakes" (895): "Doth not Christ himselfe teach the highest things by the similitude of old bottles and patcht cloaths?" (898). The defense of "sanctifi'd bitterness against the enemies of truth" (901), including vehement laughter, dominates these pages, enlisting "only . . . such reasons and autorities, as religion cannot except against" (899)—authorities like John the Baptist, Ezekiel, John of Patmos, and the author of the Book of Numbers.

Milton continues to seek a wide audience, omitting nothing "which may furder satisfie any conscionable man," for "in the teaching of men diversly temper'd different wayes are to be try'd" (899). Again, the model is Christ's:

> Our Saviour . . . was Lord to expresse his indoctrinating power in what sort him best seem'd; sometimes by a milde and familiar converse, sometimes with plaine and impartiall home-speaking regardless of those whom the auditors might think he should have had in more respect; otherwhiles with bitter and irefull rebukes if not teaching yet leaving excuselesse those his wilfull impugners. What was all in him, was divided among many others the teachers of his Church. (899–900)

The flouting of a hostile audience, the quirky need to leave them "excuseless," is familiar to readers of Milton, who here openly claims a divine model. This attempt to reach a wide and varied auditory, while implicitly condemning an elite one, should prepare the reader for the soon-to-appear radical analysis of Christ's response to the Pharisees in the *Doctrine and Discipline*. Milton's relish in putting down the favorite is like the "bespurting" of the Bishop in *Animadversions* (662), not very admirable, but understandable. Milton's excuse is that God Himself allows the teachers of His Church their various styles:

> no man being forc't wholly to dissolve that groundwork of nature which God created in him, the sanguine to empty out all his sociable livelinesse, the cholerick to expell quite the unsinning predominance of his anger; but that each radicall humour and passion wrought upon and corrected as it ought, might be made the proper mould and foundation of every mans peculiar guifts, and vertues. (900)

"That groundwork of nature" allows the speaker his own voice and requires of him the recognition of the varied needs and linguistic levels of his audience. John Preston had found fault with those who preached "University Sermons to the people, which they had made for a more learned auditory" (see chapter 1, n. 42); Milton adds the nature of the speaker to the definition of preacherly decorum. The villains are still the elite group, the "carnall, and false Doctors" (900) who insist on set forms and impressive rhetoric. Milton's rhetoric of zeal scorns and disallows such display, while urging regard for—and something like gentleness toward—those auditors needing an accommodated style. The aim is finally a broader audience, necessarily one "lower" in terms of class and education.

To combat the "Doctors," Milton now invokes a version of the Chariot of Paternal Deity:

> Zeale whose substance is ethereal, arming in compleat diamond ascends his fiery Chariot drawn with two blazing Meteors figur'd like beasts . . . the one visag'd like a Lion to express power, high autority and indignation, the other of count'nance like a man to cast derision and scorne upon perverse and fraudulent seducers; with these the invincible warriour Zeale shaking loosely the slack reins drives over the heads of Scarlet Prelats, and such as are

insolent to maintaine traditions, brusing their stiffe necks under his flaming wheels. (900)

For the proud, the "coole unpassionate mildnesse of positive wisdome" is wrong. Zeal has two faces—one accommodating, the other "galling and vexing"—like Christ with the "Prelaticall Pharisees" (900–901). In this last-to-be-printed of this group of tracts, Milton insists on the right of a wide range of people to be taught in language appropriate to their capacities; and he continues to insist on his own right to gall and vex the Pharisees.

Classical, biblical, Rabbinic, and Christian examples demonstrate God's accommodation to human capacities, His freedom and liberality of expression. In their "insuls rule," the Targumists would change God's obscenity into "more civill words" (903); "I will cut off from Ieroboam him that pisseth against the wall" becomes "I will cut off all who are at yeares of discretion," in the translation of Jonathan and Onkelos (902). "Fools, who would teach men to read more decently then God thought good to write." Language is absolutely free in its ultimate serviceability to God. "All words and whatsoever may be spoken shall at some time in an unwonted manner wait upon [virtue's] purposes" (903). Much of Milton's construction of decorum in the prose, including the later exclusion of "tolerated popery" from freedom of the press, must confront that "unwonted manner."

Socrates' daemon, the Stoic Hegemonicon, and Christian "inward witnesse" are inner voices to which good men accede; God provides an inward Christian decorum for those "who had forsaken all other doctrines for his"; they have no "need to measure themselves, by other mens measures how to give scope, or limit to their proper actions" (904–5). The typical progression from classical to Christian is a small history of the inner light upon which rests Milton's confidence of his connection to God. This knowledge enables him to imagine the loss of that connection in *Samson Agonistes*.

The defense of the "benevolence of laughter and reproofe" (905) as accompaniment to the rhetoric of zeal has not been heard so clearly since the *Of Reformation;* "Sir Francis Bacon . . . is match't and overmatcht" by Eliah and the Martyrs, which proves "what force of teaching there is sometimes in laughter" (903). The attack on specious moderation, which "cannot any where be but in Paradise" (910) becomes practical, a political demonstration of the Reveltion 3.16 text. The "manifest crimes" of the hard-line prelates "serve to bring forth an ensuing good and hasten a remedy against themselves," but the "seeming good" of the Moderate (that is, Bishop Hall) "tends to reinforce their selfe-punishing crimes and his owne, by doing his best to delay all redresse" (911). The case against moderation is startling. There are no innocent bystanders: "he that is not with me is against me, and he that gathers not with me scatters" (911–12). Hall is Pilate holding the scourgers' garments—"does he think to be counted guiltlesse?" (913–14).

In what he labels a digression, Milton turns to praise of Parliament, "those publick benefactors of their country" (922). The class consciousness cuts two ways: "most of them being either of ancient and high Nobility, or at least of knowne and well reputed ancestry," have "a great advantage towards vertue one way, but in respect of welth, ease, and flattery, which accompanies a nice and tender education, . . . as much a hindrance another way." The "temptation of riches, high birth, and that usuall bringing up" is poised against imitation of "the worthiest of their progenitors" and "the strength of an inbred goodnesse"—their Hegemonicon. Parliament, "wiser then their teachers," has *survived* the universities, "nurseries of superstition, and empty speculation" (923). Superior educations come from individual wills and talents, not from institutions.

After a cruel image of Strafford "groveling upon the fatall block" (924), Milton again urges Laud's death. The lurid gloating by Puritans over the execution of Strafford and the prospective execution of Laud matched the earlier Anglican gloating over the maiming of Bastwick, Burton, and Prynne. In July of 1641, Thomas Case had preached to the House of Commons, "Behold, he *lies grovelling at your feet,* there wants nothing but the *cutting off his head,* which you may do with his *own Sword"* (*Two Sermons,* A2v). As in the Fable of the Wen, Milton urges violence. Civil liberty and religion are parallel concerns of Parliament; with one archenemy down, there is one to go. "And meeting next . . . with the second life of tyranny (for she was growne an ambiguous monster)" they "neither were taken with her miter'd hypocrisy, nor terrifi'd with the push of her bestiall hornes." In the wash of Apocalyptic imagery, Laud becomes the Whore of Babylon and Strafford the Beast, "to be slaine in two shapes" (924). Two kinds of tyranny, two kinds of obedience, and, not far behind, two kinds of heroism. The civil hero of old freed men from external tyranny, but Parliament has "freed us from a doctrine of tyranny that offer'd violence and corruption even to the inward persuasion" (925).

The excitement increases. Great exploits are for Milton almost always linked with a vision of the praise of those exploits, the hero and his celebrator, separated yet equal in their separate respective categories, rather like the patron and poet in Jonson's "To Penshurst." In this fascination with "true" and "false" heroism, with internal and external mastery, Milton is developing his own idea of what epic is, how it relates to a truly laudable moral performance by its heroes, and how it must emerge from a necessary interaction of public and private virtues. The "poem-in-praise-of" is seen as the authenticating climax of heroic and virtuous action. In the process of defining heroism, as the promise of a solution is being made, Milton's language becomes resonant with powerful rhythms, alliterations, allusions, and richer images.

Here, perhaps because of its plural vehicle, the heroism emphasizes availability: "the Fathers of their country . . . sit as gods among daily Petitions and publick thanks flowing in upon them. . . . to whom] the meanest artizans and labourers, at other times also women, and often the younger sort of servants . . . have gone with confidence" (926). The presence of the underprivileged is celebratory, inclusive, not exclusionary. The language takes on the glow of the agoraphilia which will climax in *Areopagitica.* In poetry, Milton was an eminent pastoralist; in these tracts, and in *Areopagitica*, he is the prose-poet of the crowded city.

Is God's inspiration at the heart of Milton's politics? Or does *he* place himself in God's hands? The process would appear to be one of cooperation:

> if we neglect not this early pledge of Gods inclining towards us, by the slacknesse of our needfull aids. . . . God himselfe condescends, and workes with his owne hands to fulfill the requests of men. . . . [God] seems to have thus cov'nanted with them, that if the will and the endeavour shall be theirs, the performance and the perfeting shall be his. (927–28)

The construal of heroic virtue in this praise of Parliament is an early stage of the long, rich meditation which ends in the creation of *Samson Agonistes*, the text in which Milton most profoundly explores the creation, fall and recreation of the Godly political man. The strategies of delay and silence of the great tragedy are being developed in these tracts.

The wrong kind of praise is "sonnetting." (928) As it does in *Eikonoklastes* (*CPW*, 3:421), the word implies inappropriate, perhaps even "effeminate" (in the modern sense), rhetorical excess. Defense of self must eschew such softness and combat the charges of vanity, venality and fraud. Against the manly truth-teller, the returned adversary becomes "wizzard. . . . Gipsy . . . Fortune-teller . . . Chaldean," summoning up false information from his familiar, "a lying feind" (*CPW*, 1:928–29). Among the "feind's" lies are those pertaining to Milton's marital hopes; he "would choose a virgin of mean fortunes honestly bred, before the wealthiest widow"; anyway, "providence . . . hath ever bred me up in plenty" (929).

Commenting specifically on his process, Milton dismisses the charges against the "big-mouthed, astounding prayer" (*Confutation*, 22):

> It was theatricall, he sayes. And yet it consisted most of Scripture language; . . . It was big-mouth'd he sayes; no marvell; if it were fram'd as the voice of three Kingdomes: neither was it a prayer so much as a hymne in prose frequent both in the Prophets, and in humane authors; therefore the stile was greater then for an

ordinary prayer. It was an astounding prayer. I thank him for that confession, so it was intended to astound and to astonish the guilty Prelats. (930)

The "theatricality" of the hymn Milton attributes to its spontaneous, inspired use of Scripture. "It had no Rubrick"; unlike the *Book of Common Prayer*, it was not prescribed. Its magniloquence, (that is, bigmouthedness), was a function of the size of audience. "Astonishment" and "astounding" are functions of the vehement style, the adversarial style. The "terrible" of Demetrius Phalereus—*deinos*—had always been an available category of style for Milton, and this passage is one of the proofs of it. The *deinos*—terrible grandeur— immobilizes the open-mouthed enemy.

Mouths—"astonied," open, eating, singing, preaching, dumb—are everywhere in these tracts, mouths and their diverse functions. Prelacy has failed in its primary purpose, to proclaim to the people the Christian truth for which they were hungry, a congregation competent not only to receive that truth, but also to choose the proclaimers. Bishop Hall denies that fitness, but "the Apostles ever labour'd to perswade the Christian flock" of their worthiness to teach. The Prelates consider the people as "the very beasts of Mount Sinai . . . suppressing the frequency of Sermons, and the printed explanations of the English Bible" (931–32). The antiprelatical tracts can be seen as huge distentions of the "blind mouths" digression of "Lycidas."

An Apology ends by summarizing the arguments on kerygmatic authority, on the gaping throats, and on the mouths which are to deliver the good news. From Isaiah come again the images of the false teachers: "dumbe and greedy dogs that can never have anough, ignorant, blind, and cannot understand, who while they all look their own way every one for his gaine from his quarter, how many parts of the land are fed with windy ceremonies instead of sincere milke" (932, citing Isa., 56.10–11).

The freely adapted passage is one of the longer Scriptural quotations in these tracts. In Christian readings, Isaiah's chapter 56 is an admonition and a promise of the Apocalypse. Milton puts the passage to immediate political use. There are many waste places in the kingdom "without preaching Minister, without light" (932); the Prelate-Pharisees foster ignorance and cultivate a complex bureaucracy of ceremonies and rights that perpetuate their interests and starve the sheep.

Against this leadership is set the meanest Christian, now enfranchised as proper elector of his own minister, one who "may easily attaine to know when he is wisely taught and when weakly. . . . not the wise only but the simple and ignorant may learne [by the best books]." The prelates "who have put out the peoples eyes reproach them of their blindnesse" (933); they have "famish't" the island, "or wholly perverted with Prelatick leven"; their professional claims are seen as "the lofty nakednesse of your Latinizing Barbarian, and the finicall goosery of your neat Sermon-actor. And so I leave you and your fellow starres."[28] The passage drips with contempt for the Establishment "stars" and with sympathy for "the divers plaine and solid men" who naively listen to them. The Blind Mouths have betrayed their mission. In the face of that failure to speak Truth, all prelatical claims to primacy, or even priority, are "sinking, and wasted to the snuffe in their westerne socket" (935).

Commonplace Puritan reiterations include the attacks on the *Book of Common Prayer*, on the burdens of Indifferency which is really Scandal, on the dryness and foolishness of set forms, "tautologies, impertinences"; the attacks include a contemptuous view on the churching of woman after childbirth, "for her delivery from Sunburning and Moon-blasting, as if she had bin travailing not in her bed, but in the deserts of Arabia" (939). Sonnet 23 reminds us that, on occasion, Milton can eschew ideology; in referring to his "late espoused Saint" he summons the churching image: "Mine as whom washt from spot of child-bed taint, / Purification in the old Law did save" (*Riverside Milton*, 259). The lines are a fine example of Milton's capacity for *discreteness* in its original sense, the capacity to present words separate and clear in their identity, strictly limited to the particular usage. Allusiveness bows to decorum.

A few pages earlier, Milton had the Prelates turning Mother Church into an institutional Circe: "by their sorcerous doctrine of formalities they take the way to transforme them out of Christian men into Judaizing beasts." (932) Now the English Church—"is this your glorious Mother of England . . .?"—has been "conceav'd and infanted by an idolatrous Mother . . . the retaining of this Romish Liturgy a provocation to God" (940–41); and her claim to "decency" is denied. The Remonstrant's "What no decency in God's worship?" is answered again, fervently:

> Certainly Readers, the worship of God singly in it selfe, the very act of prayer and thanksgiving with free and unimpos'd expressions which from a sincere heart unbidden come into the outward gesture, is the greatest decency that can be imagin'd. (941–42)

Devotion comes from the inside. Prescribed gestures for personal devotion are, for the Puritan polemicist, particular targets, especially those at the celebration of the Eucharist: "no Wine, bowing, creeping, crawling, cringing, whipping, slashing, beating, thumping, sighing, howling, and the like."[29] The "Beauty of Holiness" is rejected as "deform'd ugliness."

Behind the fear of gesture is the fear of Rome, and Rome is presented, dramatically, as a crafty divorced woman, as Dalila, as Queen Henrietta Maria. Milton deplores the Romish vestiges of the Church of England: "If we have indeed given a bill of divorce to Popery and superstition, why do we not say as to a divors't wife; those things which are yours, take them all with you, and they shall sweepe after you? Why were not we thus wise at our parting from Rome?" Then he gives a small, tight drama of sexual politics:

> Ah like a crafty adultresse she forgot not all her smooth looks and inticing words at her parting; yet keep these letters, these tokens, and these few ornaments; I am not all so greedy of what is mine, let them preserve with you the memory of what I am? No, but of what I was, once faire and lovely in your eyes (*CPW*, 1:942).

"Let me approach at least, and touch thy hand." Here is, I suspect, the kernel of the scene of Dalila's return in *Samson Agonistes*, starting with the imagery of whoredom and ending with a subtle campaign for winning, almost compelling, forgiveness: "Thus did those tender hearted reformers dotingly suffer themselves to be overcome with harlots language. And she like a witch . . . [whose] whoorish cunning should prevaile to work upon us her deceitfull ends" (942). The absolute necessity of extirpating Roman influence is like Samson's absolute and shocking rejection of Dalila's hypocritical courtesies: "Out, out Hyaena." Root and Branch—even the Creed—"if it be hers let her take it. We can want no Creed, so long as we want not the Scriptures." The strong anti-Roman passage leads to a renewed attack on the prelate-martyrs, a reminder of their continued iconic relevance in these controversies; "their negligence and halting" is blamed for "all that following persecution" (943).

In this most personal of his attempts to reach the reader, Milton has used the direct address "Readers" or "Reader" some 35 times, far more than in any other of his prose works. Now that this teachable audience has, with the speaker, "the Port in sight" (943), they will recognize in God's providence that Milton has guided them not to have read amiss. The need to address directly intensifies; it reflects the need to defend, which is always there. For all the conventions of levels of style, all the political allowances, for all the community of a rhetoric of zeal, Milton was regularly criticized for impropriety. His vehemence violated the expectations that his initially elegant and erudite style would raise in a reader; for some of his Presbyterian colleagues he was dangerously expanding the language of controversy into new and uncontrollable areas. Steadily, and necessarily, he prefaced his tracts, interlaced his arguments, and powerfully digressed to argue another real propriety, the decorum of kerygmatic authority, of a revived Christian truth delivered to a new and expanded audience, which Milton attempts here to clutch and hold fast.

An Apology ends with a valedictory to the antiprelatical matter, with relief at the promised end and gathered strength for the finale. The imagination has tired a little, the contempt thinned down, as in the description of the prelatical summonings of the Fathers, "ye shall see their great heape shrink and wax thin beyond belief." (945) Milton is learning control, distance, and conservation in the handling of his argument, as we can see, if we compare this passage with the gorgeous contempt toward the same matter in *Of Prelatical Episcopacy* (see chapter 3). Now he can easily confess to not having read "more of the Councils" (944), and he passes quickly through the corruption of the universities, the impressive defense of Christian sovereignty by law, the citing of Gower against the Donation of Constantine, the acceptance, and reinforcement of the Confuter's backhanded praise. All these are now subordinated to the final statement against prelates, including reminders of the earlier arguments against Bishop Hall.

The wealth of the Church provokes Milton's final passion and alliteration. The "prizes" invite "avarice and ambition"; "they are most apt to blind, to puffe up and pervert the most seeming good" (948). As at other moments of synthesis, the figure of Christ is summoned, here to reject dignities: "Christ refus'd great riches, and large honours at the Devils hand. . . . why then should the servant take upon him those things which his master had unfitted himselfe to use." The "teaching labour of the word" has been debased into "the unteaching ease of Lordship over consciences and purses" (949).

These last pages condense images of both the ideal and the betrayed mission of the ministry: teaching and misinforming; Israel and Egypt; the Gospel and the Law; Christian manhood and Jewish childhood; Jacob and worse-than-Simon-Magus; Christian and Infidel. Christian ministry is to be defined within the Gospel, not in terms of perquisites of office: "the Gospell is our manhood, and the ministery should bee the manhood of the Gospell. . . . their calling is spirituall, not secular." Like the Jesus of *Paradise Regained*, the minister should be a hero of "speciall warfare" without "many impediments," working "by meane things and persons to subdue mighty ones" (950–51).

The idea of the hero has inhabited this text, sometimes peripherally or analogously, sometimes directly. The discussions of inner and outer selves, of misspent selves, and of specious authority flow into the problems of portraying the Christian hero, problems that Milton was struggling, and failing, to postpone from consideration. Under the description of the good minister was the good poet; under that, the hero. Under the description of the bad prelate was the abuser of language; under that the Adversary of the Word.

The piece ends with powerful images of the present corruption by worldliness of the great office. True and false feeding enter in dense array: "Prelats are mute . . . and yet they eat. . . . They . . . bring in a dearth of spirituall food . . . sending heards of souls starvling to Hell, while they feast and riot, consuming and purloyning even that which by their foundation is allow'd and left to the poore, and to reparations of the Church" (952). The mute prelatical mouth slobbers over food and drink in Puritan polemic and throughout these tracts. It neglects the poor, and it, muting truth, preaches false doctrine. It does not speak the Word that feeds souls, that leads people to salvation. This betrayal is the contrapuntal theme to Milton's main theme: the search for kerygmatic authority for his party and for himself. This is not a theoretical excursus or a precocious or precious convolution of certain interesting possibilities in contemporary polemical vocabulary. The Word gives life: the Minister's function is to speak that Word and expound it. By implication, the good poet's vocation is to further infuse the nation with knowledge of the Word and to celebrate that knowledge. The corruption or suppression of the Word is the ultimate perversion; those corruptors are no easy enemy, and they must be removed or destroyed.

Milton urges action, the action he had left his "deepe and retired thoughts" (*Of Reformation, CPW*, 1:519) to urge. The King himself is advised to be a "true defender of the Faith" (952). The relative casualness of this suggests how far parliamentary prestige had come. And yet some dark lessons had been learned too:

if yee thinke that soundnesse of reason, or what force of argument
soever, will bring them [the false ministers] to an ingenuous silence,
yee think that which will never be . . . ye shall soon discerne that
Turbant of pride which they weare ùpon their heads to be no helmet
of salvation; . . . and that they have also this guift . . . to have their
voice in their bellies, which being well drained and taken downe,
their great Oracle, which is only there, will soon be dumbe, and
the Divine right of Episcopacy forthwith expiring, will put us no
more to trouble with tedious antiquities and disputes. (953)

Rhetorical closure and a demand for political closure. The
"Helmet of Salvation" recalls "the sword of the Spirit, which
is the word of God" (Eph. 5.17). It is with this sword that Bishop
Hall—"their great Oracle"—is dispatched, "drained and taken
downe," along with his *Episcopacie by Divine Right*, which
launched the whole Smectymnuan controversy. Milton makes
terminal statements on the specious uses of antiquity; on the
true and false word, on true and false food; on Canterbury's
relation to Rome, and on the "irrational" persistence of prelacy.
Simon Magus reappears in these last pages (950) to remind
the reader of the venality traditionally associated with church
office.

Blind mouths fall before the kerygma, false word before true.
But the violent suggestion of cure, within weeks of the Bishops
Exclusion Bill, shows that this pamphlet and this wing of the
pamphlet wars are deadly serious political statements, as well
as hymns of personal religious and ethical commitment.

Six

Kerygmatic Authority in *The Reason of Church-Government*

The *Reason of Church-Government Urg'd against Prelaty* is the longest of the antiprelatical tracts, the first to be acknowledged by its author, and the most carefully read of Milton's early prose pieces. The autobiographical essay at the head of book 2, with its resplendent promises for the future, suggests a new stage of awareness of his career, a public declaration of the writing self. Ralph A. Haug, editor of the Yale edition, dates the piece as between August 4, 1641, and January 1, 1642, and conjectures that Milton signed it "because he felt that here, at length, he had written something that might live" (*CPW*, 1:736). I would add that it is a "signing off," planned as a termination of the prelatical matter, as well as a "signing in" and announcement of things to come. This intended exit from the tract wars was disrupted by the attack from the Modest Confuter, necessitating *An Apology*. So *Reason*, for all its dignity and control, shows Milton's equilibrium under unusual stress. He wants to terminate his part in the Smectymnuan campaign and announce his plans for the future. And he wants to fulfill his duty in the present, urgent arena. The role of Proclaimer that Milton has been envisaging as his personal destiny is at issue. In *Reason*, two often conflicting yet vital functions of that role are discussed— poet and prophet of the national destiny and pamphleteer in the Wars of Truth. There is no clearly maintained demarcation between the two roles. There are conflicts, contradictions, imbrications—and delays. The intended conclusion of the antiprelatical tracts becomes penultimate; the lofty tone is impaired. But the thrust toward a definition of kerygmatic authority, and a powerful claim on that role by the speaker, is clear enough to make the piece a major work of intellectual autobiography. The advertisement of the great poet to come is a finial on the end of the antiprelatical struggle.

Critical attention has looked rather intently at Milton's failure to respond adequately to the collection *Certain Briefe Treatises, Written by Diverse Learned Men, Concerning the Ancient and Moderne Government of the Church* (Oxford, 1641). It is true that Milton assays "to prove" Presbyterian- ism; that he assures us he will bring "reason," that the "question . . . is so needfull to be known at this time chiefly by every meaner capacity" (*CPW*, 1:749). But it is also true that Milton's attitude toward the five bishops is a little unserious, and condescendingly good-natured. These "profound Clerks . . . are so earnestly meting out the Lydian proconsular Asia . . . whilest good *Brerewood* as busily bes- tirres himselfe in our vulgar tongue to divide precisely the three Patriarchates of Rome, Alexandria, and Antioch, and whether to any of these England doth belong" (748–49). This view of the Bishops as benign Laputans subverts the claim for serious response, as does the statement at the end of the Preface that the reasons—here clearly the particulars of *evidence*— for Church government are not "formally, and profestly set downe, because to him that heeds attentively . . . they easily imply themselves" (750). Milton's failure to address the arguments of the bishops has been overemphasized. The main purpose of *The Reason* of *Church-Government* is, first, to proclaim "a heavenly structure of evangelick discipline so diffusive of knowledge and charity," and then to argue Milton's right to proclaim that structure. Milton claims and proclaims kerygmatic authority.

Animadversions had brilliantly chanted the praises of the great office: "there is no imployment more honourable, more worthy to take up a great spirit, more requiring a generous and free nurture, then to be the messenger, and Herald of heavenly truth from God to man, and by the faithfull worke of holy doctrine, to procreate a number of faithfull men, making a kind of creation like to Gods" (721).

This glowing conception of ideological procreation pervades both of the last two tracts in the series. Both proclaim closure, and both exhibit a quite elaborate defense of self. Yet the autobiographical digression in *An Apology* is *occasional*; in *Reason*, it is clearly a set piece, a transitional mechanism announcing what was expected to be the next phase of the career of the new poet-proclaimer. Milton's plan for a more or less dignified exit from the debates gave way to the need to defend himself from the slanders of *A Modest Confutation*.

Yet one of the purposes of *Reason* was immediately polemical, a response to the collection of pamphlets by an influential group of prelates, including the great and respected Ussher and Andrewes, to both of whom Milton had earlier shown significant deference. Even sympathetic readers have found this response to *Certain Briefe Treatises* unsatisfactory. Don M. Wolfe finds the tract "a weak presentation of Presbyterian claims" (*CPW*, 1:199). K. G. Hamilton finds Milton "jumping up and down in one place";[1] and Stanley Fish calls the deliberate failure of linear development "something of a joke, which functions at the expectations its title encourages."[2] Fish identifies two co-existing structures: the first "promises rational deliberation, progressive clarification, and encapsulated knowledge," but is in fact "circular and tautologous"; the second is at the expense of the other's promises: in it "the real argument inheres in the reinforcing and expanding of the oppositions and associations established in the preface, especially the opposition of reason to intuition and the linking of the one with the Prelates and of the other with the clear-eyed adherents of Presbyterianism" (272). One of the problems with Fish's astute reading is his construal of the word *reason,* which here, in several critical instances, means "evidence," the *reasons for,* not *the intellectual process of arriving at.*[3] The difference is proclaimed in the contrast between Genesis and Exodus that Milton immediately proposes: "Moses . . . knowing how vaine it was to write lawes to men whose hearts were not first season'd with the knowledge of God and of his workes, began from the book of Genesis as prologue to his lawes" (*CPW,* 1:747). Gratitude for God's gift of Creation stems from the plenitude of His "universal goodnesse"; it precedes the logical instruction of the Law.[4] The contrasts between gratitude and obedience, between example and precept, ultimately help to shape the different modes of *Paradise Lost* and *Paradise Regained.* Adam provides the model; his first response to creation is the awe that precedes gratitude: "Straight toward Heav'n my wond'ring Eyes I turn'd" (*PL,* 8.257). In this tract, the good Christian reader starts with gratitude and proceeds to understanding.

The disparagement of the wrong uses of the reasoning process is here, too, by now a familiar part of Milton's prose and of Puritan rhetoric generally. Here the mockery of "good Brerewood" and "other profound Clerks" is benign as "they make good the prime metropolis of Ephesus" (*CPW,* 1:748). But the preface ends unconvincingly, given the fury of the contemporary debate, with its claim that the Scriptural reasons for presbytery are easily deduced, even if "not formally and profestly set down" (750).

The lack of parallelism in chapter headings and the "illusion of logical movement" which Fish notes in support of his 1972 argument (*Artifacts,* 279) are by now familiar lapses in these tracts. In *Of Reformation,* the promise of "orderly proceeding" in the division of "inquiries into our *Fore-Fathers dayes* and into *our Times*" (*CPW,* 1:528) is not fulfilled. In the same tract, the implicit promise of regularity, roughly proportional treatment of "*Antiquitarians . . . 2. Libertines, 3. Polititians*"

(541) is not fulfilled; the first category is discussed in 24 pages (in the original edition), the second in one scant page, the third in 48. *Animadversions* proceeds section by section through Hall's *Answer*, but Hall's sections 6 through 8 are omitted without comment.[5] In the near future, *Areopagitica* will also promise a regular pace through the history of censorship, but linger over some historical periods, while ignoring others, climaxing in what Milton signals us to identify as a digression. In these cases one perceives neither strategy nor deception, but failure. The architectonic skill for which Milton is often praised simply does not apply to his prose. I am not alone in seeing this; Don M. Wolfe and William Alfred have commented that "Milton's prose is singularly chaotic and capricious in organization" (*CPW*, 1:109). But these claims neglect the other unities of images and rhythms, juxtapositions and recoveries, "the reinforcing and expanding of the oppositions and associations" which Fish has noted. They ultimately provide cohesion.

Yet Milton's eminent concerns now are for discipline, the ordering power of scripture delegated to God's elect speakers, the concern to establish promulgative authority, from which will devolve power in matters ecclesiastic and political. The arguments are rational but not systematic. Despite lacunae, repetitions, and initially curious emphases, like the auto-biographical digression, the argument accumulates, and channels the reader toward the dismissal of the false authority of prelacy and the validation of kerygmatic authority in an already radicalizing Presbyterianism. Who may proclaim? God's still reforming Englishmen—for one, John Milton, who will again discuss the validity of his claims to authenticity.

In chapter 1 discipline is the axle upon which "all the movements and turnings of humane occasions are moved to and fro." Discipline is socially useful, removing disorder: it is "the very visible shape and image of virtue. . . . [Her] golden surveying reed marks out and measures every quarter and circuit of new Jerusalem" (751). Discipline leads to a happiness not "confin'd and cloy'd with repetition" but full of motions and paradoxical tensions: "a thousand vagancies of glory and delight," "an invariable Planet of joy and felicity." Ralph A. Haug notes the oxymoron (753), one which injects joy, motion, irregularity into the discussion of discipline—"a kinde of eccentricall equation" (752–53).

This symbiosis of discipline with naturally endowed freedom is critical to Milton's thinking at this stage and, after painful revisions, throughout the later stages of his career. But nature without God, the source of discipline, is frightening, "our darke voyage." After the celebration of natural freedom, there is need for retreat into God. Or is it the need to search for a true leader? Does Milton have Lord Brooke in mind when he extols

> a true knower of himselfe, and himselfe in whom contemplation and practice, wit, prudence, fortitude and eloquence must be rarely met, both to comprehend the hidden causes of things, and span in his thoughts all the various effects that passion or complexion can work in mans nature; and hereto must his hand be at defiance with gaine, and his heart in all vertues heroick. (753)

The rhythms here remind one of the descriptions of the poet in both book 2 of this tract and in *An Apology*. And the foil of "wretched projectors who bescraul their Pamflets every day" suggests an antithetical writing hero. Lord Brooke was that, as *Areopagitica* was sadly to remember, a spokesman for the serious antiprelaticals. His attack on indifference has been noted; it must have affected and pleased Milton. Brooke's death in March of 1643 was widely lamented, and I would suggest that Milton felt the loss of the rare one who had the breadth and style to lead a Miltonic revolution, a hero with an inside as well as an outside. Ten years before the Cromwell sonnet, Milton has redefined the hero, not as "ideal Renaissance statesman," as E. M. W. Tillyard suggests,[6] nor as orator, as Annabel Patterson has argued,[7] but as the politically effective and eloquent Christian *proclaimer*, an immediately viable spokesman.

The argument on authority takes a curious private detour. Though many "deepe counsellors" and "worthy Preachers" are successful in public affairs, "how deficient they are in the regulation of their own family" (*CPW*, 1:754). Family dynamics and the dieting of virgins are distracting here, signs of that serious consideration of marriage which surfaces in these last two tracts.

Eloquence is not the whole issue: "discipline is the practick work of preaching directed and apply'd as is most requisite to particular duty," with pastoral service now seen as more immediately to the "benefit of souls" than preaching (755–56). The source of that Baconian plea for immediacy is the authority of God in his role of father-tutor, and of Christ as husband-leader of the church.

The reasons of church government do not "easily imply themselves" despite the off-handed assurance (750); there must be explanations which unfold, as Fish has suggested, in visions not reasons. Christ is "golden survaying reed" (752) and "husband" (755); the Temple is regenerated in us as "the lovely shapes of vertues and graces, the sooner to edifie and accomplish the immortall stature of Christs body which is his Church." The habit of incarnational and incorporational thinking encourages, and assumes, complexity, despite its immediacy as image; the church is inward Temple *and* Christ's body simultaneously. The rejected Temple is not the body but the failed body, "under a vaile" (758), "patch't afterwards, and varnish't over with the devices and imbellishings of mans imagination" (757).

Motion and heat are generated by the idea of a godly unity, and the excited speaker becomes the architect: "And there was given me a reed like unto a rod: and the angel stood, saying, Rise, and measure the temple of God, and the altar, and them that worship therein" (Rev., 11.1). Milton assumes "the office of a great Evangelist and the reed given him from heaven": Christ himself bids him "take his Reed" (*CPW*, 1:761, 760). *The Reason for Church-Government* becomes Milton's preeminent claim for kerygmatic authority *now*: "Doctrine indeed is the measure, or at least the reason of the measure, tis true, but unlesse the measure be apply'd to that which it is to measure, how can it actually doe its proper worke" (760–61). Milton proclaims his right to use his reason/

reed/rod: his right to judge, to write, and, as we shall see, to marry.

Yet the second part of his title is "Urg'd against Prelaty"; God's measurement demands the rejection of the evil ones: "But the court which is without the temple leave out, and measure it not; for it is given unto the Gentiles" (Rev., 11.2). And Milton restates the ban: "yet in as much as it lyes thus unmeasur'd he leaves it to be trampl'd by the Gentiles, that is to be polluted with idolatrous and Gentilish rites and ceremonies" (*CPW*, 1:761). The right to prophesy includes the right to exclude, as Sanford Budick notes: "[Milton's] idea of a spiritual architecture is a unity that includes division and separation and distance."[8]

Sacred space is real and communal yet also interior. "Christ's body which is his Church, in all her glorious lineaments and proportions" (*CPW*, 1:758) is the holy community of complete persons building from the inside out. Protestant interiority both absorbs and is absorbed into the external glory of Ezekiel's temple vision: "it cannot be wonder'd if that elegant and artfull symmetry of the promised new temple in *Ezechiel*, and all those sumptuous things under the Law were made to signifie the inward beauty and splendor of the Christian Church thus govern'd" (758).

This is different from Archbishop Laud's sacred space. I cite again from the *Relation of the Conference:* "Ceremonies are the *Hedge* that fence the Substance of Religion from the Indignities, which *Prophaneness* and *Sacriledge* too commonly put upon it" (B2V). Puritans attack this sacredness of physical space: "all *Places* are equally *holy,* no one Place being holyer than another: and consequently, the Church is not more *holy* than other places, nor one part of it more *holy* than another . . . [bowing toward the Table] is a *breach of order,* and so of decencie, in the service of God, which is so much pretended for it."[9]

One can now better understand the polemics of this memorable passage from *Of Reformation:*

> The Table of Communion now become a Table of separation stands like an exalted platforme upon the brow of the quire, fortifi'd with

bulwark, and barricado, to keep off the profane Laicks whilst the obscene and surfeted Priest scruples not to paw, and mammock the sacramentall bread, as familiarly as his Tavern Bisket. And thus the people vilifi'd and rejected by them. (547–48)

The table, a place designated for *communion,* here *separates;* it becomes a secular excrescence—"exalted platforme"—a barrier rather than a communing space. It distances the ironically described "profane"—not clerical, hence profane—Laity. While the not ironically described Priest—obscene, surfeited, pawing, mammocking—*transubstantiates* the sacramental bread into his "Tavern Bisket." In a final inversion, the speaker pronounces his contempt for those who would vilify and reject, and urges that they themselves be vilified and rejected. This is Milton at his most harshly effective.[10]

That virulent irony, present to some extent in all of the preceding tracts, now reemerges as a loathing of specious hierarchy, of the wrong kind of exclusion. The strategies are populist. The worldly space to which Milton lays claim is a commons, fenced in by the usurpation of the prelates; the space of his imagined religious practice is demarcated but always gives access to the individual conscience. Church-discipline is set down by God in Scripture, "hedg'd about with such a terrible impalement of commands, as he that will break through wilfully to isolate the least of them, must hazard the wounding of his conscience even to death" (760). Yet the end of the commandment is charity, the violence of the language is ultimately the defense of the individual. Laud's liminalizing injunctions are full of communal weights, his italics are for institutional values. Milton's commands are those of a discipline to be obeyed by, as construed by, the individual. His hedge keeps in; Laud's keeps out. Laud's truth is final and maintained *in place.* Milton's truth, his Church, is real, even corporeal, and yet a vast, loose confederation of individual consciences: an early version of the paradise within.

Fear of domination by tradition is related to the fear of being "tutored." The "tutor" is not only the memory of the Cambridge experience; it is the Law itself. The Hebrew type invoked by the prelates is mocked; Lucifer was the first prelate, not Adam. Nature, not "ceremony or type," is the ground for Apostolic imitation of the Hebrews; and resentful youthfulness asserts itself as ripeness: "How then the ripe age of the Gospell should be put to schoole againe, and learn to governe her selfe from the infancy of the Law . . . will be a hard undertaking to evince from any of those principles which either art or inspiration hath written" (*CPW*, 1:763). The bristling worry over those who would disallow his ripeness recurs in the early works of this usually assured aspirer to immortality. Milton does not abjure his tutors, but he seems to conceive of himself as largely self-taught. The letters to Thomas Young, "best of Teachers" (*CPW*, 1:311) "most excellent Teacher" (*CPW*, 1:315) are evidence that, involved with all the conventional praise, there is a real gratitude for Young's teaching—and this praise is missing in the letters to Alexander Gill, who is clearly a closer friend. The defensiveness gets less personal in later prose, but it does persist: "I hate a pupil teacher" (*CPW*, 2:533).

Teaching authority is writing authority, in man and Gospel, self-engendered, not borrowed. *Imitation* is a word of caution, perhaps even of slight distaste here, as later in *Eikonoklastes:* "the Gospell, as stands with her dignity most, lectures to us from her own authentick hand-writing, and command, not copies out from the borrow'd manuscript of a subservient scrowl, by way of imitating" (764; compare *CPW*, 3:361, 464, 555). Mere imitation is unwilling submission to authority, yet "laborious teaching in the word and doctrine" is enjoined by the Apostles (765). Milton continues to divide his text.

Here, Gospel moral law is original not imitative; its links with the past are in nature, not the Hebrew Testament. The emphasis on Christian liberty diminishes the authority of Mosaic law, even in the face of a Nature which has engraved in us "those unwritten lawes and Ideas" (764). Restricting the polemical and literary use of types, Milton asserts the concept of what will appear, after more strenuous oppositions, in *Tetrachordon*, as "our manhood in Grace" (*CPW*, 2:636). The Gospel does not "imitate the law her underling, but perfect her" (*CPW*, 1:764). From infancy and subservience, from veiled speaking and imitation, "which engender'd to bondage the sons of Agar," we arrive at free utterance by "the children of the promise, the heirs of liberty and grace" (765).

The *originality* of Christian liberty is the center of chapters 4 and 5. Origins—blood lines, traditions, investitures, deductions, birth rights—are reviewed and evaluated. Some claims are respected, some not fully entertained. Andrewes's "little treatise" is scolded rather than attacked for claiming that Aaron and his sons were types of the prelacy. In an unusual passage Milton comments:

> the priests were not chosen out of the whole number of the Levites, as our Bishops, but were borne inheritors of the dignity. Therefore unless we shall choose our Prelats only out of the Nobility, and let them runne in a blood, there can be no possible imitation of Lording over their brethren in regard of their persons altogether unlike. (767)

The exclusion of the Bishops from the House of Lords may be the primary issue here, but one can also recognize reservations in the shrugged off "unlesse" and in "running in a blood . . . Lording over"; *and* there is conventional anti-Laudian snobbery. The Archbishop, like Becket and Wolsey before him, was seen as a classic usurping churchman,[11] "one of the Lordly prelates raised from the dunghill equal commonly in birth to the meanest peasant," "a little Hocus Pocus in a velvet jerkin."[12] Milton's passage is ambiguous; it carefully separates priestly hierarchies from kingly, rejects imitation, type, and tutoring as vehicles for the claims of legitimacy; and it again problematizes the claims of heredity.

These layers of attitude toward the problems of class and caste show Milton as republican and a snob, truly both and truly discrete, but not always discrete. Populist enthusiasm and enthusiasm for the populace can coexist with contempt for their stupidity, and for the stupidity of the rich and famous, especially pretentious stupidity. Contempt for stupidity can cut across class lines. Perhaps treatments of these class attitudes and sympathies have not been supple enough to describe accurately Milton's participation in the politics of his day.

Puritan attacks on the Bishops show this complexity, with the sneer at the low-born aspirers to status a virtual commonplace. Lord Brooke had noted in the famous *Discourse*, "For the most part [a bishop] is *Ex Faece plebis; humi serpent;* of the lowest of the people (an old complaint)" (in Haller, *Tracts*, 2:47). Milton concurs in *An Apology* with his "Prelats of meane birth, and oft times of the lowest" (*CPW*, 1:950). This snobbery is heightened by his own quest for acceptance by his peers and superiors, and an anger at their neglect. In the *Apology* and especially in the *Colasterion*, he sees himself as confronted by second stringers who are insultingly beneath his capacities. The demand that he be taken seriously, that he be seen as an intellectual aristocrat, will later bring out the cries of "Serving-man" and "Pork" (*CPW*, 2:726, 737). This is related to—but not equivalent to—the simple demand for an earned polemical respectability, a claim he puts on the Parliamentary majority especially, as represented by the Smectymnuans: "Give me my due!"

The scorn, even disgust, for inferior educations is not always associated with low social status, as the attack on the educated gentry at the end of this tract will show. Prelatical pride of place had been an issue with radical Protestantism from the beginning, a seeming contradiction of the humility of Christ as an example for His church. When humility is advertised by a churchman whose pride in his education is publicly proclaimed, Milton becomes enraged—as with Bishop Hall.

An early passage from John Bale illustrates Puritan treatment of these contradictory attitudes toward ecclesiastical pride and personal social status. In a comparison of the deaths as martyrs of Protestant Sir John Oldcastle and Catholic Thomas Becket, Bale comments:

> Conferre [i.e., compare] the causes of this godlye mannys death with poyntes that Thomas dyed for and other Popish martyrs besides & ye shall fynde them farre dyfferent and unlyke. Thomas Beckett was slayne at Caunterburye in his Prelates aparell in the

head churche before the high aultre among relygyouse Monkes and Prestes and in the holy tyme of Christmas by his owne sekynge. And all this is gloryouse unto worldlye judgements. Syr Joyn Oldcastle was brent in cheanes at London in saynct Gyles felde under the galowes among the laye people upon the prophane workynge daye at the Bysshopes procurement. And all this is ungloryouse yea & very despicable unto those worldlye eyes what though Jesus Christ his mastre were handed after a very lyke sort.[13]

The Lord Cobham is compared to the "Cheapside brat" as every reader would know; but the scene of his dying establishes Oldcastle as partaker in the genuine humiliation of Christ and His identification with the common folk. Like Milton's passage on Laud, Bale's passage is a snobbish, social, attack on presumption *and* a pious, religious, attack on lordly distance from the humility that Jesus Christ had validated for His church.

On intellectual nobility, Milton is harsher. The serving man is intellectually inferior, as are the young graduates he is berating. (I call attention to the opposing kinds of snobbery the academic establishment by and large expresses toward the intellectual standards of our current president—"Alfred E. Newman"—and the "behavioral" standards of our former President—"Billy Bob.")[14] Citing Paul's caution about "fables and endless genealogies" (1 Tim. 1.4; a favorite text in these discussions), Milton now complicates the construal of Scriptural history. In some cases historical precedent provides a model, in others only a limited analogy. In a brutal and puzzling passage, Milton appears simply to dismiss the argument: "I shall not refuse therefore to learne so much prudence as I find in the Roman Souldier that attended the crosse, not to stand breaking of legs, when the breath is quite out of the body, but passe to that which follows" (*CPW*, 1:774). Is this merely inept, or subversive? Andrewes is Christ, Milton, the Roman soldier?[15] Is this an almost positivist separation of the functions of interpretation and the limits of allusion? Or is it a denial of typology? The analogy is mere analogy—no more than a verbalism. The argument is dead, why pursue it?

Andrewes is no more heir to an office typologically accredited than Milton is heir to the role of Roman soldier. Perhaps a bold common sense has its privileges.

Long ago Perry Miller said of the American Puritan that "he demanded only that conflicts be joined on real and explicit issues."[16] Milton would make the same demand. Against the prelates' claims from typology, he finds church government "a matter of eye sight, rather than of disquisition" (*CPW*, 1:775). Faith in the clarity of Scripture always coexists with the necessity of human interpretation. Prelacy at once complicates the text and suppresses the reading: "Doe they keep away schisme? if to bring a num and chil stupidity of soul, an unactive blindnesse of minde upon the people . . . be to keep away schisme, they keep away schisme indeed" (784–85). Prelacy ceases the "stitches and paines" of man by putting down the spiritual Spring of reformation, "when the gentle west winds shall open the fruitfull bosome of the earth . . . the flowers put forth and spring . . . the Sunne shall scatter the mists and the manuring hand of the Tiller shall root up all that burdens the soile without thanks to your bondage" (785). The speaker celebrates the new freedom for a people who are "no rabble sir Priest, but a unanimous multitude of good Protestants" (787–88). The banalities of censorship are dispersed by the motions toward Christian and political liberty, toward productiveness, intellectual and natural. The logic, the "reasons," are subsumed in visions.

Censorship proceeds by misnaming. Milton, continuously engaged in creating a serviceable history of Puritanism, insists that the prelates invented schisms by "scandalous misnaming," trying to juggle the people "out of their faith and religion by a mist of names cast before their eyes." The English people will, however, see through the mist, "knowing that the Primitive Christians in their times were accounted such as are now call'd Familists and Adamites, or worse" (788). This debunking of the labels put on radicals has consequences. Milton's toleration of individual liberty is expanding, and his points of political contact are changing. The man who condemned Anglican decency in *Of Reforma-*

tion found broad support from the dominant Parliamentary center. The man zealous for the expanding capacities of the individual human consciousness now invites new, politically narrower, alliances.

Milton wittily opposes the four-square church, his "one great cube, the main phalanx, an embleme of truth and stedfastnesse" (789) to the prelatical pyramid. The Westminster Assembly is imminent, and the conveners get some clear advice: the model of the Church should be from Acts 15, where "no faithfull Christian was debarr'd, to whom knowledge and piety might give entrance" (789). The inclusiveness of the "main phalanx" contrasts with the comically alliterative pyramid of prelacy: "Lordly ascendent in the horoscope of the Church, from *Primate* to *Patriarch,* and so to *Pope.* I say *Prelaty* thus ascending in a continuall *pyramid* upon *pretence* to *perfect* the Churches unity" (790; my italics). Tower of Babel? The alliteration suggests some such play. As with the passage on the Roman soldier, Milton is having his way with the image that Sharon Achinstein has identified as an Anglican icon against the sects (*Revolutionary Reader,* 71–101). Traditionally a ziggurat, the Tower of Babel was the emblem of absurd pride and presumption and of the corruption of language. The ziggurat overlays and overrides the pyramid, which is according to Sir William Temple "of all figures the firmest" (see *CPW,* 1:790, n. 78); it here becomes "the most dividing, and schismaticall forme that Geometricians know of," one that "aspires and sharpens to ambition, not to perfection, or unity."[17] Through a metamorphosis that is like a military maneuver, the pyramid of prelacy "must be faine to inglobe, or inscribe her selfe among the Presbyters" (*CPW,* 1:790). Again commandeering the opposition's images, Milton transforms the pyramid from an emblem of stability to one of sharpness, the sharpness of the prelatical mitres of ambition that gore as they aspire. "Go to, let us build a city and a tower whose top may reach unto heaven; and let us make a name, lest we be scattered abroad upon the face of the whole earth" (Gen. 11.4). The prelates would inscribe themselves in prideful *goring* and *naming* upon the structure of the church.

Even in the poem to Shakespeare, the pyramid is "weak witnes" (*Riverside Milton*, 61). Fame is no plant that grows on mortal soil, and those who seek to make a name, inscribed on, or in the shape of, the lasting monument, are wrong.[18] The real builders of the church saw themselves not as inscribers but as scaffolding that would fall away after the completion of the church. The architectural metaphor fulfills itself; that is, it self-destructs, when Milton turns to Peter and John, "hasting to lay downe their dictatorship, they rejoys't to call themselves and to be as fellow Elders among their brethren. Knowing that their high office was but as the scaffolding of the Church yet unbuilt, and would be but a troublesome disfigurement, so soon as the building was finisht" (*CPW*, 1:791). That is rather a fine way of looking at founding fathers and at theology generally. It complements the treatment of post-Apostolic authority in *Of Prelatical Episcopacy*. And it provides a kind of metaphor for Milton's canon: the prose pieces as scaffolding for the poetry. But not *quite* self-consuming artifacts, because they point to a stable, if articulated and internally dynamic, textual base. So I return to Stanley Fish's argument in order to disagree: "the relationship between the plan of the building and what is inside it is seen to be accidental. No matter what the chapter heading says, no matter what label is put on the container, the import of what is asserted is always the same" (*HMW*, 279). Milton's scaffolding is temporary but not accidental; his discourse moves toward an end: service to his God; it is not tautological or accidental or hopelessly ambiguous. At the center of this text is an idea of God and his Church—Christ's Body comprising all believers. The scaffolding of theologies builds toward recognition of that Church and then falls away. Goal-directed, aiming *in*, the consumption is not self-consumption, not autonomous. Is it maturation? or "lively sacrifice"? In any case, the argument for the proper vehicle toward truth is absolutely related to the central truth it has earned the right to celebrate. There still remain the ironic counterstatements: Milton excluding the excluders; the arguer for self-effacement proclaiming his authority to proclaim.

Issues of class return with the review of levels of language. The "lofty minds" of the post-apostolic ages "thought it a poore indignity, that the high rear'd government of the Church should so on a sudden, as it seem'd to them, squat into a Presbytery." The homely return is just right, the theme is the old one of pastoral communication: "the timeliest prevention of schisme is to preach the Gospell abundantly and powerfully throughout all the land, to instruct the youth religiously, to endeavour how the Scriptures may be easiest understood by all men" (*CPW*, 1:791). Having failed their broad audience, the prelates are commanded to self-destruct, first in tones of ironic imprative ("Cling fast to your Pontificall Sees"), then with real threat. Twelve bishops in the Tower would not read these lines as abstract: "For certainly of all those lesser souls which you have persecuted, and those miserable ones which you have lost, the just vengeance does not sleepe" (793).

I have not read the first book systematically, but I have read it as a cumulative argument. The evidence is inductive, and full of oppositions that define. It directs the reader toward the dismissal of prelaty, and of its arguments against schism, and toward validation of Presbyterian claims to kerygmatic, and hence to ecclesiastical, authority. So the last chapter of book 1, just preceding the self-conscious debut as poet-potential, summarizes "the throws and pangs that go before the birth of reformation" (795). Aesthetic and theological examples entwine and oppose. Prelatical government in *Animadversions* was a "livelesse *Colossus,* that like a carved Gyant terribly menacing to children, and weaklings lifts up his club, but strikes not" (699). The "statue" of Presbyterial government is more effectively process and involves the "struggl of contraries" (795):

> No Marble statue can be politely carv'd, no fair edifice built without almost as much rubbish and sweeping. . . . No wonder then in the reforming of a Church which is never brought to effect without the fierce encounter of truth and falshood together, if, as it were the splinters and shares of so violent a jousting, there fall from between the shock many fond errors and fanatick opinions. (796)

Statue, Church, poem are not to be won easily; the process may be messy, "not without dust and heat" (*CPW*, 2:515). It is not the energy of repression, but of an exuberant and assured confrontation.

Milton continues to invoke the about-to-be achieved Kingdom of God on earth, never achievable until the end of time, at once the hope and erasure of the hopes of millenarianism. The fullest statement of this is in *Areopagitica*, but the images of Apocalyptic judgment and wholeness occur throughout the English prose, images of imminence, of *emergency* in the Donnean sense, and yet of ending, with no connection between the two. Fully participating in the icons of Apocalyptic discourse, exploiting the trope of Laodicean lukewarmness, Milton rejects the calendar. Any account of Milton's use of the Book of Revelation as chart and source must recognize his refusal to play the numbers game with Apocalypse, a game in which his contemporaries enthusiastically engaged, from famous eccentrics like Lady Eleanor Davis, to the eminently respectable Joseph Mede.

This commitment to building toward wholeness *here,* while expecting completion only at the last day *there,* contributes to the argument that Milton's prose is inconsistent. The journey with all its assertive trappings of circumstance will not end in time, but on the threshold of time and eternity. The speaker must both stand and wait, *with*stand evil by *under*standing kairos (as Carol Barton has strongly argued in "They also perform the Duties"),[19] but yet be busy about his Father's business. Perhaps this *is* a kind of jumping up and down in one place, after all, but to recognize accumulation, the spectrum of repetitions, is not to negate the ultimate cohesion; nor does it obviate the necessary final leap.

Book 1 ends with consideration of the Irish question, which now becomes another argument against prelacy. The bishops who boast themselves "the only bridlers of schisme" have failed totally in Ireland, where the murderous Irish "revenge upon English bodies the little care that our Prelats have had of their souls" (798). With another long citation from scripture, Milton urges the "reformers" to violent action: *"let not your hands be weake for your worke shall bee rewarded"* (*CPW*, 1:799, citing 2 Chron. 15.3, 5–7). The Scriptural context is violent, Asa's suppressing of the abominable idols out of all the land of Judah and Benjamin. There is a great assembly and sacrifice, and entrance "into a covenant to seek the Lord God of their fathers." The violence is aimed against both general—"whosoever would not seek the Lord God of Israel" (the Irish) and specific: "And also concerning Maachah the mother of Asa the king he removed her from being queen because she had made an idol in a grove" (2 Chron. 15.12, 13, 16). Milton's assumptions of Scriptural literacy amongst his readers would suggest a reference to an idolatrous queen, one like Henrietta Maria.

The first book closes with the beleaguered Protestants in Ireland waiting for relief from the "populous and mighty nation" (799) that has so far failed them. With the reformation of the Church, the settling of the Irish question will be easy; the contest with the sects will test and ultimately strengthen the true faith. On the authority of scripture and from the experience of the immediate past, rebellion will collapse only when the Church is settled. The solution of foreign problems will follow. In the body politic, there must now be a national spiritual self-reform. This swift, dense summary provides transition to the plans for individual self-reform and to the plans for a glorious self-fulfillment, plans which now open the second book.

BOOK 2

The preface to book 2 can be seen first as a nine-page autonomous essay, then as part of the larger structure of the tract. The essay centers on the burden of vocation, the talent which is death to hide, the gift of prophetic utterance which I call, with increasing assurance, kerygmatic authority. The Preface is syndecdoche for the whole tract; it considers, passionately, the vocation of prophet-poet within the framework of Milton's personal terror of the parable of the talents.[20] His conflicts between public and private rhetorical concerns include his own private clashes between arrogance and humility, between startling candor and defensiveness. It is the *locus classicus* of the struggle between Milton's commitment to the political prose and his aspirations toward a monumental poetry.

The burden of knowledge comes first: "How happy were it for this frail, and as it may be truly call'd, mortall life of man . . . if knowledge yet which is the best and lightsomest possession of the mind, were as the saying is, no burden, and that . . . it did not with a heavy advantage overlay upon the spirit" (801). A gloomy opening, especially with its dismissal of Baconian "contemplation of naturall causes and dimensions" as a "lower wisdome." Yet the higher wisdom suddenly charges the rhythms with something like gaiety; joy in knowing of "God and of his true worship, and what is infallibly good and happy" separated out from the cumbersome in life, "in it selfe evil and miserable, though vulgarly not so esteem'd." But the resonances of *burden* remain foremost in the mind of the steward of God's gifts, who, remembering "that God even to a strictnesse requires the improvement of these his entrusted gifts, cannot but sustain a sorer burden of mind . . . how and in what manner he shall dispose and employ those summes of knowledge and illumination, which God hath sent him into this world to trade with" (801). Milton is a "trader" with the ordinary problems of merchandizing his product. The joy comes from knowing the value of the product: "certain pretious truths of such an orient lustre as no diamond can equall" (801). The "sorer" burden is the necessity of improving these "entrusted gifts"—how else but by promulgation? Milton's burden is to out-proclaim the opposition. Like a good salesman, he denounces the competition: "the great Marchants of this world fearing that this cours would soon discover, and disgrace the fals glitter of their deceitfull wares . . . practice by all means how they may suppresse the venting of such rarities and such a cheapnes as would undoe them, and turn their trash upon their hands" (802). "This cours" creates, by the very greatness of his good news, a prophet, unabashedly a salesman for the message which he is to "improve." The only improvement for the pretious-truths-orient-lustre-pearl-greater-than-diamond Gospel is the manner of promulgation, and the timing. So *kairos* becomes a critical concern of Milton's evangelic decorum, another reason for worry about his age; in his anxiety about the kerygmatic moment, he fools himself, and tries to fool his readers, about his youth.

The "great Marchants" are powerful purveyors of junk ("deceitfull Pedleries" in *Of Reformation* [592]), abusing the people "like poor Indians with beads and glasses."[21] They have at once sold goods dearly overpriced to the abused people and bought the people by "gratifying the corrupt desires of men in fleshly doctrines." These bribes are intended to lure the people from the "selected heralds of peace, and dispensers of treasure inestimable without price to them that have no pence" (*CPW*, 1:802). Part of the burden of the heralds of peace is the contumely of these false merchants, who label them "the greatest variance and offence." Like Jeremiah and John and Sophocles' Tiresias, Milton knows that "although divine inspiration must certainly have been sweet to those ancient profets, yet the irksomenesse of that truth which they brought was so unpleasant to them, that everywhere they call it a burden" (802–3). The burden follows the gift, the burden helps to define the gift, as it did for the great prophets of the past. Yet interlaced with the grand historical identification is the need for accommodation; decorum, even the decorum of preaching the Word, is, to a critical extent, merchandizing.

Burden appears four times in powerful positions on these first two pages of the preface, absorbing meaning from a whole group of other powerful words: *knowledge, wisdom, gifts, toil, weight, illumination, precious truths, pearl, Truth, heavenly traffick, divine illumination, book, eye brightning electuary.* Burden—which is also song—is the necessity to proclaim these riches, to speak these hard, radiant truths. The OED is useful; see *burden*, definition 3.8: "Used in the Eng. Bible (like *onus* in the Vulgate) to render Heb. massa, which Gesenius would translate lifting up (of the voice), utterance, oracle; the

Septuagint has ῥῆμα, λῆμμα, ὅραμα. But it is generally taken to mean a burdensome or heavy lot or fate." A contemporary English-Hebrew dictionary has "load, burden, oracle, prophecy."

Onus and song, bitter and sweet, like the scroll in Revelation 10, the burden of prophecy is both urgent in this world and yet on its own autonomous time system. It is Christian knowledge, radical and reformed, which necessarily evolves into kerygma, the burden of dispensing that Truth whose essence is clarity and brightness, but whose purity can be, has been, polluted in transmission these 1,500 years. Again, commentary here is seen as largely corrupt and corrupting. In scouring off that corruption, Milton still believes that he must use vehemence: "But when God commands to take the trumpet and blow a dolorous or a jarring blast, it lies not in mans will what he shall say, or what he shall conceal" (*CPW*, 1:803). Jeremiah suffered for his silence: "*his word was in my heart as a burning fire shut up in my bones. . . .* Which might teach these times not suddenly to condemn all things that are sharply spoken, or vehemently written, as proceeding out of stomach, virulence, and ill-nature" (803–4).

The criticism of the prelates is conventional compared to the stunning emphasis on Milton's personal career decorum. First the fear of repressing or neglecting one's talent, of missing or misreading God's cues (Samson's problem). But what is the talent that is death to hide? Is it the creation of the magni-loquent canon he is about to announce? Or is it the burden of God's propaganda now? If not now, when? And *what*? Second, and continually nagging, is the concern for the construal of his vehemence, for the "endeavour to impart and bestow without any gain to himselfe those sharp, but saving words which would be a terror, and a torment in him to keep back."

The only solution to the problems here bristling is to view the life whole: "I have determin'd to lay up as the best treasure, and solace of a good old age . . . the honest liberty of free speech from my youth" (804). God's condemnation for failure or delay of that honest liberty is fearfully imagined: "Timorous and ingratefull, the Church of God is now again at the foot of her insulting enemies: and thou bewailst, what matters it for thee or thy bewailing? when time was, thou couldst not find a syllable of all that thou hadst read, or studied, to utter in her behalfe" (804). Privileges are burdens, like Milton's own ivory tower, paid for "out of the sweat of other men." He knows the extent and solidity of his education and that he has used it for the adornment of "vain subject[s]" (805). He *must* now use that God-given, father-subsidized, quite extraordinary power of speech: "when the cause of God and his Church was to be pleaded, for which purpose that tongue was given thee which thou hast, God listen'd if he could heare thy voice among his zealous servants, but thou wert domb as a beast; from hence forward be that which thine own brutish silence hath made thee" (805). This extended scene of Milton's presence before God, a God who listens for his creature's serviceable voice, is severe, circumstantial, colloquial: "where canst thou shew any word or deed of thine which might have hasten'd her [the Church's] peace. . . . Dare not now to say, or doe any thing better then thy former sloth and infancy" (805). At the center of Milton's model for participation is reverence for speech as life. Speaking responsibly is maturity; shirking that speech is infancy, with its full etymological resonance. In claiming his "right of lamenting the tribulations of the Church" he establishes his "charter and freehold of rejoycing" to himself and his heirs (806). *Infancy* is tutelage, here totally rejected.

The digression in *The Reason of Church-Government* arises out of a concern embedded in most of Milton's early writing, the direction, the timing, and the character of his literary energies. For Milton these energies must be in the service of the kerygmatic force of English Protestantism. These imagined debates with God, always implied in his comments on his style, are serious, and deeply conscious of the fragility and tenuousness of scheduling one's life, even a life in the service of God Himself.

Having claimed the community of saints, he turns to defining his claim on the "charter and freehold of rejoycing." The professional question defers to the personal issue of the talents: "neither envy nor gall hath enterd me upon this controversy, but the enforcement of conscience only, and a preventive fear least the omitting of this duty should be against me when I would store up to my self the good provision of peacefull hours" (806). This examination of personal motive begins with the controversial issue at hand—the critique of *Certaine Briefe Treatises*—but moves to address a fitter audience, one which can comprehend his discussion of the severe decorum of the inspired:

> So lest it should be still imputed to me, as I have found it hath bin, that some self-pleasing humor of vain-glory hath incited me to contest with men of high estimation, now while green yeers are upon my head, from this needlesse surmisall I shall hope to disswade the intelligent and equal auditor . . . although I would be heard only if might be, by the elegant & learned reader, to whom principally for a while I shal beg leav I may addresse my selfe. (806–7)

Visions of a broad audience are suspended "for a while"; and interesting distinctions are implied amongst the "intelligent and equal auditor," "the elegant & learned reader," and those to whom "it were a folly to commit any thing elaborately compos'd" in these "tumultuous times" of "carelesse and interrupted listening" (806–7). The learned will now be addressed; therefore, the second part of the preface is more narrowly focused, but, under the pressure of the parable of the talents, more personal drama than boast. He is confident of his own talents and aware of his reading audiences, present and potential; and he is quite frank about his ambitions: "if I were wise only to mine own ends, I would certainly take such a subject as of it self might catch applause, whereas this hath all the disadvantages on the contrary . . . not deferring is of great moment to the good speeding" (807). *Now* is as essential to Milton's discipline of conscience as it is to the Puritan politicians' agenda. Charles Herle's *Abrahams Offer Gods Offering* was published two years after *Reason*, but it is relevant: "It is this one word *now*, now we may, or else never. . . . I say in vaine *shall you have the high-sounding praises of God in your mouthes, unless you have a two edged sword in your hands.*"²² "This one word *now*" is essential to the rhetoric of zeal, a rhetoric of urgency.²³ Milton's adherence to *Now* is expressed in the "speedy redress" of *Areopagitica* (*CPW*, 2:487), and in this propitiatory analysis of his career plans.

Afraid of his own temporizing, Milton provides links between the discussion of genres he is contemplating and the duties of the Protestant Englishman in a time of violent disruptions. He identifies two audiences, two styles, two levels of his abilities, two hands:

> I should not chuse this manner of writing wherin knowing my self inferior to my self, led by the genial power of nature to another task, I have the use, as I may account it, but of my left hand. . . . For although a Poet soaring in the high region of his fancies with his garland and singing robes about him might without apology speak more of himself then I mean to do, yet for me sitting here below in the cool element of prose, a mortall thing among many readers of no Empyreall conceit, to venture and divulge unusual things of my selfe, I shall petition to the gentler sort, it may not be envy to me. (*CPW*, 1:808)

Italianate snob or primitive Christian? Both. Milton the prose writer is "a mortall thing among many" who eschews the prerogatives of the soaring Poet; yet he petitions "the gentler sort" to hear his "unusual" ambitions. For some time to come he retains the dream of at least partial popular enlightenment, and hence he must maintain contact with and recognition of a populist aesthetic as complement to both his practical politics and his aesthetics of grandeur. That prose aesthetic is different from, and inferior to, the poetic; but it is essential now.

The questions of genre that Milton poses have received generous attention previously.²⁴ Here, I emphasize the literary and theological positioning. While demonstrating astute and comprehensive literary training, and stopping to address an elite audience, the poet must also demonstrate his separation from mere poetasters or merely professional poets and his usefulness to the nation: "not to make verbal curiosities the end, that were a toylsom vanity, but to be an interpreter &

relater of the best and sagest things among mine own Citizens throughout this Iland in the mother dialect" (*CPW*, 1:811–12). Comparing his potential with the "greatest and choycest wits" of the past he stakes his carefully immodest claim, "I in my proportion with this over and above of being a Christian" (812). "Time servs not now" to consider the possibilities, but he takes the time, and, indulging himself, affectionately names the great genres and their masters, here acting out the laureate role as described by Richard Helgerson (see chapter 1).[25]

The next section of the genre passage speaks of poetic ability: "the inspired guift of God rarely bestow'd, but yet to some (though most abuse) in every Nation" (816). The halting in those four phrases and the nervous parentheses take us back again to poetic burden, with the added and curious distribution of equal opportunity to every nation. A sudden shift and the uses of the great genres are put magniloquently; the poet's abilities fuse with the poem, "of power beside the office of a pulpit, to imbreed and cherish in a great people the seeds of vertu, and publick civility" (816). The language ignites into high titles, great circling overviews, reckless aspirations. Homer, Job, Tasso, Sophocles, *glorious and lofty Hymns, high providence, exemplary, majestick, stately, hallelujahs, magnifick, the laws and prophets, celebrate, victorious agonies, the whole book of sanctity and vertu, solemn Paneguries*. The passage exhales the great promise.

Yet questions arise. Who needs the sugar-coated pill—the superior reader, to whom Milton has directed these comments? If so, is it *superior* to need the sugar coating? If Milton is addressing himself to the "Italianate" poetry lovers why are they damned lightly as "those especially of soft and delicious temper who will not so much as look upon Truth herselfe, unlesse they see her elegantly dressed" (817–18; a far cry from *Of Reformation*, 557)? This concern for the capacities of the individual, "tender and mild consciences," "softer spirited Christians" (*Animadversions, CPW*, 1:662, 664) is a regular theme of the early English prose. On the one hand Milton has difficulty imagining an audience of cobblers and weavers; his special help is extended usually to the "softer," and "milder."

On the other hand he calls himself to account and proclaims universal educability, condemning prelatical neglect of the common people. The toleration is equal for both audiences, though the tolerated weaknesses are different. Milton's intellectual agoraphilia is an admittedly occasional but populist high, buzzing throughout the digression on career. Admitting his "honest haughtiness," he accommodates both audiences.

Another question: If Truth is obvious, why does she need interpreting, softening, sugar-coating? If grace is the only vehicle of real saving knowledge, all the rest is verbal curiosities, and the end of Milton's 65 pages is only self-consumption. Is this process of "self-consumption" itself a teaching that provides the necessary way to knowledge through grace? That argument is itself self-consuming as set over against the agonistic self-analysis of John Milton (and later of his Samson); it does not answer the data of physical, emotional and psychological energies of the text, a text which, among other things, expresses faith in the possibility of human and hence rational exploration *toward,* and adjustment *to,* the immense mystery-gift of God's grace—situationally understood, as it were, and approachable if ultimately unfathomable. It also recognizes, to an unusual extent, the availability of grace.

Milton is a monist, and that heresy gets him into difficulties; but it also releases him into visions of final participation (I use Owen Barfield's term advisedly)[26] that include an intense image of self and of community, both irradiated with God's recovered meaning. *Of Reformation* had provided the image of apocalyptic identity for Milton, "amidst the *Hymns* and *Halleliuahs* of *Saints*" (*CPW,* 1:616). His "elaborate Song to Generations" (706) has a circumstantial life of its own, and as part of his vision of the Final Day. I've already noted that almost always the image of ravishing ascending unity in the prose is attended by a recording secretary, clearly Milton himself; and it includes the falling bodies of his enemies. The autobiographical digression splits the image of the last day's music—"the victorious agonies of Martyrs and Saints"—from the present day image of a Milton struggling for his church party. But the ultimate goal of the poet is to perform *as if* at Apocalypse, and the covenant he makes with his readers connects revelation and revolution:

> Neither doe I think it shame to covnant with any knowing reader, that for some few yeers yet I may go on trust with him toward the payment of what I am now indebted, as being a work not to be rays'd from the heat of youth, or the vapours of wine, like that which flows at wast from the pen of some vulgar Amorist, or the trencher fury of a riming parasite, nor to be obtain'd by the invocation of Dame Memory and her Siren daughters, but by devout prayer to that eternall Spirit who can enrich with all utterance and knowledge, and sends out his Seraphim with the hallow'd fire of his Altar to touch and purify the lips of whom he pleases. (820–21)

Like the threshhold passage in the Nativity ode, this passage summons Isaiah:

> Then flew one of the seraphim unto me, having a live coal in his hand, *which* he had taken with the tongs from the altar:
> And he laid *it* upon my mouth, and said, Lo, this hath touched thy lips; and thine iniquity is taken away, and thy sin purged.
> Also I heard the voice of the Lord saying, Whom shall I send, and who will go for us? Then said I, Here *am* I; send me.
> And he said, Go, and tell this people. (Isa. 6.6–9)

The mouth is purified and empowered. The speaker is a ready recipient and then volunteer—*send me*.[27] The Lord gives, and the Lord receives service. The message Isaiah is to hear is not a happy one, presumably less promising than Milton's, but the point of the installation for both is rather powerful necessity than pleasure or even choice.[28] Jeremiah's reception of God's message is even more difficult, yet again relevant:

> My bowels, my bowels! I am pained at my very heart; my heart maketh a noise in me; I cannot hold my peace, because thou hast heard, O my soul, the sound of the trumpet, the alarm of war.
> Destruction upon destruction is cried; for the whole land is spoiled. (4.19, 20)

In Ezekiel's version there is the same mixture of radiance and burden, an intimate circumstantiality attendant on the majesty of God, who selects him as his voice:

> Son of man, I send thee to the children of Israel, to a rebellious nation that hath rebelled against me . . . *they are* impudent children and stiff hearted. I do send thee unto them; and thou shalt say unto them, Thus saith the Lord GOD. And they whether they will hear, or whether they will forbear . . . yet shall know that there hath been a prophet unto them. (2.3–5)

The prophet is then given a scroll written with "lamentations, and mourning, and woe" (2, 10), and ordered to eat it;

> Then did I eat *it*; and it was in my mouth as sweet as honey for sweetness. And he said unto me, Son of man, go, get thee unto the house of Israel, and speak with my words unto them. For thou *art* not sent to a people of a strange speech and of an hard language, *but* to the house of Israel. (3.3–4)

Though in the *Reason* passage the force of Jeremiah and Ezekiel is muted, all three of these utterances are powerful influences on Milton's kerygmatic voice, a voice he will carry into the great poems, a voice which, in the words of Michael Lieb, provides "a sense of what it means to be overwhelmed by the *ganz andere,* to be imbued with the numinous in all its resplendency, . . . a testament to all that the holy represents."[29] The author assumes the public will understand and that it will be responsible, except of course for the prelates, persons of a strange speech and a hard language. The additions to the numinous here are moderate, optimistic, unglamorous; to the touch of the Seraphim "must be added industrious and select reading, steddy observation, insight into all seemly and generous arts and affaires." The suddenly mundane scene causes the tongue again to thicken: "I refuse not to sustain this expectation from as many as are not loath to hazard so much credulity upon the best pledges that I can give them" (*CPW,* 1:821).

Milton discriminates. The present task is a burden, from God, an essential and seamless part of his career. But this polemic is not as worthy as the poem that he honestly expects himself to write. A reassertion of the left hand image—but here not in terms of his own talents: rather, of the worth of the discourse. Wittily, he writes of the polemical marketplace:

> I trust hereby to make it manifest with what small willingnesse I endure to interrupt the pursuit of no lesse hopes then these, and leave a calme and pleasing solitaryines fed with cherful and confident thoughts, to embark in a troubl'd sea of noises and hoars disputes, put from beholding the bright countenance of truth in the quiet and still air of delightfull studies to come into the dim reflexion of hollow antiquities sold by the seeming bulk, and there be fain to club quotations with men whose learning and beleif lies in marginal stuffings, who when they have like good sumpters laid ye down their hors load of citations and fathers at your dore, with a rapsody of who and who were Bishops here or there, ye may take off their packsaddles, their days work is don, and episcopacy, as they think, stoutly vindicated. (821–22)

Compared with the attacks on Hall this is mild, but the sentence, loaded with absurdity, identifies his difference from the professional, the academic, polemicists.

The idea of *stooping* to this present task, of debating with his inferiors calls up once again his "higher" audience: "Let any gentle apprehension that can distinguish learned pains from unlearned drudgery, imagin what pleasure or profoundnesse can be in this, or what honour to deal against such adversaries" (822). He has earned the right to speak these truths, following his honorable refusal to perjure himself by acceding to the so-called Et Cetera Oath:

> I thought it better to preferre a blamelesse silence before the sacred office of speaking bought and begun with servitude and forswearing. Howsoever thus Church-outed by the Prelats, hence may appear the right I have to meddle in these matters, as before, the necessity and constraint appear'd. (823; for the oaths that offended Milton, see footnote 161)

The "sacred office of speaking"—kerygmatic authority—is flanked by "blamelesse silence" and "servitude and forswearing." That tableau is comfortable, self-righteous; it is marred, happily, by the urgent, indecorous figure of the budding poet who has a right to—*meddle* (a word that Milton uses in our modern sense in the prose). That interaction between the monumental static timeless with the nervous, incongruous present progressive is familiar to the readers of Milton's prose, and continues into the later career, perhaps even into the great last poems. Here the monumental is personal, the "progressive" is public; the preface to book 2 ends with this firm claim on their interrelationship.

The grandiosities of the digression were, Milton must have known, open to criticism if not ridicule, or to cooption by the prelatical party. "After this digression . . . I must confesse . . . that I shall endanger either not to be regarded, or not to be understood" (823–24). "The sacred office of speaking" could be claimed by Laud or Hall; the attack on prelatical corruption must be renewed, even if much is repetitive. Prelacy is corrupt and worldly, unlike the suffering servant, whose image Milton now summons to re-establish his rhythm of assurance: "who is ther almost that measures wisdom by simplicity, strength by suffering, dignity by lowlinesse, who is there that counts it first, to be last, somthing to be nothing, and reckons himself of great command in that he is a servant?" (824). Milton feels that "mystery" deeply and derives energy from it. St. Paul feared to "affect the wisdom of words in his preaching"; the prelates, Milton proclaims, debase language and their mission in the search for *titles*, "nullifying the power and end of the Gospel," and seeking temporal precedencies in "the galanteries of *Signore* and *Monsignore*, and *Monsieur*" (824). Titles reify the sacred offices of speaking. Titles point outward toward "the pompous garb, the Lordly life, the wealth, the haughty distance of Prelaty" (826); but "the form of a servant was a mean, laborious and vulgar life aptest to teach; which form Christ thought fittest" (825). The movement into hierarchical religion is not decency; it is corruption. And so Milton emerges from the personal digression, separating clerical from poetic ambition.

Though the headnote claims that he will discuss doctrine, Milton attacks discipline, deploying an obsessive set of oppositions, unitary truth against multiple errors: the Bible against "unweildy volumes of tradition"; Christ's ordinance against "the pervers iniquity of sixteen hunderd years." The rhetorical climax enacts K. G. Hamilton's famous phrase, "jumping up and down in one place," yet powerfully supports faith over reason: "But let them chaunt while they will of prerogatives, we shall tell them of Scripture; of custom, we of Scripture; of Acts and Statutes, stil of Scripture, til the quick and pearcing word enter to the dividing of their soules, & the mighty weaknes of the Gospel throw down the weak mightines of mans reasoning" (827). Isaiah's words thread the political issue into focus: "Are the feet so beautifull, and is the very bringing of these tidings so decent of it self? what new decency then can be added to this by your spinstry" (828).

The images of acceptance are not mere submission; they are illumination, an illumination which activates, as in *Paradise Lost:*

> So much the rather thou Celestial Light
> Shine inward, and the mind through all her powers
> Irradiate, there plant eyes, all mist from thence
> Purge and disperse, that I may see and tell
> Of things invisible to mortal sight. (*PL*, 3.51–55)

In *Reason* the scriptural images are associated with an illumination which activates: "angelic brightnes . . . unclouded serenity." Naked Gospel truth motivates, is obvious, is not elusive of human comprehension, but available. It is no more opposed to pure reason than the Lady of the Masque is opposed to human flesh.

There is an attendant horror which misleads, or obscures, of baroque excess and fleshiness, in language as well as gesture, the "gaudy glisterings" of ceremony, to which the good minister must provide a cleansing opposite. "If the multitude be rude, the lips of the Preacher must give knowledge, and not ceremonies" (*CPW*, 1:828). An ostentatious tutelage is loathsome; even for children, "the sincere milk" (932) of the Gospel is the only nourishment (828–29).

But the chapter headings continue to deceive. Chapter 3 announces the topic as jurisdiction, but the emphasis again is on the carnality of the Church, a rather dark discussion of language and its susceptibility to corruption; Milton confronts the ambivalences of language. Truth has a "fatall" unhappiness; to reach the understanding, she must be led through the "many little wards and limits of the severall Affections and Desires" sometimes "habited and colour'd like a notorious Falshood"; and falsehood itself may be made to "counterfeit the very shape and visage of Truth . . . [by] inchantresses with such cunning . . . the suttle imposture of these sensual mistresses" (830–31).

Despite these ambiguities, the discussion of jurisdiction begins firmly. "Ecclesial jurisdiction" is "a pure tyrannical forgery . . . jurisdictive power in the Church there ought to be none at all" (831). That is plain speaking, with added contempt for censorship and a concern for tender persuasion, a concern which will reappear at the end of the *Areopagitica*. If the Church has the "use of her powerful Keies" (that is, of judgment), she needs not "the beggarly help of halings and amercements." The separation of Church and State is essential to the health of both. The Church of England "thinks to credit and better her spirituall efficacy, and to win her self respect and dread by strutting in the fals vizard of worldly authority" (832–33).

Liberty of conscience is beginning to be discussed everywhere, and Milton's opinions are already nearly formed. His contempt for the prelacy should not obscure his reverence for liberty of conscience, apparent from the beginning of his career. The Lady celebrates it; so do the Prolusions. Here it begins to assume an important role.

The Magistrate has jurisdiction over the body and over "the mind in all her outward acts," but it was God who added "that which we call censure" first in the father of the family, then in wise men and philosophers, Priests, Levites, Prophets, Scribes, Pharisees. The Gospel, "the straitest and dearest cov'nant" decrees that such censure—"this blest efficacy of healing"—should be in the hands of "the minister of each Congregation . . . who . . . hath best reason to know all the secretest diseases likely to be there." Patriarchal indeed, the passage is nevertheless sweet with compassion and intimacy, reflecting God's "sweetest and mildest manner of paternal discipline" (837).

Spiritual censure is not punishment, it is cure, a "loverlike contestation" (*CP* 1, 603). Milton's concern for the strayed sheep regularly "contests" with his virulent contempt for the excommunicators, as in this almost feverish passage from *Of Reformation:*

> the sacred and dreadfull works of holy *Discipline, Censure, Penance, Excommunication,* and *Absolution,* where no prophane thing ought to have accesse . . . but sage and Christianly *Admonition,* brotherly *Love,* flaming *Charity,* and *Zeale* . . . Paternall *Sorrow,* or Paternall *Joy,* milde *Severity,* melting *Compassion* . . . [violently opposed to] sordid fees . . . the truccage of perishing Coine, and the butcherly execution of Tormentors, Rooks, and Rakeshames sold to Lucre. (591)

This concern reemerges even at *Areopagitica's* notorious exemption from freedom of "tolerated Popery," which "it self should be extirpat, *provided first that all charitable and compassionat means be us'd to win and regain the weak and misled*" (*CPW,* 2:565; my italics).

The concern for shielding the spiritual errant from harshness of judgment compares interestingly with that of Henry Hammond, chaplain to Charles I, who attacks the savage voluptuousness of certain kinds of censure:

> There is not a sinne that hath more of our *flesh* powred out upon it, more of our *wits,* then that of *judging* and *censuring* other men, one of the richest *voluptuousnesses* and *sensualities* of our life, a kind of *savage rejoycing* in the *shame* (as inhumane as in the *blood*) of others . . . the setting up of a perpetuall *inquisition* upon our brethrens actions, hunting for *faults* and infirmities in other men . . . I mean the *hearing* or *reporting* the *shame of dissenting* Brethren.[30]

It is an eloquent passage, too late to bear directly on Milton's text. But it illustrates sharply the two sides of Milton's behavior in the judging of individual error in church discipline: on the one hand *voluptuously* and precipitously condemnatory; on the other patiently solicitous of the limits and weaknesses of the human condition. The latter attitude has been neglected in Milton studies.

Loving Father is now set against pompous schoolmaster. Ten pages of the sixty-five are devoted to what is essentially a celebration of lay sanctification as children of "a most indulgent father," as members of Christ's body, "with all those glorious privileges of sanctification and adoption" as "the best of creatures" whose "nature . . . God hath not only cleans'd, but Christ hath also assum'd" (837, 844, 845). The celebration interacts with bristling specifics. All Christians are Clergy according to the title Saint Peter gave them, "a chosen generation, a royal Priesthood to offer up spiritual sacrifice in that meet place to which God and the congregation shall call and assigne them." No longer will they be separated in the Church by "partitions" and "vails" that exclude " the members of Christ from the property of being members, the bearing of orderly and fit offices in the ecclesiastical body" (838–39). Using echoes of the Church's own Canons (*CPW*, 1:992), Milton redefines Holy Decency to contain all Christians as equal participants. God's glorious creature has been condemned by prelacy as "so unpurifi'd and contagious, that for him to lay his hat, or his garment upon the Chancell table they have defin'd it no lesse hainous in expresse words then to profane the Table of the Lord" (845). The chapter seethes with outrage at *exclusion,* at the uses of "the scornfull terme of Laick . . . of a repugnant and contradictive Mount Sinai" (843). Dishonoring God's masterpiece is next to denying God: "And if the love of God as a fire sent from Heaven . . . be the first principle of all godly and vertuous actions in men, this pious and just honouring of our selves is the second . . . the radical moisture and fountain head, whence every laudable and worthy enterprize issues forth" (841). This celebration of man's worth pervades Milton's work and triumphs, after enormous testing, even at the close of his three last great poems. One must hold "himself in reverence and due esteem, both for the dignity of Gods image upon him, and for the price of his redemption" (842).

Church-outed by the prelates? Perhaps not; but the passion of these pages suggests the personal refusal to be excluded from God's service. Again one notes the ways by which, and the distances across which, Milton makes connections. The digression on career is sharply reinforced by the argument for liberty of conscience; that argument is reinforced by the authority gained in the digression.

The main issue remains kerygma. Bad teaching, prelatical of course, is schoolmasterly; the good is fatherly; the praise of "paternal discipline" echoes the praises of the digression and the praise of John Milton senior in the "Ad Patrem." Paternal discipline encourages and includes; prelatical schoolmasterliness condemns and excludes. The first honors God's image in man, "God's living temple" (843); the second condemns man, putting "a wide and terrible distance between religious things and themselves [lay Christians]" (843). Revulsion at prelatical discipline succumbs to the promise of the Christian community on this earth: "the congregation of the Lord . . . the household and City of God" (844).

The solemn and often corrupted processes of excommunication mirror Milton's own polemical choices. If a "vitious appetite" is unaffected by the ministrations of Elders and friends," such engines of terror God hath given into the hand of his minister as to search the tenderest angles of the heart." If this does not avail, the sinner is to be "wip't out of the list of Gods inheritance" by the "dreadfull sponge of excommunication." Milton can argue for the death of Archbishop and later of King, but here the very aim of excommunication is salvation: "a rough and cleansing medcin, where the malady is obdurat; a mortifying to life, a kind of saving by undoing" (847). This is a saving in this world. And the reclamation of the excommunicant, after assurances that he has indeed been reclaimed, has the homely joy of the return of the prodigal son and of the two preceding parables of forgiveness in Luke 15: "if he bring with him his bill of health . . . then with incredible expressions of joy all his brethren receive him, and set before him those perfumed baskets of Christian consolation with pretious ointments bathing and fomenting the old and now to be forgotten stripes" (848). In the middle of this passage Milton cites Paul's severe description of *"spirituall weapons of holy censure"* (2 Cor. 10.4–5), but the frame of his commentary softens the censure. The individual soul is infinitely precious, "that divine particle of Gods breathing" (848); and the description of the new dispensation is purposefully humane:

> how can the Prelates justifie to have turn'd the fatherly orders of Christs houshold . . . those ever open and inviting dores of his dwelling house which delight to be frequented with only filiall accesses. . . . these domestick privileges into the barre of a proud judiciall court where fees and clamours keep shop and drive a trade, where bribery and corruption solicits. (848–49)

Son of a moneylender, Milton is turning the money-lenders out of the Temple. He is also celebrating the family in which there are no servants.

The anger is real, but so is the goal of holy and humane community: "those fornicated arches which she [Prelacy] cals Gods house" (845) will be turned into "filiall accesses." The style itself is "a mortifying to life, a kind of saving by undoing" (847). Not mere rhetorical antithesis, this concept of good-out-of-evil, of *felix culpa*, is already deeply imbedded in Milton's thinking, surely in his epistemology, penetrated into his way of viewing moral and physical reality. One knows Truth by knowing evil, but one can still identify and reject evil after its epistemological function is complete, after one has been shown the sanctity of human conscience, the fervency and delicacy of its correction, and the dangers of a contemptuous infringement of that sanctity.

Following the discussion of jurisdiction, the subtle dissection of his own personal motives, the analysis of audiences, the frank exposure of personal plans and of the kinds of time in which the writer lives and works, Milton returns to something like sheer traducing. The subtitle of the Conclusion is "The mischiefe that Prelaty does in the State."

The images of carnal feeding on the one hand and servility on the other take over the text. The blind mouths still horrify, and contact with the corruption that issues forth from their tongues defiles like contact with the dead bodies in open, unwhited sepulchres in the fields around the city of Jerusalem before the feast of Passover:[31] the liberty of the English spirit is about to be "subdue[d] . . . by a servile and blind super-stition," enthralled

> under the swelling mood of a proud Clergy, who will not serve or feed your soules with spirituall food . . . But when they have glutted their ingrateful bodies, at least if it be possible that those open sepulchers should ever be glutted . . . will they yet have any compassion upon you [?] What will they do then, in the name of God and saints, what will these man-haters yet with more despite and mischief do. . . . by their corrupt and servile doctrines boring our eares to an everlasting slavery. (851)

Those who willingly "subscribe slave" to the preaching of false prophets are like the bondsman in Exodus 21:2–6 who rejects his proffered freedom out of love for his master: "Then his master shall bring him unto the judges; he shall also bring him to the door or unto the door post; and his master shall bore his ear through with an aul; and he shall serve him for ever." The corrupt word bores, that is mis-instructs, the ear into servility. Speaking God's truth is the highest function of the inspired; perverting God's truth in pulpit or poem must then be the lowest. Hearing God's truth and acting on it is the highest function of the ordinary Christian; listening to the perversion of that truth and accepting it is slavery. Paul's words from Romans 3 throb through these passages:

> Their throat *is* an open sepulchre; with their tongues they have used deceit; the poison of asps *is* under their lips:
> Whose mouth *is* full of cursing and bitterness:
> Their feet *are* swift to shed blood.

There is too a fear of the tyrant—"God turn such a scourge from us" (*CPW*, 1:852)—who might too easily suborn a corrupt Prelacy. There is passing parody of Psalm 121 and then again the celebration of Truth as public and political benefactor, no abstract idea: "the property of Truth is, where she is publickly taught, to unyoke & set free the minds and spirits of a Nation first from the thraldom of sin and superstition, after which all honest and legal freedom of civil life cannot be long absent" (853). In the attack on the universities, the corrupting of Truth and of potential truth-tellers is again given in terms of mouths, with an almost kinesthetic effect:

> honest and ingenuous natures . . . fed with nothing else, but the *scragged* and *thorny* lectures of monkish and miserable sophistry, were sent home again with such a *scholastical burre* in their throats, as hath stopt and hinderd all true and generous philosophy from entring, *crackt* their voices for ever with metaphysical *gargarisms,* and hath made them admire a sort of formal outside men prelatically addicted. (854, my italics)

The "sincere milke of the Gospell," which is also the "childrens food . . . we know to be no other then the sincerity of the word that they may grow thereby" (649, 828–29), hovers as antithesis to the excesses of the prelates. Milton gathers the people about him to condemn the mouths who want us "to fat them . . . cramme them as they list," "greasy sophisters" who would "snore in their luxurious excesse . . . ravenous and savage wolves," who "took upon them to feed, but now clame to devour . . . fatn'd with virgins blood" (855–57). They have become Spenser's "sailewing'd monster that menaces to swallow up the Land, unlesse her bottomlesse gorge may be satisfi'd with the blood of the Kings daughter the Church" (857). The monster is boldly collated with the classical Python, "a fenborn serpent . . . shot to death with the darts of the sun, the pure and powerful beams of Gods word" (858). Apollo's bow becomes the sword of the spirit.

Even bolder is the comparison between Samson and Charles. The "state and person of a King" is likened to "that mighty Nazarite *Samson*" who "grows up to a noble strength and perfection with his illustrious and sunny locks the laws waving and curling about his god like shoulders" (858–59). The passage suggests again that early interest in the Samson story, but more importantly it shows the desanctification of the King's image that Milton has gradually been introducing into the prose. I have discussed above the possibility that Milton sees Samson as a type of Charles I and Delilah as a type of Henrietta Maria (chap. 6, "book 1"). The passage here is clearly pointed. Samson/Charles may

> with the jawbone of an Asse, that is, with the word of his meanest officer, suppresse and put to confusion thousands of those that rise against his just power. But laying down his head among the strumpet flatteries of Prelates. . . . they wickedly shaving off all those bright and waighty tresses of his laws . . . deliver him over to indirect and violent councels, which as those Philistims put out the fair, and farre-sighted eyes of his natural discerning, and make him grinde in the prison house of their sinister ends and practises upon him. (859)

The "indirect and violent councels . . . Philistims" who blind the king are the Queen and her advisors. Otherwise why "indirect"? The "grinding" is the sexual act producing Catholic heirs, "their sinister ends."[32] This demonizing of Queen Henrietta Maria has been cumulative since her first entrance into the kingdom.[33]

Samson revives and rains "thunder with ruin" upon the evil counselors and upon himself, with no particular respect for the king's body. To the prelatical claim that the king is the Lord's anointed (with its corollary, the necessity of anointers), Milton replies: "if Kings be the Lords Anointed, how they dare thus oyle over and besmear so holy an unction with the corrupt and putrid oyntment of their flatteries; which while they smooth the skin strike inward and envenom the life blood" (*CPW*, 1:859–60). Provisionally accepting anointment, he dilutes the holiness of the oil, not very reverently. The piece ends with the preeminent authority not of King but of Parliament. It is " your selves, worthy Peeres and Commons" whose "glorious and immortal actions" have opposed the prelates.

The punishing hand of Parliament, not of a reformed King, ends *The Reason of Church-Government*. Parliament will punish a prelacy whose condemnation has been the stated business of this tract. Prelacy is worse than contemptible—it is disgusting, Solomon's harlot, Sodom. It is Parliament, not Charles, who becomes King Solomon and renders judgment: "let your severe and impartial doom imitate the divine vengeance; rain down your punishing force upon this godlesse and oppressing government: and bring such a dead Sea of subversion upon her, that she may never in this Land rise more to afflict the holy reformed Church, and the elect people of God" (861). Thirteen bishops and one archbishop are in the Tower. With his left hand self-consciously but vigorously engaged, the future singer of songs to generations has described what he sees as the dire corruptions of Episcopal Church government and its perversion of the Good News he here proclaims, and which he promises to proclaim more splendidly in the future. Firmly, sometimes ruthlessly, Milton asks for the destruction of those who would hinder his vision of a godly community, hinder his kerygmatic voice, Sword of the Spirit, straining to proceed from confrontation to celebration of a glorious national destiny.

Rhetoric and Revolution

The Eccentrical Equation

> *Grant I may never rack a Scripture Similie, beyond the*
> *true intent thereof, Lest instead of Sucking Milk, I squeez Blood*
> *out of it.*[1]
>
> —*Thomas Fuller*

I joined the faculty at the State University of New York at
Stony Brook in the summer of 1968. It was an exciting move
for me and my family, from the beautiful and dignified campus
of the University of Delaware to the raw, new community
emerging from the mud of Long Island with enormous energy
and stridency. At Newark, Delaware, I had felt like a radical
in opposing the expelling of students for protesting against
ROTC on campus. In Stony Brook I was a suspect, "somebody
over 30," in the midst of an activist student body protesting
the war, racism, sexism, and the "famous" campus drug bust.
It was a remarkable time of real debate and communal activity,

204

full of sincere attempts at reforming practically everything. I thought I had come to Eden for liberals.

I had been interested in Milton's rhetoric of zeal since the early sixties, when J. C. Maxwell responded to a note submitted to *Notes & Queries* by pointing out the Greek behind the Revelation 3.16 text. The essay "Milton and the Rhetoric of Zeal" had been published in 1965 (but not included in my book *The Fierce Equation*—though so described in some bibliographies), and the idea at the heart of that essay was a major source of my continuing interest in Milton's prose. But two events occurred that summer that not only intensified my interest, but made the topic seem very important, very contemporary, very "engaged." The first was a conversation with my 13-year-old son, Tommy, who was, like me, a dedicated activist against the Viet Nam war. (I remember the conversation if not precisely at least accurately.) During that summer of 1968, he and I attended a talk on campus by Paul O'Dwyer, the maverick Democratic candidate for the U.S. Senate. O'Dwyer spoke well and passionately against the war in Viet Nam, against racism, against poverty—those topics that absorbed so many of us that summer after the assassinations of Martin Luther King, Jr., and Robert Kennedy— the summer also of the Chicago convention and its disgraceful repressions. On the way home, Tommy and I were discussing the campaign and O'Dwyer's chances against the incumbent Senator Javits. I cautioned, fatuously I suppose, against attacking the senator because he was "a good decent liberal" who had voted the right way on a number of issues. My son exploded; "It's just those good decent liberals I can't stand! They think they're something because they voted for the civil rights bill in 1964." The anger was intense. And I recognized the tone; it was the tone of the Puritan activists of the 1640s, the haters of *moderate* virtue, outraged moralists who demanded the extreme.

The second episode occurred during the first week of the new semester on my new campus. The university administration had declared a moratorium on classes for that week, during which the entire campus community would devote itself to discussion of the vital public issues facing the campus, the nation, and the world. An ambitious schedule of meetings, discussions, lectures was to help define the university's role in society, with quite specific attention to how the community could serve to ameliorate social ills, to improve living conditions for the poor; there was even much discussion of how the community could force the university to stop participating in war-related research, to stop supporting the "military-industrial complex." An important part of the discussion was to be devoted to the possibilities for radical reform of the university itself. The first meeting of the first day was a plenary session in the gym. Most of the (then fairly small) campus population was there. The opening remarks were made by Professor Bentley Glass, academic vice president, the man who, probably more than any other, was considered responsible for Stony Brook's high intellectual aspirations, a distinguished scholar and teacher. Dr. Glass started out with an optimistic if sober welcome to this important event and an intense plea for rational discussion. Before he finished his first paragraph, a student from the front row of the bleachers set up for the convocation yelled out, "Bull-*shit!*" That was my second shock of recognition: Radical violation of Liberal decorum.

That first year at Stony Brook and the two years following, when I was "Master" of Woody Guthrie College (we shared a quad with Jimi Hendrix, Bela Lugosi, Harpo Marx and John Steinbeck—all the names but Steinbeck have been changed), confirmed my initial equation of the radical rhetorics of the 1640s in England and the 1960s in the United States. The strategies of both these lexical sets aimed at destroying the decorum of the Establishment. That strategy arose from an overwhelming sense of moral outrage, outrage at the injustice and cruelty of a power structure that claimed authority through a more or less elaborate façade of traditional practices and dogma. In 1640s England the traditional framework was hierarchical, in civil government monarchical and aristocratic;

in church government, prelatical and authoritarian. In the United States, the traditional view of ourselves was of a nation benevolently tolerant, egalitarian and democratic. Both cultures had carefully articulated recent history. In the 1630s and 1640s, England saw herself as God's elect nation, guardian of the theological golden mean, *via media* between the extremes of doctrine and discipline in God's Christian world. In America, the mythical heritage was that of a nation that had never fought an unjust war and never lost one (these self-deceptions were commonplace). As the 1960s moved into the 1970s, and as the moral outrage peaked and receded and peaked again, as President Nixon somehow withstood the passionate theaters of the antiwar demonstrations, as Kent State came and went, I found myself charting similarities between the two historical periods even as I joined in the demonstrations, swept along by something like an angry euphoria of political righteousness. After the years of Kissinger/Nixon, after the bitter irony of Dr. Kissinger's Nobel Peace Prize; after getting teargassed in peace demonstrations in Washington, D.C. (and nursing the lingering smell in my beard for an extra day); after bailing my older son out of jail several times for his part in the demonstrations; after conviction that in fact I *was* a part of the military-industrial complex (no longer in quota-tion marks); and, surely, by the late seventies, I began to recognize that I was not of this time or of this place . . . too tied to the past, too tenured, too mortgaged, perhaps too old.

In 1972 I had been lucky enough to get a Guggenheim grant to London, where I read Thomason Tracts for a year. For many years following, the study of these materials tended to confirm and extend the propositions I had pondered after reading Brightman and Bastwick at the Huntington Library in 1962, questions and provisional answers concerning the origin and career of the rhetoric of revolution. At a certain stage of literacy and intellectual commitment, a large reading public became convinced of a serious abuse of power, of exploitation of a politically unaware populace, and of a curtailment of reli-gious or intellectual freedom. The original response was an intellectual one, in fact a pedagogical one. In England, it was the buying of posts for preaching the truth to the public, the feoffees. In America it was the teach-in. The origins of these ultimately subversive movements were in highly prestigious intellectual communities—communities like Emanuel College, Cambridge and the University of California at Berkeley. In the 1960s anger and euphoria fed each other in the best universities in the country, and a (now) surprising range of people were attracted to the cause. In a letter to *The New York Times Magazine*, January 19, 1969, Martin Peretz attacked Walter Goodman's report on the New Left Conference at Princeton:

> I did not conclude that reasonableness is not preferable to political hysteria. I said that cool reasonableness is not always or necessarily preferable to hysteria. I would go further: there are times of moral enormity when cool reasonableness is a more pathological and unrealistic state than hysteria—that is when hysteria is constructive and creative and when reasonableness is evasive and irresponsible.[2]

The teach-ins and preach-ins didn't work; sometimes they were suppressed because they showed early signs of success; sometimes the rebels lost patience at their own slow progress. The teach-in gave way to the demonstration, then to the riot. The sermon gave way to the serious, even physical, protests in the churches against ceremony, then to street demonstrations, then to riots, then to war.

Steadily, systematically, often in inspired ways, the rebels attacked the *decorum* of the Establishment. In England, with Marprelate and his heirs, or Bastwick's description of a stately ecclesiastical procession; in America, with the Free Speech movement and its strongly capitalized "Freedom Under Clark Kerr" banner, or Abbie Hoffman's fright-wig parody of the judge in his Chicago trial. Talk of moderation and reasonableness was burnt up in the chants of "Peace *Now*" and "Do it *Now*." Campus protests may have been welcomed, but they most certainly were not led, by good, graying liberals. Contempt for academic deliberations and their *Roberts Rules of Order*

were everywhere. The author of *The Liberal Imagination* was
a chief villain to the antiwar, antiracism demonstrators at
Columbia University. The "good liberals" were fakes who
presented soft hypocrisies in the face of truth and expected
the young to be taken in. Humphrey and Johnson were worse
than Nixon. The "all deliberate speed" of the school
antisegregation ruling became a laughing-stock phrase.
Impassioned urgency was the only truth. My older son was
reading Jerry Rubin's *Do It!* and I was reading injunctions to
act: "*Now*, this minute, this very moment"[3] and powerful
sermons like that of Joseph Symonds to the House of
Commons on the text from 1 Chronicles 28.10: "Take heed
now for the Lord hath chosen thee to build an house for the
Sanctuarie. Be strong and doe it."[4] With particular energy and
brevity Symonds expresses the Puritan ideal of polemical style
with its emphasis on *Now:*

> My purpose is to speake chiefely of the *charge,* In which two things
> are required of Solomon   resolution   .   { *Be strong*
>   execution   .   { *Doe it.*   (B2)

Immediacy of action is almost the prime virtue:

Your resolutions must be 1) firme 2) spirituall . . . 3) willing
4) Speedy. For

> 1. It's the greatest worke you   { Priority
>   have to doe. Therefor give it   { Quick dispatch
> 2. Delayes are dangerous
>   Doe it well
>   Doe it now

>   (Symonds, D2–D4v)

Living in and reading the late 1960s and early 1970s was
uncannily mirrored in reading the 1640s.

This is ancient history, and it is of course a simplified view
of two historical periods whose differences outweigh their
similarities. But I will maintain the comparisons. Zeal redefined our era as it did the mid-seventeenth century in
England. I still remember those days as thrilling, somewhat
scary, and finally exhausting. They ended with a whimper.

The Establishment wore down the movement, suborning some members, cutting off some from the necessary resources, while channeling others into abstract speculation, coopting the radical style of flamboyant freedom into the marketing of clothing, entertainment and the arts, and making it a good investment. By the mid-1970s, the revolution was chiefly remembered in the nation's shopping malls, which marketed "protest" style. Torn jeans were chic. By the 1990s Marxism, queer theory and feminism were tenured and thriving in the American university; but the reform of the university as a whole was minimal, and class disparities widened and would continue to widen, among individuals, and surely among institutions.

In the 1660s the Church of England returned to hegemony, perhaps more solidly than ever, with careful, limited expressions of tolerance and with a lingering fear, and the proper kinds of fearful contempt for the "Good Old Cause." Mark Kishlansky writes,

> The revolution. . . . left a legacy that nourished two political traditions. The first—conservative and loyal—kept the memory of the Revolution alive so that glimpses of the dark, churning underside of British society could always be seen. . . . The other . . . long lived underground—their touchstones remained distrust of the monarchy and dissent from the established church. Liberty was their shibboleth, and they became torch-bearer to the great revolutionary movements of the late eighteenth century— one of the few examples of to the losers belong the spoils. (341–42)

Without worrying the point too much, the energies *and* the disappointments of the two periods are similar. Nostalgia for the 1960s as a "style" coexists with disappointment and a lingering hope, not quite underground, that some of the benefits of that zealous redefinition of rights will accrue to something other than the abstracting think tanks of our humanities institutes.

The English radicals established a literature of individual rights that fed the American Revolution as well as the long history of reform in England. Eloquent opposition to the suppression of dissent was an essential part of that literature.

In England, it surfaced early and not only in Milton. This opposition may backtrack in order to protect its new-won authorities; it can move to its own repressions, to moments of meanness and a vulgar sobriety. Parliament can find the celebration of Christmas a subject for new ordinances, chastising and *directing* those "who have turned this Feast, pretending the Memory of Christ, into an extreme forget-fulnesse of him, by giving liberty to carnall and sensuall delights."[5] But zeal can also mature, and it can develop and expand, groping toward another kind of political and social idealism, movingly tolerant and vulnerable in the midst of political realisms that argue for irony, especially in the great debate on Liberty of Conscience. In the mid-1640s, from both sides, the attractions of moderation as tolerant and partici-patory are rephrased and represented after the experience of zeal. The quite eminent moderate, Thomas Fuller, is accused of lukewarmness from both sides—he ends up of the King's party—but his claim for moderation is heard. The title itself speaks of shifting values of rhetorical currencies: *Truth Maintained, Or Positions Delivered in a Sermon at the Savoy Since Traduced For Dangerous: Now Asserted For Sound and Safe.* Fuller makes the distinction that had been made before: "Moderation [is] an wholesome Cordiall to the soule: whilst lukewarmness (a temper which seekes to reconcile hot and cold) is so distastefull, that *health it selfe* seems sick of it, and vomits it out."[6] More strikingly, Henry Robinson speaks for moderation *and* freedom:

> men of moderation which endeavour to qualifie or decline the precipice of extreams, ought not to be accounted newtralls or luke-warme . . . it is the freedome of their owne conscience which they desire, not to be indifferently of any Religion, or prophanely of none at all, but that they might enjoy alwayes peaceably that Religion which they examined and found to be the true one. . . . I plead not against, but for liberty, and that the best of all liberties, the Liberty of Conscience.[7]

The zeal of the early 1640s fiercely denounced the "moder-atours" and the "tolerationists"; later its very volatility contributed to the environment for moral assertion in which Robinson can speak. By 1644, an anonymous Independent can calmly and firmly ask for consideration by the Presbyterian leadership: "We have set you down, as it were where you should be; We have dislodged the *Canaanites* before you, we are necessitated to passe on further; it were but your duty to march on before us, and give us quiet possession with you."[8] The plea for moderation advances from a plea for peace to a plea for liberty. Zeal has provided a habit of release which can also lead to toleration.

Congealed, zeal also provided the licensed stridencies of repression, at its ugliest when it turns on itself. An attack on five tolerationist pamphlets (including Roger Williams's *The Bloody Tenent*)[9] bludgeons the zealots for "their pernicious, God-provoking, Truth-defacing, church ruinating, & State-shaking toleration."[10] The hypocrisy of zeal is regularly seen as a cover for self-indulgence, or for the seizing of power: "they plead for libertie, but it is licentiousnesse: . . . it would soon appear whether or no they would rage and swell and get over, or beare downe afore them all that should stand in their way."[11] At another stage of his career and of his personal life, Milton will echo this: "license they mean, when they cry Liberty" (Sonnet 12), but to a different end, one which does not contradict his earlier investment in the rhetoric of zeal. In its dotage, Puritan zeal becomes "quaint"; but the power and the stridency can be remembered with some fear by everyone from Swift to Dickens and Hawthorne, and even to Flannery O'Connor, Philip Roth and Toni Morrison.

It is the stridencies that have been overemphasized in English and especially American literary history. "Puritanism" is the bondage against which American writers have been proclaiming rebellion, for at least these 150 years. For most of my 50 academic years, literary historians, from Parrington on, oversimplified the definition of the zeal that propels the growth and maintenance of radical Protestantism. Happily there have been powerful correctives to this simplification, including the work of twentieth-century eminences like William Haller and Perry Miller. By now, William

Prynne and Jonathan Edwards are no longer the major models of a Puritan style. But my teaching experience has firmly argued that the American academy still uses the Puritan as a scapegoat model of repression. My study has attempted to show the complexity, the power and, frankly, the value of a zeal that helped to energize and reform English society.

Hugh Trevor-Roper, no sentimentalist of liberal hypotheses, eloquently identified "the ideological force which, at least for a time gave to [Milton's] 'Whig' ideas their historical, even metaphysical power and inspired his greatest eloquence, and the weakening of which left him, in the end, like so many of his generation, disillusioned and sour" (*Catholics,* 235). I do not accept Trevor-Roper's description of Milton's later career as "a sterile and often discreditable career of violent, and in the end, futile polemic" (236); but his description of the summer of 1641 serves as a virtual epigraph for what I have been trying to demonstrate here: "The excitement, the exhilaration and expectancy of those months is audible still" (250). I write this after September 11, 2001, when the dangers of zeal, foreign and domestic, need not be expounded.

Milton does not express nostalgia for the "revolution"; nor does he turn on it. He absorbs its failure and moves on, as in the remarkable *Readie and Easie Way,* the only piece in which he cites, with some emotion, the phrase "*the good Old Cause*" (*CPW,* 7:462). He reviles license in his sonnets on the divorce tracts, but he remembers the lessons of enfranchisement taught by the rhetoric of zeal. Sharon Achinstein puts it strongly:

> [Milton's] political engagement required a rhetorical opportunism at times. Yet from a rhetorical perspective, Milton was surprisingly committed to a single goal, that of making his public fit to achieve self-governance through training in virtue. He persisted in his attempts to formulate an image of the public. (*Revolutionary Reader,* 8)

Milton cherishes his independence and that of his community in establishing the decorum of the modern man, a truly situational decorum that dismisses the strictures of the past and assumes the surpassing of example. From that surpassing emerges the continuous redefinition of precept. In *Paradise Lost, Paradise Regained,* and *Samson Agonistes,* Milton proclaims the potentialities of the Emergent Christian Hero.

Notes

Notes to Preface

1. The findings of the Committee on Tenure and Academic Freedom and the recommendations of President Raymond B. Allen were published in *Communism and Academic Freedom: The Record of the Tenure Cases at the University of Washington* (Seattle: University of Washington Press, 1949). There is a retrospective look at these events in Nancy Wick, "Seeing Red," *Columns, The University of Washington Alumni Magazine* 17, no. 4 (December 1997), 16–21.

Notes to Chapter One

All works cited are published in London unless otherwise noted. All references to Milton's prose are taken from *The Complete Prose Works of John Milton*, 8 vols., ed. Don M. Wolfe et al. (New Haven: Yale University Press, 1953–1982). All biblical citations are from the Authorized King James Version (KJV).

1. Stephen Marshall, *A Divine Project to Save the Kingdome* (1644), 5; hereafter *Divine Project.*

2. For an overview, see Elizabeth Eisenstein, *The Printing Press as an Agent of Change*, 2 vols. (Cambridge: Cambridge University Press, 1985). For a description of the period's "revolution in reading," see the introduction to Sharon Achinstein, *Milton and the Revolutionary Reader* (see note 72 for full citation). See also Nigel Smith, *Literature & Revolution in England, 1640–1660* (New Haven: Yale University Press, 1994), esp. chaps. 1 and 2.

3. Quoted in William Haller, *Foxe's Book of Martyrs and The Elect Nation* (London: Jonathan Cape, 1963), 110.

4. See my *The Fierce Equation: A Study of Milton's Decorum* (The Hague: Mouton, 1965), chap. 1.

5. Walter J. Ong, S.J., *Ramus, Method, and the Decay of Dialogue* (Cambridge, Mass.: Harvard University Press, 1983), 16.

6. As indicated above, all biblical citations are from the KJV, though I have consulted other editions, especially William Tyndale's New Testament (1534) and the Geneva Bible, 1560 edition.

7. *CPW*, 6:697. Where there are numerous contiguous citations from volume 1 and a clear common source of text, I will cite only page numbers or volume and page numbers. I am aware of the important challenges of the provenance of the Latin treatise, especially the work of W. B. Hunter Jr., *Visitation Unimplor'd: Milton and the Authorship of "De Doctrina Christiana"* (Pittsburgh: Duquesne University Press, 1998). Despite the arguments of the foremost scholar of the work, I remain, with a number of other Miltonists, uneasy about the "deaccessioning." In some of the chapters to come, I will point out passages in the early prose that at least reflect the attitudes of the *De Doctrina*.

8. *The Compact Edition of the Oxford English Dictionary: Complete Text Reproduced Micrographically*, vol. 2 (New York: Oxford University Press, 1971), 3868.

9. I use the terms *Anglican* and *Puritan* brazenly, despite John N. King's warning about the "anachronistic terms *Anglicanism* and *Anglican*." See his *English Reformation Literature: The Tudor Origins of the Protestant Tradition* (Princeton: Princeton University Press, 1982), 3, and his suggestion that the more accurate terms are *Formalist* and *Nonconformist*. I'm aware of the multiple overlaps in theological and political views during this period. My distinction between rhetorics should help reinforce the ordinary and unsophisticated, but nevertheless clear and useful, view of two opposed camps that disagreed on serious fundamentals, a disagreement which obscured many of the positions they had in common. *Anglican* in this study will refer to supporters of the Established Church of England as constituted in 1640 and as administered by the canons of that year, its doctrine and discipline as established, however fluidly, since the time of Elizabeth I; *Puritan* will refer to those Protestants who opposed that church at that time because they rejected major portions of its doctrine and/or discipline. I hope these designations will serve the subject as well as they have served Barbara K. Lewalski in her *The Life of John Milton: A Critical Biography* (Oxford: Blackwell, 2001). Archbishop William Laud and John Milton stand near the poles of the arguments. Bishop Joseph Hall, a serious case in point, is initially a mediator in doctrine who moves toward the right in matters of discipline during the period I discuss. I treat him as *Anglican* and as opposed to *Puritan*. I am emphasizing discipline over doctrine in my ascriptions and therefore working outside of a good part of the important research of recent years by, among others, Georgia Christopher, Joan Bennett, Dennis Danielson and John N. King.

10. Stephen Marshall, *Meroz Cursed, or A Sermon Preached To The Honourable House of Commons At their late Solemn Fast*, 1641. An early biography writes, "Himself has boasted, that he preach'd one Sermon (I believe that was *Curse Ye Meroz*) three-score times" (*The Godly Mans Legacy to the Saints upon earth exhibited in the life of . . . S. Marshall*, 1680), 26. This anonymous account was written (despite its title page) "to undeceive such well-meaning Persons as are still unhappily misled in the same way, and miserably gulled and abused by the usual Artifice and Cunning of those grave Sinners, who would needs call themselves the *Saints*, the *People of God*, the *Secret Ones*, and take Pride in many such fine Names" (sig. A2r). The publication date may have something to do with the contradiction.

11. *Paradise Lost* 5.896–99, in *The Riverside Milton*, ed. Roy Flannagan (Boston: Houghton Mifflin, 1998), 503.

12. Arthur Salwey, *Halting Stigmatiz'd in a Sermon Preached to the Honourable House of Commons on the monethly Fast day, Octob. 25, 1643. At Margarets Westminster* (1643), 8.

13. John Weigand [Johanaes Wigandus], *De Neutralibus, & Mediis: Grosly Englished Jacke of both sides* (1620) [first English edition, 1562], 33.

14. Thomas Hill, *The Militant Church Triumphant Over THE DRAGON AND HIS ANGELS, Sermon, July 21, 1643* (1643), 9, hereafter *Militant.*

15. Norman Perrin, *The New Testament: An Introduction* (New York: Harcourt Brace Jovanovich, 1974), 18.

16. In *Helter Skelter*, Vincent Bugliosi and Curt Gentry write that both Charles Manson and The Process, also known as The Church of the Final Judgement, "preached an imminent, violent Armageddon, in which all but the chosen few would be destroyed. . . . The three great gods of the universe, according to The Process, were Jehovah, Lucifer, and Satan, with Christ the ultimate unifier. . . . Manson had a simpler duality; he was known to his followers as both Satan and Christ." (Vincent Bugliosi with Curt Gentry, *Helter Skelter: The True Story of the Manson Murders* (New York: W. W. Norton, 1974; reprt. 1994), 612.

17. See C. A. Patrides and Joseph Wittreich, eds., *The Apocalypse in English Renaissance Thought and Literature* (Manchester: Manchester University Press, 1984). See especially the essays by Jaroslav Pelikan, Bernard Capp, and C. A. Patrides, and the bibliography. See also Janel Mueller, "'Embodying Glory': The Apocalyptic Strain in Milton's *Of Reformation*," in David Loewenstein and James Grantham Turner, eds. *Politics, Poetics, and Hermeneutics in Milton's Prose* (Cambridge: Cambridge University Press, 1990), hereafter *Politics.*

18. Henry More, *Apocalypsis Apocalypseos of the Revelation of St John the Divine unveiled* (1680), 35–36.

19. John Bale, *The Image of bothe Churches after the moste wonderfull and heavenly Revelation of Sainct John* (1551), 49–50.

20. John Jewel, Bishop, *A Sermon Preached Before Q Elizabeth By That Learned and Reverend Man John Jewel Bishop of Sarisbury* (1641), 7, 15. In most cases, I will cite the early reformers from The Parker Society Reprints; occasionally, as here, I use early editions, especially those reprinted during the period on which I am focusing. Elizabeth herself comments sourly on the political dangers of the Revelation text: "Some of [my Protestants] of late have said that I was of no religion—neither hot nor cold, but such as one day would give God the vomit." Quoted in Elizabeth Plowden, *Elizabeth Regina: the Age of Triumph 1588–1603* (New York: New York Times Books, 1980), 42.

21. William Perkins, *Lectures Upon the Three First Chapters of the Revelation* (1604), 306–7.

22. Edward Hyde, Earl of Clarendon, *The History of the Rebellion and Civil War in England Begun in the year 1641,* 6 vols. (Oxford: Clarendon Press, 1969), 1:263, hereafter *Rebellion.*

23. On the Marprelate tradition and its influence on the controversies of this later period, I have found the following most useful: James Egan, "Milton and the Marprelate Tradition," *Milton Studies,* vol. 8, ed. James D. Simmonds (Pittsburgh: University of Pittsburgh Press, 1975), 103–21; Peter Auksi, "Milton's 'Sanctifi'd Bitterness': Polemical Techniques in the Early Prose," *Texas Studies in Literature and Language* 19 (1977): 363–81; Raymond A. Anselment, *"Betwixt Jest and Earnest": Marprelate, Milton, Marvell, Swift & the Decorum of Religious Ridicule* (Toronto: University of Toronto Press, 1979); Nigel Smith, "Richard Overton's Marpriest Tracts: Towards a History of Leveller Style," in *The Literature of Controversy: Polemical Strategy from Milton to Junius,* edited by Thomas N. Corns, 39–66 (London 1987).

24. *The Works of the Right Reverend Joseph Hall, DD.,* ed. Philip Wynter, 10 vols. (Oxford: Oxford University Press, 1863), 6:444.

25. Francis Bacon, *A Wise and Moderate Discourse, Concerning Church-Affaires. As it was written, long since, by the famous Authour of those Considerations, which seem to have some reference to this. Now published for the common good* (1641), 16–17.

26. In his essay entitled "'Mediocrities' and 'Extremities': Francis Bacon and the Aristotelian Mean," Joshua Scodel demonstrates Bacon's "transformation and subversion of the Aristotelian doctrine of the mean" (90) and shows that "Bacon promotes himself as a simultaneously Christian and worldly man of virtue who pursues the mean of truth guided by a praiseworthy 'extremity' of love for his fellow man" (126). See *Creative Imitation: New Essays on Renaissance Literature in Honor of Thomas M. Greene,* ed. David Quint, Margaret Ferguson et al. (Binghamton, N.Y.: Medieval & Renaissance Texts and Studies, 1992).

Bacon's political decorum includes this shrewd evaluation and use of both concepts, moderation and zeal; yet it seems clear to me that the printing of these texts in 1640–1641 is an effort to enlist them for the Church of England.

27. First circulated in 1589, but not published in full until 1641. For the relationship between *A Wise & Moderate Discourse* and the next citation, see *CPW*, 1:450–51.

28. Francis Bacon, *Certaine Considerations Touching the Better Pacification, and Edification of the Church of England* (1604; reprint, 1640), A4; hereafter cited as *Certaine Considerations*.

29. Robert Bolton, *Generall directions for a comfortable walking with God*, 4th ed. (1634), 50–51; hereafter cited as *Directions*.

30. Another Latin edition appeared in 1612, and three English editions followed between 1611 and 1616.

31. Thomas Brightman, *The Revelation of S John illustrated with an Analysis & scholions. Wherein the sence is opened by the Scripture, & the event of things foretold by Histories. The third Edition corrected & amended, with supply of many things formerly left out* (Leyden 1616), 170; hereafter cited as *Revelation,* and the edition from which I cite throughout.

32. Thomas Hill, *The Trade of Truth Advanced, Fast Sermon (July 27, 1642)*, 8.

33. Matthew Newcomen, *The Craft and Cruelty of the Churches Adversaries* (1643), 15.

34. Robert Baillie, *A Parallel or Briefe Comparison of the Liturgie with the Masse Book* (1641), A2–A2v; hereafter cited as *Parallel.*

35. Francis Quarles, *Observations concerning Princes and States, Upon Peace and Warre* (1641), 2.

36. Daniel Featley, *The Dippers Dipt* (1645), 212–13.

37. David Loewenstein, *Milton and the Drama of History* (Cambridge: Cambridge University Press, 1990), notes Brightman's criticism of the Church of England, but emphasizes his focus on England as the Elect Nation (see 9–11).

38. George Gyffard, *Sermons upon the Whole Booke of the Revelation* (1596), 103.

39. John Fowler, Clement Saunders, and Robert Bulwarde, *A Shield of Defence Against the Arrowes of Schisme Shot abroad by Jean de l'Eglise in his advertisement against Mr Brightman* (Amsterdam 1612), 17.

40. William Cowper, Bishop of Gallaway *Pathmos; or, A Commentary on the Revelation of Saint John* (1619), 22–23.

41. See, for example, *A true and perfect Copie of the Protestation of the Archbishops & Bishops of Ireland Against the Tolleration of Poperie* (1626; reprint, 1641).

42. John Preston, "The Pillar and Ground of Truth," in *Sermons preached before his Majestie, and upon other occasions* (1630), 19; hereafter cited as "Pillar."

43. Brightman had seen the Church of Scotland as but one of a consort of contemporary churches that were prefigured by the Church of Philadelphia: "Helvetia, Suesia, Geneva, France, Scotland" (*Revelation*, 139).

44. *A Glimpse of Sions Glory* (1641), 32, attributed to Hanserd Knollys by William Haller (*The Rise of Puritanism*, 270, 396); however, it is also attributed to Thomas Goodwin in 5.12 of the *Works of Thomas Goodwin* (1861), and John F. Wilson, "A Glimpse of Syon's Glory," *Church History* 5, no. 31 (1962), disputes Haller's theory (223–41).

45. Jeremiah Burroughs, "Mr. Jeremiah Burroughs his speech in Guild-Hall," in *Four Speeches Delivered in Guild Hall . . . sixth of October 1643* (1643), 27–38.

46. Nicholas Ardron, *The Ploughmans Vindication* (1646), 46.

47. Nathaniel Rogers, *A Letter, Discovering The Cause of Gods continuing wrath* (1643), 3.

48. Thomas Edwards, *Gangraena*, 2nd part (1646), 200–207.

49. Samuel Gibson, *The Ruine Of The Authors and Fomentors Of Civill Warres:* A Sermon before the House of Commons (1645), 33.

50. See Henry Burton, *The Sounding of the Two Last Trumpets the sixt and seventh, or, Meditations by way of paraphrase upon the 9th, 10th and 11th chapters of the Revelation as containing a prophecyie of these last times* (1641), 28; Edward Calamy, *Gods Free Mercy to England presented in a Sermon before the House of Commons at their fast* (1642), 47; Lewis Hewes, *Certain Grievances or the Errours of the Service Booke; Plainly Layd Open* (1640), 39; hereafter cited as *Grievances;* John Lilburne, *The Christian Mans Triall; or, A True Revelation of the Apprehension and Examinations of John Lilburne* (1641), 28; hereafter cited as *Triall;* Marshall, "Preface," in *Divine Project*, passim.

51. John Halsted, *Brightman Redivivus; or, The Post-Humian Of-Spring of Mr Thomas Brightman in IIII Sermons* (1647).

52. In J. Max Patrick, ed., *The Complete Poetry of Robert Herrick* (New York, 1963).

53. *Papisto-Mastix or Deborah's Prayer against Gods Enemies* (1641), 12.

54. Wilkinson's claim of persecution in *A Sermon against luke-warmnesse preached at Saint Maries in Oxford, the sixth of September, 1640* [1641], is corroborated by Sir Edward Dering, *A Collection of Speeches* (1641), 43–48. Dering's reliability and his involvement in the same issues that engaged Milton are discussed in two essays by Jason P. Rosenblatt—"The Plot Discovered and Counterplotted," *English Literary Renaissance* 15 (Autumn 1985): 318–52, and "Sir Edward Dering's Milton," *Modern Philology* 79, no. 4 (1982): 376–85.

55. Richard Byfield, *The Power of the Christ of God; or, a Treatise of Power* (1641), 10.

56. In C. A. Patrides, ed., *The English Poems of George Herbert* (Totowa, N.J.: Rowman and Littlefield, 1974), 122–23.

57. For two contrasting views, see Jeanne Clayton Hunter, "'With Winges of Faith': Herbert's Communion Poems," *Journal of Religion* 62 (1982): 57–71; and Stanley Stewart, *George Herbert* (Boston: Twayne, 1986), esp. chaps. 2 and 3.

58. William Laud, *A Speech Delivered in the Starre-Chamber XIVth of June MDCXXXVII* (1637), 39; hereafter cited as *Star Chamber.*

59. Richard Hooker, "The Holiness of Churches," in *Of the Laws of Ecclesiastical Polity. The Fifth Book,* ed. Ronald Bayne (London: Macmillan, 1902), 5:61; hereafter cited as *Ecclesiastical Polity.*

60. William Laud, Archbishop of Canterbury, *A Relation of the Conference Between William Laud, Then Lord Bishop of St. Davids; Now Lord Arch-Bishop of Canterbury; and Mr.* [John] *Fisher the Jesuite . . .* (1639), 21–22. I have eliminated running italics; hereafter cited as *Jesuite.*

61. Richard Hooker, "A Discovery of the Causes of the Continuance of these Contentions concerning Church-Government," in *Certaine Briefe Treatises Written by Diverse Learned Men, concerning the ancient and Moderne government of the church* (Oxford: 1641), 5.

62. Charles Carlton, *Archbishop William Laud* (New York: Routledge & Kegan Paul, 1987), 190.

63. William Laud, Archbishop of Canterbury, "Canons and Constitutions Ecclesiasticall Gathered and put in forme, for the government of the Church of Scotland, Aberdeen" (1636), printed in *The Works of the Most Reverend Father in God, William Laud DD.,* vol. 5, part 21 (Oxford, 1847–1850).

64. Joseph Hall, "A Common Apology of the Church of England" (1610), in *Works* 9:92.

65. For a warning about ascribing "indecorum" too easily to the diction of Milton's polemical prose, see Thomas N. Corns, "Obscenity, Slang and Indecorum in Milton's English Prose," *Prose Studies* 3 (1980): 5–14.

66. Thomas Cheshire, *A True Copy of that Sermon Which was preached at St. Paul's the tenth of October last* (1641), 13.

67. Martin Mar-prelate [pseud], *Hay Any Work For Cooper; or, A Briefe Pistle* (1642; reprint, 1589), 14; hereafter cited *Hay.*

68. John Bastwick, *The Letany of John Bastwick, Doctor of Physick,* 2nd ed. (1637), 6; hereafter cited as *Letany.*

69. One notes the paradox of Puritan sainthood, which tends, perhaps accidentally, to be etymologically sophisticated: martyrs are really *witnesses* as in the Greek original. Puritan martyrs from Sir John Oldcastle and Mistress Anne Agnew to Bastwick, Burton, Prynne and

Lilburne tend to be very garrulous. Catholic martyrs suffer; Puritan martyrs preach. I do not mean this flippantly.

70. *Triall,* 26.

71. John De La March, *A Complaint of the False Prophets Mariner upon the Drying up of their Hierarchicall Euphrates* (1641), 36. The reference is to Revelation 15:2.

72. The topic is discussed throughout Sharon Achinstein, *Milton and the Revolutionary Reader* (Princeton: Princeton University Press, 1994), but see esp. 24–25. Achinstein cites a notorious later authority, Hitler's Joseph Goebbels, "we do not talk to say something, but to obtain a certain effect" (150).

73. *Vox Borealis, Or the Northern Discoverie: By Way of Dialogue between Jamie and Willie . . . Amidst the Babylonians, by Margery Mar-Prelat, in Thwackcoat lane* (1641).

74. Not all of the attacks on decency were comic or merely symbolic. *The Brownists Synagogue or a Late Discovery* (1641) describes a congregation as "laying violent hands upon the Minister, rending his Hood from his neck, and tearing the Surplice from his back, he hardly escaping in his own person, from being torne in peeces, and even when the Psalme is singing . . . as likewise rending the Railes from before the communion Table, chopping them in peeces, and burning them in the church Yard" (2).

75. John Finch, Baron Finch of Fordwich, *L. F., Lord Keeper, The Kings Majesty and . . . Parliament* (1641), A2v; hereafter cited as *Speech.*

76. Lucius Cary, Viscount Falkland, *A Speech made to the House of Commons concerning Episcopacy* (1641), 3, 4.

77. Henry Burton, *A Replie To a Relation Of The Conference Between William Laude and Mr Fisher the Jesuite* (1640), 83, hereafter *Replie.*

78. SMECTYMNUUS, *An Answer to a Booke Entituled, An Humble Remonstrance* (1641), 69, hereafter *An Answer.*

79. Joseph Hall, *A Defence of the Humble Remonstrance, against the frivolous and false Exceptions of SMECTYMNUUS* (1641), 145.

80. This includes some sneering at "effeminacy" in the modern sense: an anonymous pamphlet *Canterburies Pilgrimage. In the testimony of an accused conscience for the bloud of Mr. Burton, Mr. Prynne and Doctor Bastwick* (1641) mentions "[Laud's] large family of *Rotchet Prelates;* which comely *Matrons,* have curbed the mouthes of faithfull Ministers, whilst this great Goat Keeper himself, *hath destroyed the grasse upon the Mountaines, prepared to feed the sheepe*" (sig. A3v).

81. Henry Robinson, *Liberty of Conscience; or, The Sole means to obtaine* <u>Peace</u> *and* <u>Truth</u> (1644), A3v.

82. *The Iniquity Of The Late Solemne League, Or Covenant Discovered* (1644), 1.

83. George Gillespie, *A Sermon Preached before the Honourable*

House of Commons At their late solemn Fast March 27, 1644 (1644), A2.

84. Willam Tyndale, *An Answer to Sir Thomas More's Dialogue* (1530), first reprinted by The Parker Society, Parker Society Publications, 55 vols. (1841–1855; reprint, New York: Johnson Reprint Corp, 1968), 45:126; hereafter cited as Parker Society Reprints.

85. William Tyndale, *Exposition Upon the Fifth, Sixth, and Seventh Chapters of Matthew* (1532), in Parker Society Reprints, 43:43.

86. Thomas Cranmer, "Appendix XXIX [Proclamation of 6th day of Feb 1548]," in Parker Society Reprints, *Miscellaneous Writings and Letters of Thomas Cranmer, Archbishop of Canterbury* (Cambridge: Cambridge University Press), 1847, 16:509.

87. Martin Bucer, *Mynd and Exposition of Bucer Uppon These wordes of S Matthew: Woe be to the Worlde because of offences. Math. Xvii* (Emden, 1566), Civ–v, Dv.

88. John Whitgift, Archbishop, *The Defense of the Answer to the Admonition Against the Reply of Thomas Cartwright* (1574), in Parker Society Reprints, 46, pt. 1:247.

89. Thomas Rogers, *The Catholic Doctrine of the Church of England, An Exposition of the Thirty-Nine Articles* (1579), Parker Society (Cambridge: Cambridge University Press, 1854), 52:262.

90. Thomas Wilson (1563–1622), *A Christian Dictionary*, 2nd ed. (1616), 296.

91. Sir Harbottle Grimstone, *Mr Grimstones Speech in the High Court of Parliament* (1641), 6; hereafter cited as *High Court*.

92. Henry Burton, *Jesu-Worship Confuted* (1641), 9.

93. *Doctrine and Discipline of the Kirk of Scotland*, (1641), single sheet.

94. *Confession of Faith of the Kirk of Scotland Subscribed by the Kings Majestie . . . 1580 . . . And Subsribed by the Nobles . . . And Commons, in 1638* (1638), 4.

95. Jeremiah Burroughs, *An Exposition of Hosea* (1643).

96. John Tombes, *Fermentum Pharisaeorum; or, The Leaven of Pharisaicall Wil-Worship* (1643), 11.

97. SMECTYMNUUS: *A Vindication of the Answer to the Humble Remonstrance, from the Unjust Imputations of Frivolousnesse and Falsehood* (1641), 38; hereafter cited as *Vindication*.

98. Samuel Rutherford, *The Divine Right of Church-Government and Excommunication To which is added a briefe Tractate of Scandal* (1646), 96, margin.

99. Lord Brooke (Robert Greville), *A Discourse Opening the Nature of that Episcopacie which is Exercised in England* (1641), in *Tracts on Liberty in the Puritan Revolution 1638–1647*, ed. William Haller, 3 vols., reprint (New York: Octagon Books, 1979).

100. *CPW*, 1:585; compare Brooke, *Discourse*, 2:138; for another example of possible cross-influence, see chapter 2, note 24.

101. William Fiennes, Lord Saye and Seale, *Two speeches of the Right Honourable William Lord Say and Seale* (1641), 17.

102. Lewis Hewes, *Certain Grievances or Errours of the service Booke; Plainly Layd Open* (1640), 4.

103. *The Institution of Christian Religion. Written in Latine by M. John Calvine. Translated into English according to the authours last edition. . . . By Thomas Norton* (1634), 23.

104. Weigand, *Neutralibus*, 44.

105. In *Tudor Puritanism* (Chicago: University of Chicago Press, 1939), Marshall Knappen cites Bishop Gardner from 1543: "They speak so much of preaching so as all the gates of our senses and ways to man's understanding be shut up, saving the ear alone" (68). David Nordbook examines the relations among emerging Protestant conceptions of prophecy, preaching, poetry and authority in *Poetry and Politics in the English Renaissance* (London: Routledge & Kegan Paul, 1984). In "Milton's Classical Republicanism," Martin Dzelzainis cites Hobbes in his attack on the clergy, "who were able to 'pretend' that linguistic expertise endowed them with 'greater skill in Scriptures than other men have,'" enabling them "to 'impose' their 'own sense' of Scripture on their fellow-subjects" (in *Milton and Republicanism*, ed. David Armitage, Armand Himy and Quentin Skinner [Cambridge: Cambridge University Press, 1995], 3). A useful recent addition to the literature on the subject is Jameela Lares's impressive study, *Milton and the Preaching Arts* (Pittsburgh: Duquesne University Press, 2001).

106. Kevin Sharpe, *The Personal Rule of Charles I* (New Haven: Yale University Press, 1992), 385–89.

107. Edward Symmons, *A Loyall Subjects Beliefe, Expressed in a Letter to Master Stephen Marshall* (1643), 66.

108. James I of England and Ireland and VI of Scotland, *Directions for Preachers* (1622). For background on *The Directions* and "the particulars of circumstances" for Donne's sermon and others during this period, see the introduction to volume 4 of *The Sermons of John Donne* (Berkeley and Los Angeles: University of California Press), ed. George R. Potter and Evelyn Simpson, 10 vols., 4:23–28, 33–34; hereafter cited as *Donne* by volume and page number.

109. Ibid., 4:197.

110. William Haller, *The Rise of Puritanism* (New York: Columbia University Press, 1938; pb. ed. 1957), 230; hereafter cited as *Rise*.

111. Samuel Hieron, *The Dignity of Preaching* (1616), 20, 32.

112. Robert Bolton, *Three-Fold Treatise* (1634), 15,42.

113. *A Message of Peace: In a Letter Consolatorie and Conciliatorie but principally about the use of the Liturgie* (1642), 2.

114. Irvonwy Morgan, *Prince Charles's Puritan Chaplain* (1959), 109.

115. Hugh Trevor-Roper, *Men and Events: Historical Essays* (New York: Harper & Brothers,1957), 138; hereafter cited as *Essays*.

116. John Preston, "The Pattern of Wholesome Words; or, Pauls Charge to Timothy, in A Treatise on 2 *Tim*. 13. Being the sum of sundry Sermons Preached by the late faithful and worthy Minister of Jesus Christ," in *The Riches of Mercy To Men In Misery. Or Certain Excellent Treatises concerning the Dignity and duty of Gods Children. By the late . . . John Preston* (1658), 272–309; hereafter cited as *Pattern*.

117. Cornelius Burges, *The First Sermon Preached to the Honourable House of Commons Nov. 17, 1640/1641* (1641), 72–73, 75.

118. John Fenwick, [VNV], *The Downfall of the Pretended Divine Authoritie of the Hierarchy* (1641), 6.

119. Elizabeth Warren, *The Old and Good Way Vindicated* (1646), 5.

120. Robert Harris, "Prefaces to Bradford on Repentance" (Oxford, 1652), in Parker Society Publications, *The Writings of John Bradford* (Cambridge: Cambridge University Press, 1848), 34:561.

121. Thomas Case, *Two Sermons lately Preached at Westminster, before sundry of the Honourable House of Commons* (1641), 10–11.

122. *The Tender Conscience Religiously Affected* (1646), 1.

123. John Cotton, *A Modest and Cleare Answer To Mr Balls Discourse of set forms of Prayer* (1642), 19.

124. *Directory For The Publique Worship of God . . . Together with an ordinance of Parliament for the taking away of the Booke of Common-Prayer* (1645), 28, 34.

125. *The Humble Petition Of the Ministers of the Church of England desiring Reformation . . . with the Answer Of the Vicechancellor . . . of Oxford* (1641), 31.

126. Charles Herle, *A Fuller Answer to a Treatise Written by Doctor Ferne* (1642), 4; hereafter cited as *Fuller Answer.*

127. John Taylor, *A Swarme of Sectaries* (1641), 9, 15; hereafter cited as *Swarme.*

128. John Cleveland, *Poems 1653* (Menston, England: Scolar Press, 1971), 106.

129. John Harris, *The Puritanes Impuritie; or, The Anatomie of a Puritane or Seperatist, by Name and Profession* (1641), 4.

130. John Taylor, *New preachers, New* (1641), A2–A2v.

131. Martin Mar-priest [pseud. Richard Overton?], *Martin's Eccho; or, A Remonstrance, from . . . Young Martin Mar-Priest, responsorie to the late Sacred Synoddicall Decretall, in all humility presented to the . . . consideration of . . . Sir Simon Synod* (1645?), 24.

132. Miles Corbet, *A Most Learned and Eloquent Speech . . .* (Oxford, 1645), 2.

133. *A New Discovery of the Prelates Tyranny In their late persecutions of . . . Pryn . . . Bastwick . . . Burton* (1641), 30.

134. Scott Elledge, *Milton's Lycidas Edited to Serve as an Introduction to Criticism* (New York: Harper & Row, 1966), 207–19.

135. [Anonymous], *Wren's Anatomy* (1641), 7–8.

136. *A Very Lively Portrayture of the Archbishops of the Church of England* (1640), 29.

137. Henry Burton, *The Protestation Protested* (1641), sig. B3.

138. Simon Ash, *The Best Refuge for the Most Oppressed*, sermon, March 30, 1642, 60.

139. *Abstract of some late Characters . . . Characters of L. Bishops, Dumb Dogs, Non-residenciaries etc.* (1643), Av.

140. John Ruskin, *Sesame and Lilies*, ed. Robert Kilburn Root (New York: Henry Holt and Co., 1904), 134.

141. Douglas Bush, *English Literature in the Earlier Seventeenth Century: 1600–1660* (New York: Oxford University Press), 1945, 1.

142. Carol Barton, "They Also Perform the Duties of a Servant Who Only Remain Erect on their Feet in a Specified Place in Readiness to Receive Orders": The Dynamics of Stasis in Sonnet XIX ("When I Consider How My Light is Spent"), *Milton Quarterly* 32 (December 1998): 109–22.

143. William Riley Parker, *Milton's Contemporary Reputation: An Essay together with a Tentative List of Printed Allusions to Milton, 1641–74* (Columbus: Ohio State University Press, 1940), 61.

144. Joan Webber, *The Eloquent "I": Style and Self in Seventeenth-Century Prose* (Madison: University of Wisconsin Press, 1968).

145. Michael Lieb and John T. Shawcross, eds., *Achievements of the Left Hand: Essays on the Prose of John Milton* (Amherst: University of Massachusetts Press, 1974); hereafter cited as *Left Hand*.

146. See, especially, Christopher Hill, *The Century of Revolution (1603–1714)* (New York: Norton, 1961), and Hill, *Milton and the English Revolution* (London: Faber and Faber, 1977).

147. Among the most useful of these studies for me are David Loewenstein and James Grantham Turner's anthology *Politics*, and the works of Sharon Achinstein, Martin Dzelzainis, James Egan, David Loewenstein, David Norbrook, Nigel Smith, Barbara K. Lewalski, John N. King, and especially Thomas Corns, listed in these notes. In addition, I have found both Lana Cable's *Carnal Rhetoric: Milton's Iconoclasm and the Poetics of Desire* (Durham, N.C.: Duke University Press, 1995), and Reuben Sanchez Jr., *Persona and Decorum in Milton's Prose* (Madison, N.J., 1997), valuable and informative.

148. Thomas N. Corns, ed., *The Literature of Controversy: Polemical Strategy from Milton to Junius* (London: Frank Cass, 1987), 1.

149. J. Martin Evans, "The Birth of the Author: Milton's Poetic Self-

Construction," in *Milton Studies*, vol. 38, ed. Albert C. Labriola and Michael Lieb, 47–65 (Pittsburgh: University of Pittsburgh Press, 2000), 63. Evans's essay concentrates on the poetry, but its conclusions are useful to my inquiry.

150. Annabel Patterson, *Early Modern Liberalism* (Cambridge: Cambridge University Press, 1997), 15.

Notes to Chapter Two

1. In *Davids Zeale for Zion* (1641), Thomas Wilson cites the three usual crises, "we were near going in 88. neare a blow by the Powder-treason; and how nigh was our trouble these two last yeares" (16; "1639–1640" in margin), as does D. F., *The equallity of the ministery plainly described* (1641). Some of the celebrators omit one or other of the preceding "miracles" as, for example, Ezekias Woodward's *The Churches Thank-Offering To God Her King, and The Parliament Wrought with God the first Wonderfull Yeare (since the Yeare 88) . . .* (1642). By 1645, in *A Sacred Record To be made of Gods Mercies To Zion: A Thanksgiving Sermon . . .*, Stephen Marshall advises Parliament to "looke upon it as a duty they owe unto God, and to the present and future age, to provide that these glorious and admirable works which God hath done for *England* and *Scotland*, since the beginning of our troubles, may faithfully bee transmitted to posterity" (31).

2. See the anonymous *Many Wonderful and Very Remarkable Passages* (1642).

3. William Riley Parker gives the details of Milton's return from the Italian journey and his probable recruitment by Thomas Young in *Milton: A Biography*, 2 vols. (Oxford: Clarendon Press, 1968), 1:174–97; hereafter cited as Parker. On the return, see also Lewalski, *Life*, 28.

4. The Smectymnuan controversy is most conveniently discussed in *CPW*, 1:76–86. For Milton's participation, see *CPW*, 1:123–28 and 203–8.

5. In an article kindly forwarded to me while I was copy-editing this study, David L. Hoover and Thomas N. Corns

> broadly endorse the received critical position. . . . [They] hypothesize that Milton had supplied the Smectymnuans with detailed notes that he expected them to use in the body of their text to supplement their refutation; they decided against doing so in order to retain the close engagement with Hall's pamphlet; and they relegated his material to an appendix, where it was printed more or less in the form in which he had supplied it, without the kinds of revision appropriate before publication.

See David L. Hoover and Thomas N. Corns, "The Authorship of the Postscript to *An Answer to a Booke Entituled, An Humble Remonstrance,*" *Milton Quarterly* 38, no. 2 (May 2004): 70. Their stylometric study does not, however, support my conjecture in chapter 4 of this study that the section "To the Postscript" in the succeeding Smectymnuan pamphlet, *A Vindication of the answer to the Humble Remonstrance* (1641, 216–19), is also primarily by Milton ("Authorship," 71).

6. See Parker (*Milton* 1:197) and John T. Shawcross, *John Milton: The Self and the World* (Lexington: University Press of Kentucky, 1993), 17; hereafter cited as *Self*.

7. Don Wolfe quotes Will T. Hale, the early and still useful editor of *Of Reformation* (New Haven: Yale University Press, 1916), as finding Milton "unfair to the prelates but not dishonest"; nor, says Hale, does he "misquote in order to twist an argument" (*CPW*, 1:515). I would put it more strongly: Milton is remarkably fair, certainly for his time, in using his opponents' texts, with scrupulous accuracy in quotation and proper order of arguments. The charge of wrenching out of context should be balanced by Milton's careful citation and assumption of the opposing text as before the reader. Other useful treatments of the tract: Michael Lieb, "Milton's *Of Reformation* and the Dynamics of Controversy," in *Left Hand*; Janel Mueller, "Embodying Glory; The Apocalyptic Strain in Milton's *Of Reformation,*" in *Politics*, 9–40; Joan Webber, *The Eloquent "I,"* 184–218, probably the finest commentary on the antiprelatical tracts; Thomas N. Corns, "The Freedom of Reader-Response: Milton's *Of Reformation* and Lilburne's *The Christian Mans Triall,*" in Roger Richardson and G. M. Ridden, eds., *Freedom and the English Revolution* (Manchester: Manchester University Press, 1986), 93–110.

8. "Milton's Prose," in *The Cambridge Companion to Milton,* ed. Dennis Danielson (Cambridge: Cambridge University Press, 1987), 195; hereafter cited as "Prose."

9. David Loewenstein, *Milton and the Drama of History* (Cambridge: Cambridge University Press, 1990), 14, 16, 20; hereafter cited as *Drama*.

10. David Norbrook, *Writing the English Republic: Poetry, Rhetoric and Politics 1627–1660* (Cambridge: Cambridge University Press, 1999), 112.

11. Carol Barton has reminded me of the allusion here to Arthur's "warlike shield . . . all of diamond perfect pure and clean . . . hewn out of adamant rock" in *The Faerie Queene,* 1.7.33, of which "no magic arts . . . had any might / Nor bloody words of bold enchanter's call / But all that was not such as seemed in sight / Before that shield did fade and sudden fall" (1.7.35).

12. W. Barlow, *"To a deputation of Presbyterians from the Church of Scotland, seeking religious tolerance in England,"* in *Sum and Substance of the Conference* (1604), 82.

13. Janel Mueller, "Contextualizing Milton's Nascent Republicanism," in *Of Poetry and Politics: New Essays on Milton and His World*, ed. P. G. Stanwood (Binghamton, N.Y.: Medieval and Renaissance Texts, 1995), 263–82; compare Lewalski, *Life*, 122.

14. Alexander Leighton, *An Appeal to the Parliament; or, Sions Plea against the Prelacie* (1628), 56.

15. John Bale, *King John* (ca. 1535).

16. See, for example, the following: for Becket, William Crashaw, *The Jesuites Gospel* (1610), 22; reprinted in 1641 as *The Bespotted Jesuit*; the anonymous *A Canterburie Tale Transcribed* (1641); J. M., *Newes from Hell . . .* (1641), 22; [Anonymous], *Bishops, Judges, Monopolists* (1641), 1.

For Bale's *King John* and for the anonymous *Troublesome Reign* and Shakespeare's play, see Herschel Baker, in *The Riverside Shakespeare*, ed. Anne Barton, J. J. Tobin and Herschel Baker (New York, 1997), 766, who argues that Shakespeare resisted the tradition of King John as Protestant martyr. For Wolsey and Wolsey/Laud, see Thomas Wilson, *Jerichos Downfall* (1642), 11; and the anonymous *A true Description or Rather a Parallel betweene Cardinall Wolsey . . . and William Laud* (1641).

17. *A Maske Presented at Ludlow-Castle, etc.* (1634), in *The Riverside Milton*, 132–33.

18. Thomas Fuller, *The Holy State* (1642), cited in *CPW*, 1:532, n. 56.

19. Lord Brooke in *Tracts 2*, 56; see also Smectymnuus, *An Answer*, 5.

20. John Lilburne, *An Answer to Nine Arguments Written by T. B.* (1644), 33.

21. William Haller, *Rise of Puritanism*, 66.

22. Richard Sibbes, "Violence Victorious," in *Beames of Divine Light* (1639), 251.

23. Obadiah Sedgwick, *Haman's Vanity . . . Sermon* (1643), 2. Milton is also joined by Sir Harbottle Grimstone, who echoes Milton's parable (with different medical protocol):

> it fares with a body politique, as it doth with a body naturall; It is impossible to cure an ulcerous body, unlesse you first cleanse the veines, and purge the body from those obstructions, and pestilentiall humours that overcharge Nature, and being once done too, botches, blaines, and scabs, that grew upon the superficies and outside of the body, dry up, shed , and fall away, of themselves. (*Master Grimstone His Worthy and Learned Speech . . . Shewing the Inward Symptoms and Causes of all our feares and Dangers*, 1642), 2

I suspect, too, that John Vicars had read *Of Reformation* before he wrote of the prelates as enemies of the church: "their *big-swoln tympanie* of insufferable *pride* and *arrogancie* to be turned into a *flashie ignis fatuus* of *self-deceiving subtilitie* and changing all their *vaporous-puffs* of gross impiety into *folly* and *madness"* (in *God in the Mount, Or Englands Remembrancer* [1642], 55; hereafter cited as *Remembrancer*).

Laud was not always merely "smeared'; some of his opponents offered what they construed as hard evidence of his evil nature, as in the anonymous *A Prophecie of the Life, Reigne, and Death of William Laud, Archbishop of Canterbury* (1644), 5:

> W. Is V. twice, that is 10
> I is a figure of 1
> LL is twice 50. that is 100
> L is once 50
> A is no numeral number
> V is 5. more 5
> D stands for 500
>
> which in all amounts to the just summe of 666
> And thus you see that *Will. Laud* Archbishop of *Canterbury,* both by his actions, and also by his name, appears to be the Beast here spoken of, called by *John another Beast:* verse 11. (Citing Revelation 13 and 5)

24. In "Milton's Wen," *Prose Studies* 19 (December 1996): 221–37, Roy Sellars does a theoretical excursus on Milton's use of the fable, with some serious, and I think strained, conclusions about Milton as author and as persona. He does not mention Laud; but he does cite Annabel Patterson's suggestion that the fable is "evidently a figure of the Long Parliament" and the wen itself is "Milton's representation of the Anglican Bishops in the House of Lords," in *Fables of Power: Aesopian Writing and Political History* (Durham, N.C., 1991), 129. Perhaps my reading of a single "corrupt" advisor might aid in the dating of this pamphlet. Strafford, the other chief influence on Charles, was executed on May 12, leaving Laud as the chief villain. External evidence puts the date of publication as somewhere between April 24 and May 31. The last two weeks of May might be more exact (see *CPW,* 1:514).

25. Thomas N. Corns, "Obscenity, Slang and Indecorum in Milton's English Prose," *Prose Studies* 3 (1980): 5–14; hereafter cited as "Obscenity."

26. Stanley Fish's essay on Milton's uses and "abuses" of reason in *The Reason of Church-Government,* "Reason in *The Reason of Church Government,"* in *Self-Consuming Artifacts* (Berkeley and Los Angeles: University of California Press, 1972), 265–302, was widely influential and serves as a sort of preface to *How Milton Works* (Cambridge: Harvard University Press, 2001), hereafter cited as *HMW;* the hypothesis is a critical part of Fish's whole study and will be addressed below.

27. Lord Brooke may be part of the networking here. In *A Worthy Speech Made by . . . Lord Brooke . . . at Warwick Castle, Feb. 26, 1643,* he speaks of "these vipers, who would knaw a passage to their ambitions throgh the intralls of their mother the Commonwealth"; on the following page, he notes "Refugees" who would meet you like a Roman matron and "aske if they thought to creepe againe into their mothers wombs and hide themselves" (4–5).

28. As in Keith Stavely, *The Politics of Milton's Prose Style* (New Haven: Yale University Press, 1975). Obviously I disagree with Stavely's argument that "an exalted 'poetic' texture limits the political effectiveness of Milton's prose instead of extending and enriching it" (2).

Notes to Chapter Three

1. The full title is *Of Prelatical Episcopacy, and Whether it may be deduc'd from the Apostolical times by vertue of those Testimonies which are alleg'd to that purpose in some late Treatises: One whereof goes under the Name of Iames Arch-Bishop Of Armagh.* It was published in June or July of 1641. The text cited here is in vol. 2 of *CPW.*

2. Joseph Hall, Bishop of Ely, *Episcopacie by Divine Right Asserted* (1640); "Peloni Almoni," *A Compendious Discourse, Proving episcopacie to be of Apostolical and Consequently of Divine Institution* (1641); James Ussher, Archbishop of Armagh, *The Judgement of Doctor Reignolds Concerning Episcopacy, more largely confirmed out of antiquity* (1641, after an earlier edition also published in 1641).

3. Twenty years ago I wrote that the battle was "won in the first twenty lines" ("Words," 154). I did not then nor do I now think that the rest of the text is "unnecessary and dangerous" (Fish, *HMW,* 217), nor is it even embarrassed about its presumption. Nor can I agree with Stanley Fish that sufficiency of Scripture proves, or even categorically implies, the insufficiency of Milton's arguments. One can accept Fish's demonstrations of Milton's extraordinary use of polarities and downright contradictions, yet still disallow the argument that the tract is devoted to its own ideational stasis, "all dressed up with nowhere to go" (*HMW,* 222). The arguments below suggest that the tract does in fact go somewhere: to the analysis of evidence and the making of judgments devolved from Scripture but of value in themselves. Against the brilliance of Fish's theoretical arguments one poses the brilliance and persistence of Milton's presentation of evidence for his position and against the prelatical position. We simply, and I quite gladly, subdue his contradictions within the larger argument as part of a quite normal procedure for the writing and the reading of political argument: stringent analysis of the opponent's evidence and plausible presentation of one's own. *Of Prelatical Episcopacy* is an attack on prelatical authority and the

traditional sources behind that authority. It is not a confession of the uselessness of the author's presentation or of all human language.

4. Parker, *Milton*, 1:202–4; J. Max Patrick, *CPW*, 1:618–22, and notes 624–52.

5. Hugh Trevor-Roper, *Catholics, Anglicans and Puritans: Seventeenth Century Essays* (London: Secker and Warburg, 1987), 120–65; hereafter cited as *Catholics*.

6. *Vox Hibernae; or, Rather the voyce of the Lord from Ireland. A Sermon Preached in St. Peters Westminster*, December 22, 1641. Thomason's manuscript comment in the British Library copy: "a disavowed and most false copie."

7. *The Copy of A Most Pithy and Pious Letter. . . . to James Usher to persuade our King to return to His Parliament*, 1645.

8. *The Character of an Oxford Incendiary* (1645), 4.

9. John Vicars, *Gods Arke Overtopping the Worlds Wares; or, The Third Part of the Parliamentary Chronicle* (1645), 153.

10. *True Informer*, no. 34 (December 6–13, 1645), 271.

11. *The Scotish Dove*, no. 113 (December 10–17, 1645), 895.

12. Hugh Trevor-Roper, "The Elitist Politics of Milton," *TLS*, no. 3717 (June 1, 1973), 601; Trevor-Roper drops the "obscene" when he expands this essay in *Catholics*, 253.

13. Eusebius, *The History of the Church from Christ to Constantine*, trans. G. A. Williamson (Baltimore, 1967), 227.

14. See, for example, Laurence Womock, *Beaten oyle for the lamps of the sanctvarie; or, The great controversies concerning set prayers and our liturgie, . . . Unto which are added some usefull observations touching Christian libertie, and things indifferent* (1641), sigs B and R and Hooker, *Ecclesiastical Polity*, 5:3.

15. John Bastwick, *The Answer of John Bastwick, Doctor of Physicke . . . To the Information of Sir John Bancks Knight, Atturney Universall* (1637), 13, 17.

16. Carole Kessner has pointed out to me the sophisticated verbal play and directed me to the Hebrew Testament, in which *Bosheth* has multiple meanings: "shame, blushing, ignominy; an idol." See the *Hebrew-English Lexicon of the Bible* (New York: Schocken Books, 1975), 34, 44.

Notes to Chapter Four

1. This chapter is an expansion of my earlier essay, "Style and Rectitude in Seventeenth Century Prose: Hall, Smectymnuus, and Milton," *The Huntington Library Quarterly* (Summer 1983): 237–69. At the time of publication I had not read Richard McCabe's excellent "The

Form and Methods of Milton's *Animadversions Upon the Remonstrants Defence Against Smectymnuus,*" *English Language Notes,* 18, no. 4 (1981): 266–72. Mr. McCabe precedes me in a number of important points concerning this debate, as his concluding statement will show: "The devastating style and methods of the *Animadversions,* suggested ironically by the techniques of Hall's *Apologie* of 1610, were designed to counteract the effect of the bishop's powerful rhetoric on the Episcopal debate by treating him as disrespectfully as he had treated his opponents" (272).

2. But see note 5 of my chapter 2 above.

3. A convenient summary of the Smectymnuan-Hall controversy is the introductory material in volume 1 of *CPW,* 75–86, and, for Milton's participation, 203–8.

4. See Frank L. Huntley's ascription to Robert Durkin in Huntley, *Bishop Joseph Hall, 1574–1656: A Biographical and Critical Study* (Cambridge: Cambridge University Press, 1969), 111.

5. David Masson, *The Life of John Milton,* 7 vols. (1894; new and revised edition, Gloucester, Mass., 1965), 2:124; hereafter cited as "Masson."

6. Bishop Joseph Hall, *Certaine Irrefragable Propositions* (1639), 1; hereafter cited as *Propositions.*

7. Hall, *The Reconciler An epistle pacificatorie of the seeming-differences of opinion concerning the truenesse and visibility of the Roman Church . . . enlarged . . .* (1629), 1, 37.

8. Joseph Hall, *The Honour of the Married Clergie Maintained Against . . . C.E.* (1621), in *The Works of Joseph Hall* (1634), 687, 719, 721.

9. Sir Edward Dering, *A Collection of Speeches 1641 (speech delivered 18 Dec., 1640)* (1641), 111–12; hereafter cited as *Collection.*

10. Huntley, *Bishop Joseph Hall, 1574–1656,* 67. In a review of Richard A. McCabe's *Joseph Hall: A Study in Satire and Meditation,* C. H. Sisson notes with less approval, "It is difficult to see this lump of Puritanism, chosen by Laud to defend episcopacy because of the known depth of his prejudice, was not acting with an eye on his position in the world when he made the alterations which Laud required. He was the sort of man who would—a man of moderation certainly, but liable to be confused by the complexity of the real world" ("Pervasively Prejudiced," *TLS,* December 3, 1982, 1332).

11. *A Modest Confutation of a Slanderous and Scurrilous Libell, Entituled, Animadversions* (1642); hereafter cited as *Confutation.*

12. *The seuen vials or a briefe and plaine exposition vpon the 15: and 16: chapters of the Revelation, very pertinent and profitable for the Church of God in these last times* by H. B. Rector of Saint Matthews Friday-street (1628), 28; hereafter cited as *Seuen Vials.*

13. Robert Butterfield, *Maschi; or, A Treatise to Give Instruction . . . for the Vindication of the . . . Bishop of Exeter, from the cavills of H. B. in . . . The Seven Vialls* (1629), 78–79.

14. J. A. St. John, ed., *The Prose Works of John Milton*, 5 vols. (London: Bohn, 1848–1853), 3:42.

15. This includes the general editor, Don Wolfe, as well as the editors of the individual tracts, Rudolf Kirk and Frederick L. Taft. See *CPW*, 1:123–25, 653–56, 866. Rudolf Kirk's view of Hall as "this peace-loving Bishop" is best shown in "A Seventeenth Century Controversy: Extremism vs. Moderation," *Texas Studies in Literature and Language* 9 (1967): 31.

16. For the emergence of the newspaper as a medium, see Nigel Smith, "Public Fora," chapter 2 of *Literature and Revolution*, esp. 54–70.

17. Arnold Stein, *Answerable Style* (Seattle: University of Washington Press, 1967), 67.

18. Barbara K. Lewalski, "Innocence and Experience in Milton's Eden," in *New Essays on Paradise Lost*, ed. Thomas Kranidas (Berkeley and Los Angeles: University of California Press, 1969), 117.

19. Kirk, "A Seventeenth Century Controversy."

20. Joseph Hall, Bishop of Norwich, *Episcopacie by divine right, asserted* (1640).

21. Joseph Hall, Bishop of Norwich, *An Humble Remonstrance to the High Court of Parliament* (1641).

22. Henry Burton, *The Protestation Protested* (1641), B2v.

23. *An Anti-Remonstrance to the Humble Remonstrance* (1641), 1.

24. John Vicars, *God in the Mount; or, Englands Remembrancer* (1642), 71

25. *"Dwalphintramis"* [pseud], *The Anatomy of the Service Book* (1641), A3v.

26. John Ley, *Sunday a Sabbath, 1641*, b2.

27. Joseph Hall, *A Short Answer To the Tedious Vindications of SMECTYMNUUS* (1641); hereafter cited as *Short Answer*.

28. Hall, *Christian Moderation* (1640), 122, in *Works*, 4:122.

29. An amusing but revealing instance of Hall's care for his polemical image is found in the first printing of the *Defence*. On page 52, Hall had written, "Pardon me, brethren if I thinke Mr. *Calvin* was more skilled in the harmony of Scripture then our selves." In the "Errata" (168), he had changed *ourselves* on page 52, line 6, to *themselves*. SMECTYM-NUUS shrewdly picked this up as an example of Hall's vanity: "For though we grant indeed Master *Calvin* was more skilled in the harmony *then ourselves*, (the *Remonstrant* might have let it passe so without putting it among his *Errata*, turning it to *themselves*)" (*Vindication*, 71). No fool, Hall corrected all the errata in the second printing except for the *ourselves*, which he let stand. I suspect he recognized that the

emendation would have confirmed the Smectymnuan suggestion of vanity.

Two points can be made. First, Hall moved quickly and seriously as a polemicist, reading the opposition immediately and eliminating weaknesses in his defense of self. The second is conjectural. Milton read the first printing of Hall's *Defence*, as his scrupulous citing of page numbers proves. Could the missing four pages of *Animadversions* have included an attack on Hall's fatuous erratum? In that case, the second printing of *A Defence*, with its retention of the original *ourselves*, would have gutted Milton's argument on that point. Milton canceled a passage of 1,600 words because the issue he was arguing—Hall's vanity vis-à-vis Calvin—had evaporated.

30. Frank Huntley sees the origin of the "abusive rhetoric" in Milton's exchanges with Hall and the Confuter as "Milton's original *persona* in the *Animadversions*" (160, n. 16). I see it rather in Hall's earlier pose of adversarial superiority, a mix of arrogance and false modesty.

31. Hall is mentioned only once by name in the early tracts, in a wry passage from this piece citing the Remonstrant's reference: "D. Hall whom you name, I dare say for honors sake," the Animadverter responds "Y'are a merry man sir, and dare say much" (*CPW*, 1:678).

32. J. Milton French, "Milton as Satirist," *PMLA* 51 (1936): 52.

33. Hugh Cholmley, *The State of the Now-Romane Church* (1629).

34. See *A Relation of the Conference Between William Laud, Then Lord Bishop of St Davids; Now Lord Arch-Bishop of Canterbury; and Mr. Fisher the Jesuite . . .*, cited in chapter 1, note 60.

35. Maureen Thum, "Milton's Diatribal Voice: The Integration and Transformation of a Generic Paradigm in *Animadversions*," in *Milton Studies*, vol. 30, edited by Albert C. Labriola (Pittsburgh: University of Pittsburgh Press, 1993), 3–25, argues that Milton is consciously using "a popular and literary paradigm which has escaped the attention of literary critics: that of the Cynic-Stoic diatribe" (3). The descriptions of the genre are valuable, especially for my purposes, in pointing out the differences with the Platonic dialogue (3–10). I agree with Thum that *Animadversions* is not "a spontaneous and vengeful personal attack, characterized by inconsistency and lack of control" (4); I still think there are moments of gratuitous ugliness unmitigated by generic expectations. I would agree with, and still question, the statement that the piece is not "a work to be understood solely within the relatively restricted context of contemporary polemical pamphlets." There is no *sole* context for any of Milton's works and very few claims of such. And I would hope that my study has suggested that "the context of contemporary polemical discourse" was not all that restricted.

36. Nigel Smith, *Literature and Revolution*, 41, thinks that Milton makes Hall "seem slightly nutty" by quoting him out of context; I would

answer that the "nuttiness" is shared, as in Milton's answer in the passage Smith cites. And I would still argue that Milton is closer to accuracy in citing his opponents than his opponents are in citing him.

37. Other possible echoes of this play are on *CPW*, 1:666, 669.

38. This passage seems to echo Bacon's *Wise and Moderate Discourse* (1641) which Milton had cited two pages earlier. The use of language as scalpel is common. In *Discourse*, Bacon uses it negatively on pp. 7 and 8, as I have noted in chapter 1, and positively, as curative, on p. 6: "it is meet the remedies bee applied unto them by opening up what is in either part that keepeth the wound greene." Scripture becomes retaliatory, and the ultimate probing instrument for Daniel Dyke when he praises "the anatomizing knife of the Word, and ripping up the belly of this Monster [deceitfulness]" (*The Mystery of Selfe-Deception* [1634], 12).

39. This quotation comes from section 9 of Hall's *Answer*, the only one, I believe, from sections 6–12 of the Bishop's tract. On the mysterious cancel in *Animadversions* of signature G, a half-sheet, see W. R. Parker, "A Cancel in an Early Milton Tract," *Library* 15 (1934): 243–46.

40. Ronald Brownrigg, *Who's Who in the New Testament* (San Francisco 1971), 417.

41. John Downame, *Christian Warfare*, 4th ed. (1634), 340.

42. John Calvin, *Commentary Upon the Acts of the Apostles*, ed. Henry Beveridge (Edinburgh, 1844), 1:331.

43. Exhaustively explored in John M. Steadman's "*Paradise Lost:* The Devil and Pharaoh's Chivalry: Etymological and Typological Imagery and Renaissance Chronography," in *Nature into Myth: Medieval and Renaissance Moral Symbols* (Pittsburgh: Duquesne University Press, 1979), 185–212.

44. Fish's whole discussion of these tracts is so brilliantly assured that it is a little risky to disagree. But the insistence on reading Milton's "carnal" as subsuming Milton's total conception of the human allows for too many omissions of pity, concern and sensitivity in these very tracts. There are too many *sheer* judgments of opposed conceptions, too little accommodation to the spectrum of ideas and feelings in Milton's presentation of human rationality, human experience. See especially part 2 of *How Milton Works*, for example, pp. 253–55.

45. Obviously the issue borders on Milton's potential misogyny; I will not engage that issue fully here. I will say that Milton's trouble with female authority seems to me to stem from the view of *concession* by the male rather than *usurpation* by the female.

46. Sharon Achinstein, *Milton and the Revolutionary Reader* (Princeton: Princeton University Press, 1994), 162.

47. See Isaiah 524; Jeremiah 23.28; Malachi 4.1, Matthew 3.12; Luke 3.17.

48. A check of Leighton's *Sions Plea . . .* (1628) and Prynne's *A Breviate of the Prelates Intolerable Usurpations* (1637) corroborates Milton's

claim that "the collection was taken . . . from as authentique authors in this Kinde, as any in a Bishops library" (*CPW*, 1:730).

Notes to Chapter Five

1. In Donne, of course, the "Holy Sonnets" and the "Hymns." In Herbert, see esp. "The Thanksgiving" and "The Reprisall." See *The Poems of John Donne*, 2 vols., ed. H. J. C. Grierson (Oxford: Clarendon Press, 1958), 1:322–31, 352, 368–70; *The Works of George Herbert*, ed. F. E. Hutchinson (Oxford: Clarendon, 1941), 35–37.

2. For influential arguments, see Richard Helgerson, *Self-Crowned Laureates: Spenser, Jonson, Milton, and the Literary System* (Berkeley and Los Angeles: University of California Press, 1983).

3. Andrew Marvell, *The Poems & Letters of Andrew Marvell*, 2 vols., 2nd ed., ed. H. M. Margoliouth (Oxford: Clarendon Press, 1967), 1:14.

4. Joseph Hall, *Christ Mysticall; or, The blessed Union of Christ and his Members* (1647), 9–11.

5. Mark Kishlansky, *A Monarchy Transformed: Britain 1603–1714*, no. 6, *Penguin History of Britain Series*, David Cannadine, gen. ed. (London: Penguin Books, 1997), 134–35. In chapter 4 of *Eikonoklastes*, "The Insolency of the Tumults," Milton vigorously attacks Charles's recounting of demonstrations by the *"the wild Beasts . . . that had overborn all Loyalty, Modesty Laws, Justice, and Religion."* Milton's closing comment: "God save the people from such Intercessors" (*CPW*, 3:397).

6. See Knappen, *Tudor Puritanism* and Norbrook, *Poetry*, chap. 1, n. 99.

7. Thomas Corns, "Milton and the Characteristics of a Free Commonwealth," in *Milton and Republicanism*, ed. David Armitage, Armand Himy, and Quentin Skinner (Cambridge: Cambridge University Press, 1995); see also the essays by Dzelzainis, Brown and Tuttle in the same volume. Compare this with Corns's earlier "Milton's Quest for Respectability," *Modern Language Review* 77 (1977): 769–79, and Janel Mueller, "Contextualizing Milton's Nascent Republicanism."

8. This outrage at being excluded is shared by William Prynne: "And indeed such Ceremonies hedge in and fence his Romish Religion, while in the mean time they hedge out the true Religion" (*Lords Bishops*, 1640), 54.

9. Even in the *Prolusions*, there is a rather brave exposure of self and an expectation of reaching his listeners. How ironic is the close of Prolusion 7? "[I]f I have perchance spoken at much greater length than is customary in this place, not forgetting that this was demanded by the importance of the subject, you will, I hope, pardon me, my judges, since it is one more proof of the interest I feel in you, of my zeal in your

behalf, and of the nights of toil and wakefulness I consented to endure for your sakes. I have done" (*CPW*, 1:306).

10. Hugh Trevor-Roper's attack on Milton's arrogance ignores what I have been emphasizing here: numerous attempts by the righteous man to contain his self-righteousness. See *Catholics*, 235–44. Trevor-Roper is positively Johnsonian in his attitude toward Milton. On the one hand, he admires the antiprelatical tracts: "as literature what wonderful works they are!" (253); but Milton the man is "an insufferably priggish undergraduate," who later "crow[s] at challenging Ussher" (142, 150), and "uttered no squeak of protest" at Cromwell's purges (271); "his magniloquence, alas, was never matched by his magnanimity" (267). I disagree. I disagree, too, with Stanley Fish, who finds "Milton's aggressive assertion of humility" an unresolved problem arising from his wish to be "God's mouthpiece" (Fish's term in *HMW*, 6). As I consider Fish's term, "God's mouthpiece" is not so far from the "kerygmatic authority" I claim for Milton in chapter 6. I deeply admire Fish's analysis of the ways Milton works, and I admire the ways in which Fish constructs Milton's intellectual life of strenuous distinctions. But I think he neglects Milton's serious, if sometimes awkward, attempts at accommodation, accommodation to his own limitations and to those of his readers, often construed as a broad, and certainly nonacademic, community. The "strenuous distinctions" sometimes bend to the need for accommodation to human, and humane, weakness.

11. In "Milton among the Religious Radicals," in *Milton Studies*, vol. 40, ed. Albert C. Labriola (Pittsburgh: University of Pittsburgh Press, 2001), 222–47, David Loewenstein has written that, in *The Reason of Church-Government*, Milton is "maintaining a certain aloofness with regard to contemporary radical groups and writers—and refusing to profess allegiance to any one group in his controversial writings" as possibly "an intentional tactic" (223). Loewenstein's essay works convincingly with Milton's "silence" and "aloofness" vis-à-vis radical groups. The instance of shattered aloofness that I cite is a more "personal" instance of a way of performing in the public arena with a reserve of resources and the maintenance of certain barriers. Milton, for example, will *not* plead humility.

12. F. R. Leavis, *Revaluation* (1936; reprint, London: Chatto & Windus, 1959); consider "a guileless unawareness of the subtleties of egotism," 58.

13. Milton openly chides the Confuter in the middle of the *Apology* "for having all this while abus'd the good name of his adversary [Milton himself] with all manner of licence in revenge of his Remonstrant, if they be not both one person, or as I am told, Father and Son" (*CPW*, 1:897).

14. Pierre Du Moulin, *Regii Sanguinis Clamor ad Coelum adversus Parricides Anglicanos* (The Hague, 1652). Selections from this text,

translated by Paul Blackford, are printed in vol. 4, pt. 2, of the *Complete Prose Works*, 1042–81.

15. I suspect it is Milton to whom the Bishop, identified by Thomason's manuscript note as Hall, refers in the plaintive *A Letter Lately sent by A Reverend Bishop From The Tower* (1642): "Can any man pretend to a ground of taxing me (as I perceive one of late hath most unjustly done)" (5) from "A miserably misguided zeal!" (11).

16. Stephen Fallon, "The Spur of Self-Concernment: Milton in His Divorce Tracts," in *Milton Studies*, vol. 38, *John Milton: The Writer in His Works*, ed. Albert C. Labriola and Michael Lieb (Pittsburgh: University of Pittsburgh Press, 2000), 220.

17. John S. Diekhoff, *Milton on Himself* (1939; reprint, New York: Humanities Press, 1965).

18. William Riley Parker, *Milton: A Biography*, 2 vols. (Oxford: Clarendon Press, 1968), revised by Gordon Campbell (New York: Oxford University Press, 1996).

19. David Masson's *The Life of John Milton: Narrated in Connexion with the Political, Ecclesiastical, and Literary History of His Time*, 7 vols. (London, 1881–1894; reprint, Gloucester, Mass.: Peter Smith, 1965). John Crowe Ransom's essay is available in *Milton's Lycidas: The Tradition and the Poem*, ed. C. A. Patrides (New York, 1961), 64–81; William Kerrigan, *The Sacred Complex* (Cambridge, Mass.: Harvard University Press, 1983). John T. Shawcross, *John Milton: The Self and the World* (Lexington: University Press of Kentucky, 1993).

20. Albert C. Labriola, introduction to *Milton Studies* 38, *John Milton: The Writer in His Works*, 1–2.

21. John Spencer Hill, "Poet-Priest: Vocational Tension in Milton's Early Development," in *Milton Studies*, vol. 8, ed. James D. Simmonds (Pittsburgh: University of Pittsburgh Press, 1975), 46–59.

22. This pause in the midst of scurrility to accuse the opponent of incorrect use of language is one of the Puritan weapons against the prelatical claim on a monopoly of learning. Even Marprelate accuses his opponent Bridges of "a style as smooth as a crabtree cudgel. . . . there be not three whole periods for every page that is not graced with a very fair and visible solecism." See the "Epitome" in William Pierce, *The Marprelate Tracts 1588, 1589* (London: James Clarke, 1913), 123, 124.

23. Milton did not always agree with William Prynne, but here he echoes Prynne's comments on academic "playing." In the second part of *Histrio-mastix* (1633) Prynne claims that arguments against popular plays stand also against academical. In fact, academic playing is worse in giving authority to the popular. Here Milton seems to agree with part of Prynne's argument, that "Acting of plays disables one from receiving Sacred Orders" (*Histrio-mastix; or, The Players Scourge and Actors Tragedy* [1633], 847, 867).

24. The only other early use, according to the *OED*, is from Tom

May's *Satires* (1657)—and suggestive: "Her being starv'd . . . and her Fort vanquisht by an unboned Member (the Tongue)."

25. John Leonard, *Naming in Paradise: Milton and the Language of Adam and Eve* (Oxford: Clarendon Press, 1990), 292.

26. William Kerrigan, *The Prophetic Milton* (Charlottesville: University Press of Virginia, 1974), 13.

27. Lysimachus Nicanor [John Corbet], *The Epistle Congratulatorie of Lysimachus Nicanor* (1640); *A Survay of that foolish, seditious, scandalous, profane libell the Protestation Protested* (1641).

28. Milton nowhere mentions John Donne, yet in his "correcting" of the Confuter's use of *stars* and *Horizon* (*Confutation*, 24), he may be referring to Donne's cautionary sermon on preaching, which I have noted in chapter 1, and which Milton could have heard.

29. R. P., *A True Inventory of the Goods and A true inventory of the chattels of Superstition* (1642), 3.

Notes to Chapter Six

1. K. G. Hamilton, "The Structure of Milton's Prose," in *Language and Style in Milton's Prose,* ed. Ronald David Emma and John T. Shawcross (New York: Frederick Ungar, 1967), 329.

2. Stanley Fish, *Self-Consuming Artifacts: The Experience of Seventeenth Century Literature* (Berkeley and Los Angeles: University of California Press, 1972), 271; hereafter cited as *Artifacts.*

3. The preface speaks of setting laws forth "to the people without reason or Preface"; of the Jews "knowing so good a reason of their obedience" and of "their understanding in the reason of that government" as well as "the mind where the seat of reason is" (*CPW,* 1:747). Clearly the first two uses stand for evidence, the third is ambiguous and the fourth means process.

4. See Regina Schwartz, *Remembering & Repeating: On Milton's Theology and Poetics* (Chicago: University of Chicago Press, 1995), especially the section on "Ritual Recompense" in chapter 3, 66–77.

5. I have offered a conjecture on this in chapter 2, n. 23.

6. E. M. W. Tillyard, *Milton* (London: Chatto & Windus, 1930), quoted in *CPW,* 1:753, n. 20.

7. Annabel Patterson, "The Civic Hero in Milton's Prose," in *Milton Studies,* vol. 8, ed. James D. Simmonds (Pittsburgh: University of Pittsburgh Press, 1975), 80–82.

8. Sanford Budick, *The Dividing Muse: Images of Sacred Disjunction in Milton's Poetry* (New Haven: Yale University Press, 1985), 42.

9. Daniel Cawdrey, *Superstitio Superstes* (1641), 7, 28.

10. The great Phoenix passage in *Areopagitica* (*CPW,* 2:558) executes a similar maneuver when the prelatical censors who oppose the

multiplication of opinions become themselves the cackling many: "timorous and flocking birds . . . with those also who love the twilight, flutter about, amaz'd at what she [the Eagle/Phoenix] means, and in their envious gabble would prognosticat a year of sects and schisms."

11. Charles Carlton notes that the "vast majority of bishops came from the lower and middle orders" and specifically discusses the problems of Laud's low birth in Archbishop William Laud (7, 33). See my chapter 3, n. 61.

12. *Kingdomes Weekly Intelligencer,* April 26–May 7, 1644, 426.

13. John Bale, *The great process of Thomas Arundell the Archbishop of Caunterburye and of the Papisticall clergy . . . against the most noble Knyght Syr John Oldcastle* (1544), 52.

14. Until September 11, 2001, and even thereafter, the editorials and cartoons depicting President George W. Bush as not very bright were everywhere. The snobbery directed at President Clinton is a little subtler, because it often appears "good-natured" on its surface, as in this passage from *The New Yorker.* In his discussion of the ex-president's book contract, Henrik Herzberg writes in passing: "Bill Clinton, it must be said, don't know nothin' about birthin' books" ("Comment: Book Him," in "The Talk of the Town," *The New Yorker,* August 20 & 27, 2003, 54). One snobbery is intellectual, aimed at the limited capacities of an aristocrat; the other is social and, whatever its proclaimed attitude of tolerance toward the ex-president, uses a locution that summons up, not only the casual literary reference to *Gone with the Wind,* but also condescension toward the diction associated with the poor of the South.

15. I asked John Leonard, an authority on Miltonic allusion, if he sees the same strange identifications that I do. He agreed that Milton casts himself as the Roman soldier. Milton's sensitivity to these kinds of metaphoric operations is shown in *Eikonoklastes,* where he comments on a passage from the *Eikon Basilike:* "In this Simily we have [King Charles] compar'd to Christ, the Parlament to the Devill, and his giving them that Act of settling, to his letting them goe up to the Pinnacle of the Temple. A tottering and giddy Act rather than a settling. This was goodly use made of Scripture in his Solitudes" (*CPW,* 3:405).

16. Perry Miller, *The Puritans,* 2 vols., rev. ed. (New York: Harper Torchbooks, 1963), 1:3.

17. The attack on the pyramid and its replacement by the four-square church suggests a rejection of the idea of hierarchy itself, a rejection perhaps temporary but of some relevance to Milton's political thinking.

18. This is a real issue for Milton, who thought long and hard about his own monumentality, about leaving "a song to generations," "something so written to aftertimes, as they should not willingly let it die" (*CPW,* 1:706, 810).

19. See Carol Barton, "They Also Perform the Duties of a Servant Who Only Remain Erect on Their Feet in a Specified Place in Readiness

to Receive Orders: The Dynamics of Stasis in Milton's Sonnet XIX,"
Milton Quarterly (December 1998):109–22.

20. For two stimulating discussions, see chapter 2, "The Parable of
the Talents as Milton's Uneasy Place," in Dayton Haskin, *Milton's
Burden of Interpretation* (Philadelphia: University of Pennsylvania Press,
1994), 29–53; and David V. Urban, "The Talented Mr. Milton: A Parabolic
Laborer and His Identity," in *Milton Studies*, vol. 43, ed. Albert C.
Labriola (Pittsburgh: University of Pittsburgh Press, 2004), 1–18.

21. Compare this to Abraham Cowley's "foolish Indian who sells his/
Gold for beads and bells"; Milton emphasizes the victimization—not
a big difference, but a real one. See Abraham Cowley, "The Bargain,"
in *The Collected Works of Abraham Cowley*, ed. Thomas O. Calhoun
et al. (Newark: University of Delaware Press, 1993), 50–51.

22. Herle, *Charles Abrahams offer Gods Offering* (1642), 16, 23.

23. We barely remember the chants of "Peace Now," "Do it now" of
the 1960s set over against the "all deliberate speed" of *Brown v. Board
of Education* and the paradoxically inflammatory "Let us reason
together" of President Johnson. That urgency has the same polemical
force in the radical rhetoric of two widely separated eras. See my coda
below.

24. See Ida Langdon, *Milton's Theory of Poetry and Fine Art* (New
Haven: Yale University Press, 1924); the bibliography since then is
enormous. Among the works that seem to me to preempt any need for
my treatment of classical generic theory here, these works come
immediately to mind: A. Bartlett Giamatti, *The Earthly Paradise and
the Renaissance Epic* (Princeton: Princeton University Press, 1966);
Richard S. Ide and Joseph A. Wittreich, Jr., guest eds., *Composite Orders:
The Genres of Milton's Last Poems*, special edition of *Milton Studies*,
vol. 17, ed. James D. Simmonds (Pittsburgh: University of Pittsburgh
Press, 1983); Barbara K. Lewalski, *"Paradise Lost" and the Rhetoric of
Literary Forms* (Princeton: Princeton University Press, 1987); Louis
Martz, *Poet of Exile: A Study of Milton's Poetry* (New Haven: Yale
University Press, 1980); Mary Ann Radzinowicz, *Milton's Epic and the
Book of Psalms* (Princeton: Princeton University Press, 1989); John
Steadman, *Milton and the Renaissance Hero* (Oxford: Clarendon Press,
1967); Joan Webber, *Milton and His Epic Tradition* (Seattle: University
of Washington Press, 1979); Joseph A. Wittreich, *Visionary Poetics:
Milton's Tradition and His Legacy* (San Marino: Huntington Library
Press, 1979).

25. But I have a basic disagreement with Helgerson's view of the
early prose as disengaged in the way he describes. See Richard Helgerson,
*Self-Crowned Laureates: Spenser, Jonson, Milton, and the Literary
System* (Berkeley and Los Angeles: University of California Press,1983),
249–50.

26. See Owen Barfield, *Saving the Appearances: A Study in Idolatry* (New York: Harcourt Brace, 1957), esp. chap. 20.

27. For a description of Milton's use of this passage, see Louis L. Martz, "Milton's Prophetic Voice: Moving Toward Paradise," in *Of Poetry and Politics: New Essays on Milton on His Works*, ed. P. G. Stanwood (Binghamton, N.Y.: Medieval & Renaissance Texts & Studies, 1995), 1–16.

28. See Abraham J. Heschel's analysis in *The Prophets: An Introduction*, vol. 1 (New York: Harper & Row, 1969), chap. 1, "What Manner of Man Is the Prophet?"

29. Michael Lieb, *The Poetics of the Holy: A Reading of "Paradise Lost"* (Chapel Hill: University of North Carolina Press, 1981), 328. Lieb has extended his study of the numinous back to sources in the Ezekiel vision in *The Visionary Mode: Biblical Prophecy, Hermeneutics and Cultural Change* (Ithaca, N.Y.: Cornell University Press, 1991). The Barfield, Martz and Heschel texts just cited are parts of the huge literature on the subject that are relevant here.

30. Henry Hammond, *Of Fraternal Admonition or Correction*, (1647), 2–3.

31. Carol Barton has called my attention to the background of this ritual as described in Alfred Edersheim's *The Temple: Its Ministry and Services as They Were in the Time of Christ* (London: Religious Tract Society, 1874), 216–17.

32. The tradition that Samson's grinding in the mill was stud service for the Philistines has considerable authority: see Petrus Comestor, "Historia Scholastica," in *Patrologiae Cursuus Completus*, series 1, ed. J. P. Migne, 217 vols., 190:1285: "The Hebrews . . . say that the Philistines forced him to sleep with sturdy women so that they might conceive sturdy children by him" (1285), cited in Watson Kirkconnell, *That Invincible Samson: The Theme of Samson Agonistes in World Literature with Translations of the Major Analogues* (Toronto: University of Toronto Press, 1964), 150.

33. Among the earliest accounts of the queen in England was the report of the disruption of Protestant services by her and her "Papist" retinue, "chattering and making a great noise" See Quentin Bone, *Henrietta Maria: Queen of the Cavaliers* (Urbana: University of Illinois Press, 1972), 49. See also *CPW*, 3:422, n. 14. By the time Milton wrote *Eikonoklastes*, Henrietta Maria was a favorite target.

Notes to Coda

1. Thomas Fuller, *Good Thoughts in Bad Times* (Exeter, 1645), 69.

2. Martin Peretz, "Protest Politics: Peretz vs. Goodman," in "To the Editor," *New York Times Magazine* (January 19, 1969), 4, 10, 12.

3. John Marston, *A Sermon Preached at St. Margarets Westminster* (1645), 15.

4. Joseph Symonds, *A Sermon Lately Preached at Westminster, Before Sundry of the Honourable House of Commons* (1641).

5. *Three Ordinances Of The Lords and Commons Assembled in Parliament For the better observation of the monethly Fast; and more especially the next Wednesday, commonly called the Feast of the Nativity of Christ* (1644), 3–4.

6. Thomas Fuller, *Truth Maintained; or, Positions Delivered in a Sermon at the Savoy Since Traduced For Dangerous: Now Asserted For Sound and Safe* (1645), sig C3v.

7. Henry Robinson, *Liberty of Conscience; or, The Sole means to obtaine Peace and Truth* (1644), sig A1v–A2v.

8. *Paraenetick Or Humble Addresse To The Parliament and Assembly For (Not Loose, But) Christian Liberty* (1644), 5.

9. Roger Williams, *The Bloody Tenent of Persecution for Cause of Conscience, Discussed in a Conference betweene Truth and Peace* (1644). In 1652, this becomes *The Bloody Tenent Yet More Bloudy by Mr. Cotton's Endeavor to Wash it White in the Blood of the Lambe.*

10. *Wholesome Severity reconciled with Christian Liberty* (1644), A3–A4.

11. John Ward, *God Judging among the gods Opened in a sermon before the Honourable House of Commons assembled in Parliament, upon the solemn day of monethly fast, March 26th, 1645* (1645), 26.

INDEX

rabble, 127–30, 154–55
Ransom, John Crowe, 135
Readie and Easie Way, The
(Milton), 131, 213
reason, 2, 166; appeal to, 19, 65;
faith vs., 83, 194; use to identify
truth, 78–79, 87; zeal vs., 7, 14
*Reason of Church-Government,
The* (Milton), 73, 76, 116, 197;
class issues in, 173–74;
conclusion of, 199–203;
digression in, 185–90, 192–93,
198; on discipline, 193–94; on
freedom of conscience, 195, 198;
intended to be last word on
prelacy, 89, 135; kerygmatic
authority in, 169–70; Milton's
career and, 185–93, 198; model
of Church structure in, 177–78;
organization of, 195; purposes
of, 163–65, 186; on vocation,
181–82, 190–92
rectitude. *See* righteousness
reform, 71; effects of, 180–81;
Milton's optimism about,
58–59, 86–87, 113–14; of
universities, 206, 210
Reformation, 7, 26, 28; English,
32–33, 57, 59, 101–3; optimism
about English, 71, 114; printing
press's importance in, 1–2
Relation of the Conference (Laud),
170
religion, Milton's, and politics, 155
revelation, 78–79, 190
Revelation, Book of, 6; Cowper on,
13–14; Milton's use of, 56,
65–66, 180; Puritans on, 10–11
*Reverend Mr. Brightman's
Judgments or Prophecies*
(Brightman), 13
revolutionary movements, 190,
213; rhetoric of, 205–7; urgency
of, 208–9; zeal in, 82, 208–10
Richard II, King, 52
Ridley, Bishop, 52, 61, 63
righteousness, 93, 207; criticisms

of Hall's, 95, 100, 106; vs.
self-righteousness, 3–4, 106. *See
also* tract wars, rectitude of
authors in
rights, 126, 210
Robinson, Henry, 27, 211–12
Root and Branch extirpation, 24
Royalists, 27
Rutherford, Samuel, 29

Sacred Complex, The (Kerrigan),
135
sacred space, 19, 130, 170–71
salvation, 57, 119, 198–99
Samson, 201–2
Samson Agonistes (Milton), 65,
155, 159
Saye and Seale, Lord, 31
scandals, 27, 30–31
Sclater, William, 16–17
Scriptures: adherence to, vs.
indifference, 26, 30; as Christ's
body, 138–39; church-discipline
in, 74, 171; decorum in, 5–6;
history in, 175–76; Milton's
adherence to, 81–82, 84–86;
Milton's use of language of,
113–14, 156–57; need to confirm
veracity of, 82–83; sufficiency
of, 76, 81, 160; written vs.
spoken, 35, 81–82; zeal in, 2–5
Scultetus, Abraham, 133
Second Defence (Milton), 50, 53,
58–59
self, 92, 146, 148–49
self-importance, 2
self-presentations: of Hall, 89–90,
95, 98, 109; of Milton, 67–68,
106, 109, 135–37, 145–47, 163,
189; of SMECTYMNUUS,
97–98, 109; in tract wars, 89,
109; of United States, 207
self-righteousness, 3–4, 106
Senecanism, Hall's, 89, 139–40
*Sermon against Lukewarmness
in Religion, A* (Wilkinson),
16–17

100–101, 122, 125–26; rectitude
of Hall attacked, 102–3, 105;
seriousness of, 162; style in, 92,
104–5, 166–67; tactics in, 77, 79,
115, 125; winners of, 100. *See
also* antiprelatical tracts,
Milton's; divorce tracts; *specific
authors and titles*
tradition, 75; contempt for, 44–45,
206; fear of domination by,
171–72; Milton's treatment of,
74, 76, 83–85, 87, 93, 120; vs.
Scripture, 81–82, 84
"Tradition and the Individual
Talent" (Eliot), 93
Trevor-Roper, Hugh, 67–68, 76–78,
213
"true poem," 140; self as, 92, 146,
148–49
truth: competing claims to, 124;
corruption of, 138–39, 200–201;
language of, 140; Milton's
assumptions of self-evidence of,
74, 101, 130–32; oral vs.
written, 81–82; reason's use to
identify, 78–79, 87; of
Scriptures, 82–83
Truth Maintained (Fuller), 211
tub-preachers, 24, 38–39
Tyndale, William, 27
tyranny, 200–201

United States, 207
urgency, rhetoric of, 184, 186–87,
208–9
Ussher, James (Archbishop of
Armagh), 72–73, 165; Milton's
treatment of, 74, 77–78; Puritan
ambivalence toward, 76–77

via media. See golden mean;
moderation
Vicars, John, 94–95
Viet Nam War, 204–6
*Vindication of the Answer to the
Humble Remonstrance, A*

(SMECTYMNUUS), 88–89,
97–99
violence: Milton urging, 154,
180–81; in rhetoric of tract
wars, 64, 125–26
vocation, 54, 161, 181–82

Warren, Elizabeth, 37
Wars of Truth, 1, 52, 124, 164. *See
also* tract wars
wealth, of Church, 160
Webber, Joan, 46, 125, 135–36
Whitgift, Archbishop, 28
Whiting, George W., 64
Wilkinson, Henry, 16–17, 25
Wilson, Thomas, 28–29
Wise & Moderate Discourse, A
(Bacon), 9
Wolfe, Don M., 133; on Brooke's *A
Discourse,* 30–31; on Milton's
work, 50, 120, 165; retrieval of
Milton's work by, 45–46
Wolsey, Cardinal, 52, 61
Workes of Thomas Brightman, The
(Brightman), 13
Works (Hall), 94
worldliness, 38, 161
Wren, Matthew, 41

York, Archbishop, 51–52
Young, Thomas, 50, 53, 172
youth, Milton's, 53, 136, 183

zeal, 25; Anglicans vs. Puritans on,
9–11; in the Bible, 2–5; defense
of, 80, 151–52; definitions of,
2–4; effects of, 7, 16–17, 212;
lack of, 16–17, 52; maturation
of, 211; Milton's, 10, 46–48, 109,
151–52; pleas for moderation of,
8–9, 34, 212; of Puritans, 4,
10–11, 34, 212; role in
revolutionary movements, 82,
208–10; study of rhetoric of,
45–47; true vs. inconsiderate,
3–4, 80, 82; uses of, 7, 71, 213